Rethinking Island Methodologies

Rethinking the Island

The Rethinking the Island series has sought to unsettle assumptions by comprehensively investigating the range of topological and topographical characteristics that lie at the heart of the idea of "islandness."

Series Editors

Elaine Stratford, Professor in the School of Geography, Planning, and Spatial Sciences, University of Tasmania, Australia

Godfrey Baldacchino, Professor of Sociology at the University of Malta, Malta; and Past President, International Small Islands Studies Association (ISISA)

Elizabeth McMahon, Professor in the School of the Arts and Media, University of New South Wales, Australia

Titles in the Series

Theorizing Literary Islands: The Island Trope in Contemporary Robinsonade Narratives, by Ian Kinane

Island Genres, Genre Islands: Conceptualization and Representation in Popular Fiction, by Ralph Crane and Lisa Fletcher

Postcolonial Nations, Islands, and Tourism: Reading Real and Imagined Spaces, by Helen Kapstein

Caribbean Island Movements: Culebra's Trans-Insularities, by Carlo A. Cubero

Poetry and Islands: Materiality and the Creative Imagination, by Rajeev S. Patke

Contemporary Archipelagic Thinking: Towards New Comparative Methodologies and Disciplinary Formations, edited by Michelle Stephens and Yolanda Martínez-San Miguel

The Notion of Near Islands: The Croatian Archipelago, edited by Nenad Starc

Atolls of the Maldives: Nissology and Geography, edited by Stefano Malatesta, Marcella Schmidt di Friedberg, Shahida Zubair, David Bowen, and Mizna Mohamed

Affect, Archive, Archipelago: Puerto Rico's Sovereign Caribbean Lives, by Beatriz Llenín-Figueroa

Ecocriticism and the Island: Readings from the British-Irish Archipelago, by Pippa Marland

Rethinking Island Methodologies, by Elaine Stratford, Godfrey Baldacchino, and Elizabeth McMahon

Rethinking Island Methodologies

Elaine Stratford, Godfrey Baldacchino, and Elizabeth McMahon

ROWMAN & LITTLEFIELD
Lanham • Boulder • New York • London

Published by Rowman & Littlefield
An imprint of The Rowman & Littlefield Publishing Group, Inc.
4501 Forbes Boulevard, Suite 200, Lanham, Maryland 20706
www.rowman.com

86–90 Paul Street, London EC2A 4NE

British Library Cataloguing in Publication Information Available

Library of Congress Cataloging-in-Publication Data

Names: Stratford, Elaine, author. | Baldacchino, Godfrey, author. | McMahon, Elizabeth, author.
Title: Rethinking island methodologies / Elaine Stratford, Godfrey Baldacchino, Elizabeth McMahon.
Description: Lanham : Rowman & Littlefield, [2023] | Series: Rethinking the island | Includes bibliographical references and index.
Subjects: LCSH: Island life—Research—Methodology. | Island biogeography—Research—Methodology.
Classification: LCC GT3480 .S87 2023 (print) | LCC GT3480 (ebook) | DDC 392.3/601—dc23/eng/20221207
LC record available at https://lccn.loc.gov/2022047466
LC ebook record available at https://lccn.loc.gov/2022047467

ISBN: 978-1-5381-6519-5 (cloth : alk. paper)
ISBN: 978-1-5381-6521-8 (pbk. : alk. paper)
ISBN: 978-1-5381-6520-1 (ebook)

The general knowledge of time [and space] on the island depends, curiously enough, on the direction of the wind.

—John Millington Synge, The Aran Islands, p. 32

Contents

viii   *Contents*

Acknowledgments

This work is the capstone and final contribution to a series titled *Rethinking the Island*, which we three started a decade ago. We owe a debt of gratitude to our advisory board members, starting with Ian Buchanan, University of Wollongong, Australia, who suggested our publisher for the project—and it went from there. And we recognize and thank the other members of our advisory board: Beate Ratter, University of Hamburg; Brian Roberts, Brigham Young University; Carol Farbotko, University of Melbourne; Elizabeth DeLoughrey, University of California; Eric Clark, Lund University; Ilan Kelman, University College London; James Sidaway, National University of Singapore; Jonathan Pugh; Newcastle University; Laurie Brinklow, University of Prince Edward Island; Lisa Fletcher, University of Tasmania; Michelle Ann Stephens, Rutgers University; Mimi Sheller, Worcester Polytechnic Institute in Massachusetts; Philip Steinberg, Durham University; Stephen Pratt, University of the South Pacific; and Vanessa Smith, University of Sydney.

Rowman and Littlefield has been with us the entire journey, of course. In reverse chronological order, we thank the following for their support and collegiality: Katelyn Turner, Rebecca Anastasi, Dhara Snowden, Scarlett Furness, Gurdeep Mattu, Holly Tyler, and Martina O'Sullivan—the last of whom took the initial step to sign us up and launch the series. Thanks, too, to other staff in the publishing house for work on the web, with marketing, at conferences, and in production.

Because this is a capstone work and the last in a series, we also want to recognize and warmly thank the authors who have come along with us and written such interesting and laudable works to help rethink islands: Ralph Crane and Lisa Fletcher; Carlo Cubero; Helen Kapstein; Ian Kinane; Beatriz Llenín-Figueroa; Stephano Malatesta and colleagues Marcella Schmidt Di Friedberg, Shahida Zubair, David Bowen, and Mizna Mohamed; Pippa

Marland; Rajeev Patke; Nens Starc and contributors; and Michelle Ann Stephens and Yolanda Martínez-San Miguel and contributors. We are most grateful that you all invested time, energy, intellectual and emotional labors, and faith in what have been both individual and collective projects.

Finally, all three of us acknowledge the fun and excitement of having worked together; we recognize the significant support from colleagues at our respective universities in order to complete this book; and we extend our gratitude to those who kept our home fires burning.

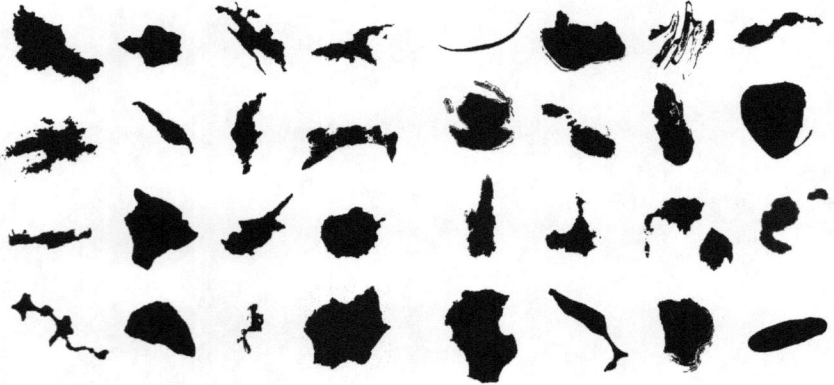

Source: Jean-Yves Vigneau.

Chapter 1

Introduction

Elaine Stratford, Godfrey Baldacchino, and Elizabeth McMahon

Introduce: To lead or bring in (a person or thing) into a place, position, state, condition, or relation to something, or into a circle or series of persons or things . . . to bring (a person) into the circle of the knowledge, acquaintance, or recognition of another or others. (OED)

The 27th of August in 2021 was a beautiful Friday morning on Prince Edward Island, Canada's smallest and only fully enisled province. It was cloudless and sunny, but a fresh wind was blowing from the west. One of us, Godfrey, and his partner, Anna, drove out from the provincial capital of Charlottetown to Canoe Cove and arrived just as the tide was coming into the sandy inlet, with waves and spray aided by the backwind. Other than us, there was just one family, its members strolling idly. One particular islet of sand had formed in the bay in the foreground, as the water slowly seeped back into the cove. Gulls and terns came by and landed to rest for a while; but they departed as the incoming water got too close for comfort. We watched the water gradually reclaim that enisled space, with the islet shrinking progressively at the edges and finding itself increasingly under water until, briefly, it was just an eddy and then disappeared completely (figure 1.1).

The image captures a short but complete story of a particular, unnamed islet. Taken by one of us—Godfrey—it may be the islet's only photograph and the only evidence of its fleeting existence. It is, perhaps, an insignificant example of an island, other than to marine and intertidal species—such as razor clams and foraging seabirds—that may depend for their survival on it and its terraqueous cycles. And yet, this story is similar to that which applies to many of the world's islands: formed by the action of water; changed by the action of water. The main differences are that some islands of the world

Figure 1.1.   Islet. Photograph by Godfrey Baldacchino.

have a size larger than our islet and tend to exist longer than a few hours or minutes and, thus, make other forms of human and more-than-human island life possible. In terms of geological time, however, islands last but the bat of an eyelid: "islands are ephemeral: created today, destroyed tomorrow" (Carson, 1951/2003, p. 84). It is perhaps the imaginative potential of this very geo(morpho)logical instability that makes islands "particularly potent landforms" to "think with" (respectively, Riquet, 2019, p. 4; Gillis, 2004, p. 1), especially if one stretches the meanings attached to contingent words such as *today* and *tomorrow*.

Of course, islands have cultural, geopolitical, literary, and other forms of significations that are more or less stable and even durable. Another of us, Elaine, is based in the capital of Australia's island state, lutruwita/ Tasmania, where she often gazes from her west windows to marvel at the ancient, massive, qualities of kunanyi (Mount Wellington). The areal extent of this large archipelago is around 68,400 square kilometers (26,409 square miles). Its Indigenous peoples—have among the longest claims to millennia-spanning occupancy of any place anywhere on Earth, having walked the peninsula from what is now the mainland, across what is now Bass Strait, over 40,000 years ago. And still, the many islands of that archipelago change daily and not just at the shoreline. There is constant shifting, too, in the vertical expression of masts and buildings, trees and mountains, interior spaces, and Indigenous and imperial settlements old and new. With those changes come others in terms of how lutruwita/Tasmania is understood as place for vastly different people who come and go over time (figure 1.2).

Figure 1.2. Transect. Photograph by Elaine Stratford.

For Elaine, continually emergent understandings of what it means to be on and off an island are tempered always by the paradox of having been born as far from the sea as one might get, in Saskatoon, in Canada, although that country, of course, has many thousands of coastal, riverine, and lacustrine islands. Either way, Elaine often equates those understandings with the turn of one of four kinds of scope, all of which have viewing apparatuses that are round, like an archetypical island. Her understandings of islands and archipelagos are sometimes kaleidoscopic—multicolored and mobile; sometimes telescopic—concentrating on scales where the particular may seem invisible; sometimes periscopic—oriented to sweeping observations by which to take in the horizon; and sometimes microscopic—hoping to capture deep nuance and detail. And she wonders: if it was possible to hold all four scopic regimes in place at one time, what might transpire?

The interconnections of place and history are meaningfully complicated by a small natural sandbar in the Cooks River, located about 10 kilometers (6 miles) south of the city center of Sydney, Australia, and close by where one of us, Elizabeth, lives. It is called Fatima Island and is the last remaining island of the river. Sitting in a stretch of the river between a railway line and a highway, Fatima Island has long provided a daily site of contemplation for commuters, as local histories document (Wheatley, 2013).

The island (figure 1.3) carries a complex and varied history for a tiny sandbar. The Cooks River is on the Country of the Bidjigal people of the Eora Nation, who have lived there for more than a thousand generations. Its Darug name has not survived. A photograph from 1880 shows two other adjacent

Figure 1.3.   Fatima Island, Sydney. Photograph by Elizabeth McMahon.

islands now gone and there is evidence that there were several more prior to the colonial period. There are middens on one side the bank, and it is thought that these sandbars provided a crossing place at that part of the river for the Bidjigal people.

Fatima Island is close to where the Cooks River flows into Botany Bay where Captain James Cook (1728–1779) lay anchor in 1770, hence its name. The First Nations people of the area were relocated in 1883 but some have returned to the area. Another layer of colonial history was added in 1901, when a retaining wall was built around the island using sandstone blocks made by transported convicts—most of these were pilfered by souvenir hunters. The island gets its name from a Catholic pilgrimage of the rosary in 1951, centering on a statue of Our Lady of Fatima, which was undertaken in response to the pope's call to prayer in response to the threat of communist Russia. Nowadays the name also resonates strongly with the local Muslim community, as it bears the name of the prophet's daughter.

Fatima Island is only just "hanging on," although there are many efforts at conservation (Blair, 2014), because it is a pest-free refuge for pelicans, egrets, silver gills, and cormorants. In radical contrast to other islands across Sydney's iconic harbor, Fatima Island is an unprepossessing shoal, but it continues to command attention and stir the imagination as we cling to its significance in this place.

OUR AGENDA

This book is a one-stop, go-to volume to prompt some rethinking about island studies and research methodologies. It fosters opportunities to reflect on and engage in comparative analysis of different approaches used across the study of islands and archipelagos. This study we sometimes describe as island and archipelagic studies, or as island studies and archipelagic studies, or as island studies: all three terms now "fail" what it is we think we are dealing with, but we are comfortable with, and excited about, what the polyvalence invites. Either way, the book is meant to support the reader's quests to apprehend and weigh the theories, philosophies, values, and techniques that underpin how we *do* island studies, and such sustained support will help to advance these research domains now and in the future.

Our chief arguments are, *first*, that for too long islands have been constituted as background, backdrop, stage setting, or case study and, *second*, that it is well past time to test whether, how, to what extent, and with what effects it is possible to *rethink* what we contingently call *island methodologies*. Like any good arguments, these two are contestable but both are based on more than a whim. Indeed, we felt compelled to write this last book in a 10-year series about *rethinking the island* to contribute to collective, ongoing labors to open the field for more reflection, scholarship, action, and advocacy.

Intrinsic to our labors are efforts to consider how research methodologies *per se* give effect to island studies. In doing so, we acknowledge the growing influence of the archipelagic imagination, obliging—at the very least—a keen sensibility for island plurality and relationality in island methodologies (see Stephens & Martínez-San Miguel, 2020). Indeed, we say *island*, but often we are confronted by *islands* in the plural: at various sizes and scales; with dynamic relations of power, trade, and migration among them; with love-hate relations between their own centers/mainlands and their peripheries; and occupying a common sea (LaFlamme, 1983). In scoping work done over a decade ago, we three authors and two colleagues suggested how the idea of the archipelago could profitably be deployed in understanding island–island relations—attempting to do so briefly in relation to Britain/United Kingdom, Canada, and Australia (Stratford et al., 2011a). In response, Philip Hayward (2012) then proposed the term "aquapelago" to emphasize the aquatic (and not just terrestrial) character of interisland associations.

Island and archipelagic studies have a long way to go—and that is a good thing because it invites more in the way of methodological innova-tion, including theoretical and empirical inventions. Certainly, fuller and deeper understandings of the role of the sea in island life are a beckoning research pursuit (Hay, 2013). So, too, are questions emerging from ocean studies (Blum, 2010, 2013), works on the Anthropocene and the oceans (DeLoughrey, 2019a, 2019b), or works on wet ontologies (Peters & Steinberg, 2019; Steinberg & Peters, 2015). And certainly, in relation to archipelagic studies—which we see as elemental in island studies—refinements continue to emerge. For example, Olga Blomgren (2021, n.p.) suggests three objectives of the field. The first is to "provide a [counter-]narrative" in relation to ideas of spatial equity such that archipelagic "thinking nullifies, rather than perpetuates, hierarchies between land masses." The second is to consider "less-studied relations between islands" not least to "emphasize histories and experiences which are not enmeshed in colonial and imperial hegemonies." The third objective, Blomgren suggests, is to prioritize "consciousness of a linked multiplicity;" in our terms, to think about and with "connection, assemblage, mobility, and multiplicity" (Stratford, 2013, p. 3).

Knowing the overlap of island and archipelagic studies, as a foundational matter we also recognize that different but related ventures inform studies of islands and archipelagos (as the aforesaid *locus* of inquiry) and island and archipelagic studies (as *focus* of inquiry) (Ronström, 2013). We acknowledge that varied research methodologies already underpin both the study of islands and archipelagos and the formal field of island studies. Yet, no single and broad-based volume of essays deals with how scholars and practitioners of island and archipelagic studies conceive, understand, know, value, and work with and for their subject matter. Few works, if any, appear to deal with *how, what, and why we know what we do* and with *how* those puzzles are then translated into research designs that become apparent and are enacted in varied sites of island inquiry. That gap exists despite growing numbers of works focused on methodological questions in relation to islands and the archive, museum, laboratory, ferry, atoll, beach, or ocean (Llenín-Figueroa, 2022; Malatesta et al., 2021; Ritvo, 1997; Steinberg, 2001; Terrell, 2020; Vannini, 2012; Walshe & Foley, 2021).

On that understanding, in the chapters that follow we use several lenses to share our thinking about disciplinary traditions, legacies, and emerging debates that inform the field of island studies; what is studied in island and archipelagic studies; and where such pursuits take place. We ponder why and how it matters that studies are located where they are; who or what is studied or studied with; and why island and archipelagic studies are pursued. We think about what methods are deployed and how are they justified; what challenges and opportunities characterize island studies; and how these may change with time. And we reflect on what strategies and tactics are used to mitigate or expand these challenges and opportunities. In one chapter we ask what future/s are foreseeable for island and archipelagic studies and include in that conversation valued colleagues from around the world. The chapters are written in our own voices but at the same time we have learned from our own and each other's efforts in the process, swapping drafts through the process. Those chapters are framed around verbs to flag the fact that we invite action from ourselves and others, elsewhere. In the work, too, there are many gaps, and we look forward to reading how others identify and respond both to those and to what we have been able to provide.

CONTINGENT BOUNDARIES

To rethink island methodologies, it is important to think about what islands are and signify; be open to existing ways of being, knowing, valuing, or applying; and be receptive to novel approaches to all of those. So, in the pages that follow, we thread together thinking about and with islands and thinking about and with research methodologies. We are sure to fail, and we are comfortable with that, too. After all, "methodological failure is both commonplace and generative . . . [and a] truly [radical] discussion of failure needs to include non-redemptive failures" (Clare, 2019, n.p.).

Either way, and perhaps ironically, both success and failure often start with a keen and instinctive appreciation of contingent boundaries. So our sense is that people understand islands intuitively: pieces of land larger than rocks but smaller than continents, surrounded by water on all sides, even at high tide. They may have been peninsulas—suggestively called *presque-îles* or *almost islands* in French. They may have come into being without fanfare: losing matter in the aftermath of dogged, eroding fluctuations of sun, rain, wind, and temperature; or gaining matter thanks to the quiet travails of millions of coral polyps in suitably warm waters. Otherwise, they come into being more dramatically: starting as seamounts—submerged hills or mountains—and eventually breaking the surface of oceans in the throes of volcanic activity. Gushing lava and raining volcanic ash identify critical events in island life: Ambrym, Vanuatu, 50 CE; Laki, Iceland, 1783; Krakatoa, Indonesia, 1883; Pinatubo, Philippines, 1991; St. Vincent, Caribbean, 2021; Tonga, Pacific, 2022. Or perhaps—and unless and until reclaimed by the sea—they are paeans to ambition and folly: artificial islands, anxious monuments to engineering prowess (Jackson & Della Dora, 2009).

Rethinking island methodologies also means being open to islands' spectacular diversity of natural and cultural forms. Islands are home to a significant part of global biodiversity resulting from high levels of species endemism, distinctive functional traits, and evolutionary patterns such as adaptive radiations. For similar reasons, islands are theatres to a dramatic number of extinctions, particularly of bird species, that often occur because of our species' encroachments. In many fields spanning diverse approaches, islands are a form of synecdoche: real-world models and systems that appeal analytically because their size *seems* manageable when compared with continents. On islands, it *seems* possible to think—at a human scale, perhaps—about complex interactions and about how multiple factors of being and doing articulate and replicate across all world regions and climate zones. Those characteristics are inherently interesting, allow for multisite comparative inquiry (Kueffer & Kinney, 2017), and are powerful because of their differential intrinsic and instrumental worth, which is perhaps why much in island and archipelagic studies is based on case studies (Stake, 1995). At the same time, there is need for both deep criticality in and from the field and more in the way of institutional advocacy for it. The latter is urgent given "growing geopolitical tensions in ocean spaces, continued adverse impacts from climate change and sea level rise, and development challenges" (Ginoza et al., 2020, p. 95).

So, then, islandness is a condition and, combined with qualities such as location, relative smallness, and distance from mainlands, that condition creates habitats that throw up cultural and social specificities in place, across spaces, and over time: distinct languages and dialects, rituals and practices, or architectures and cuisines. Certainly, distinction is not unique to islands, but it is worth noting that one-sixth of UNESCO's World Heritage Sites are either found *on* islands—Galápagos (Ecuador), Giant's Causeway (Ireland),

Ħaġar Qim Temples (Malta), Lamu Old Town (Kenya), Rapa Nui (Chile)—
or they comprise *whole* islands—Amami (Japan), Bikini atoll (Marshall
Islands), Fernando de Noronha (Brazil), Gough (United Kingdom), and Macquarie (Australia).

Such rich distinctiveness spills over into other domains. Consider jurisdictional status. Around one-quarter of sovereign states—46 of 193 members of
the United Nations General Assembly—are made up exclusively of single
islands or archipelagos (figure 1.4).

Just eight of those states share land borders with another, internationally
recognized, sovereign island state. And more than two-thirds of countries
include islands off their coasts or in their lakes and rivers. Here too, various such territories can be classified as *subnational island jurisdictions*, and
many enjoy some distinct or special administrative status: as municipalities,
regions, provinces, or special autonomous regions. Only 10 permanently
inhabited islands are shared between more than one country. How the labors
of decolonization are likely to reframe island boundaries and borders has yet
to be determined and, in any case, these are processes rather than end points
and will draw on profoundly complex ways of knowing and being in the
world (Carter, 2019; Grydehøj et al., 2021).

Rethinking island methodologies also requires a deep commitment to
curiosity about what is known about islands: their numbers, qualities, populations, or distributions, for example. Perhaps surprisingly, there have been
few attempts to accurately delineate all the islands on Earth. The Global
Islands database comes close: it is a project of the United States Geological
Survey (USGS), in collaboration with Esri (a geographic information system

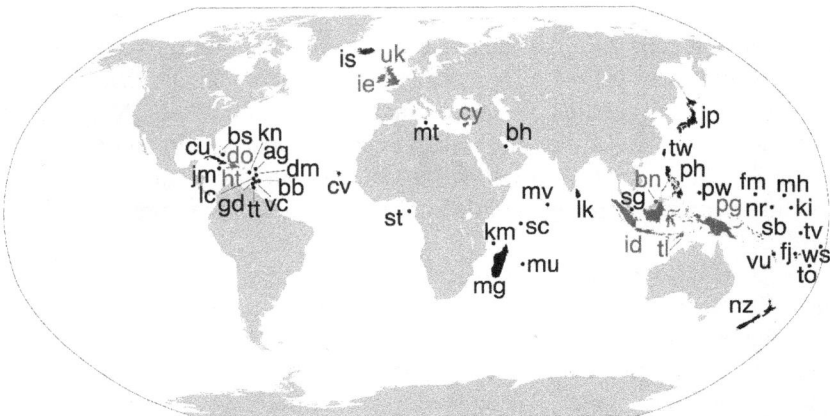

Figure 1.4. Island nations and their international internet domain names. *Source*:
Public Domain.

company) and the World Conservation Monitoring Centre (WCMC) and supported by the UN Environment Programme. It identifies five continental mainlands, 21,818 islands greater in area than one square kilometer (0.4 square miles), and 318,868 islands smaller than one square kilometer in area but larger than 30 × 30 meters (98.5 × 98.5 feet), all developed from annual composites of 2014 Landsat satellite imagery (Sayre et al., 2019; United States Department of the Interior, n.d.). These collectively make up just over 5% of Earth's land area. The world's islands are home to around 730 million people, which is more than one-tenth of the world's total population. Almost half of islanders live on just four islands: Britain (United Kingdom), Honshu (Japan), Java (Indonesia), and Luzon (Philippines).

Of the world's island and archipelago states only one—Iceland—is completely in a cold-water island location, although Hokkaido in Japan and the South Island of Aotearoa/New Zealand typically experience quite cold winters and get their share of snow and frost. These qualities are not simply literal: they enable approaches by which to interrogate, for example, tipping points for climate in the Anthropocene (Huijbens, 2021). Meanwhile, most island and archipelagic states are nested within the temperate and tropical regions of the planet, with concentrations in Southeast Asia and Central Western Pacific Ocean (19 sovereign states), the Caribbean Sea (13 states), and the Indian Ocean (six states). Southeast Asia is home to the world's most heavily populated and transnational archipelago, with Indonesia as its core, along with Brunei, the Philippines, Papua New Guinea, Timor-Leste, Singapore, and parts of Malaysia. Over half the planet's islanders reside there. In contrast, the world's largest island assemblage by land area lies in northern Canada. It includes three of the world's 10 largest islands—Baffin/Qikiqtaaluk, Ellesmere/Umingmak Nuna, and Victoria/Kitlineq—but is sparsely populated. Its main settlement—with just 7,700 residents—is Iqaluit, capital of Nunavut, the world's largest Indigenous territory. These two antipodean clusters are clearly visible on a map that shows *only* islands: that is, a map that excludes the five continental landmasses of Europe–Asia, North–South America, Africa, Australia, and Antarctica, as well as mainland Greenland (figure 1.5). If the continents still seem to appear on this "islands-only" map, it is only because so many "continental islands" hug long stretches of their coastlines.

These near islands have their destinies imbricated with adjoining mainlands (Starc, 2020a), and that has methodological implications examined in other chapters. Few such islands enjoy any distinct political status, and the closest ones would be connected to their mainlands by means of fixed links: typically, bridges, tunnels, or causeways (Baldacchino, 2007c; Cottrell & Cottrell, 2020). Land reclamation would compromise the island status of those *urban islands* that lie close to growing metropoli (Grydehøj, 2014).

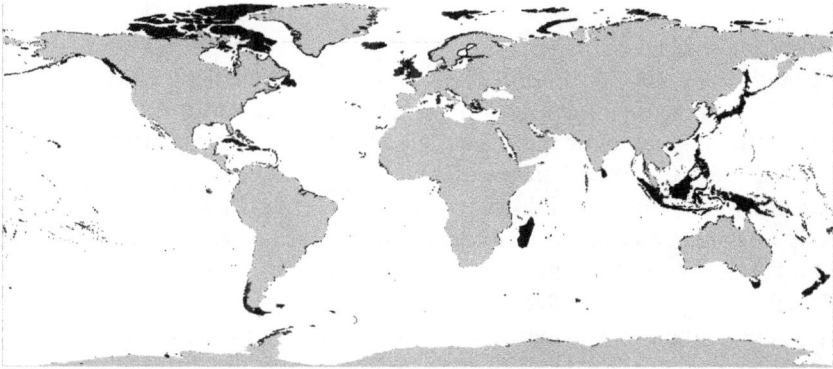

Figure 1.5. Island-only map of the world. *Source*: **Base de données Insulaires Mondiale (BIM, version 3, January 2021, https://doi.org/10.23708/T37S0K). Thanks to Christian Depraetere.**

Otherwise, the map also shows *oceanic islands* located in remote parts of the world's oceans that serve as key hotspots of biodiversity.

DESIDERATA

So far, so good. But how else do we know islands? How do we know how to approach and study them? That question is especially pertinent because none of the aforesaid maps or datasets allude to exemplars such as Atlantis—perhaps "the earliest isle of literary renown" and created by Plato (c. 427–347 BC). Not one of those maps or datasets points to Hippolyte's island, whose existence also remains uncertain (Fischer, 2012; Hodgson, 2001). Not one refers to Amity Island, a seasonal resort town in New York, United States, from the book and film *Jaws* (Benchley, 1974). None considers Neverland, a fictional, remote, and mountainous islet where Peter Pan, Tinker Bell, Captain Hook, the Lost Boys, and other beings live (Barrie, 1911). None deals with Cayo Perico, a heavily fortified Caribbean private island, owned by Juan "El Rubio" Strickler, the Colombian drug trafficker in *Grand Theft Auto Online* (Business Wire, 2020). None alludes to Catan, an imaginary island without islanders in a popular board game, *The settlers of Catan*, where it serves as "an unmitigated colonial fantasy, purified of the violence of invasion" (Fair, 2022, p. 46). None mentions *Coral Island*, the staggeringly successful novel by Robert M. Ballantyne (1857), the stage for a boys' adventure and contrasting utopian antecedent to *Lord of the flies* (Golding, 1954). None refers to Seongapdo, the small, privately owned volcanic island in Korea (excised by Google Maps) that became the set for the enactment of a series of deadly games in the hugely popular 2021 Netflix series, *The squid game* (Johnston, 2021).

Islands invariably turn up in diverse genres that challenge how we think about the real, mythological, and imaginary and that unsettle the crucial power of all of them—not to mention how they bleed into one another (Campbell & Moyers, 1988; Crane & Fletcher, 2017; McMahon 2003). Sometimes, islands are simply convenient backdrops, concocted material frames in which to nest a gripping story, movie, or video game. Recall, islands are not simply a locus but a focus, and in this vein, what gets imbricated in the plot are archetypes of their *islandness*—boundedness by water; relatively small size/scale, insularity, and isolation; remoteness and the impulse to mobility; or singularity and archipelagicity (Baldacchino, 2018a; Farbotko et al., 2016; Olwig, 2007; Ronström, 2013; Stratford et al., 2011a; Vannini et al., 2009). And while these islands may be conjured from the fertile imaginations of novelists, video game software developers, or film producers, the island traits they are gifted with can mirror and correspond to what may transpire on islands in the material world. Indeed, the island's "gradual shift from material denotation to its role in representing more abstract states, is another way that islands and archipelagos are at the heart of modernity's literary structures" (McMahon, 2019, p. 9).

Whether in fact or fiction, islands serve conveniently as high-security prisons; sanctuaries for spiritual observance and catharsis; laboratories for experimentation both useful and macabre; exotic hideouts for the rich, famous, or quirky; hidden refuges for endemic or exogenous species; or blank slates for adventures in unbridled colonialism and the exploitation of Indigenous peoples and natural settings. A theory of island *poiesis* has emerged, with fictive islands joining real islands as emblematic heterotopias and sites of counter-narratives that critically inform diverse metanarratives and practices related to, for example, depopulation, gentrification, globalization, climate change, and the Anthropocene (see Thomas, 2009). As described by one of us:

> Islands (also islets, isles)—paradoxical spaces: absolute entities surrounded by water but not large enough to be a continent, territories, territorial; relational spaces—archipelagos, (inter)dependent, identifiable; relative spaces—bounded but porous; isolated, connected, colonised, postcolonial; redolent of the performative imaginary; vulnerable to linguistic, cultural, environmental change; robust and able to absorb and modify; placed in regions, (part of) nation states and global life; paradisiacal, utopian and dystopian, tourist meccas, ecological refugia; frames within which interdisciplinary scholarship and dialogue can be constituted and deployed. (Stratford, 2003, p. 495)

Thus, there are many reasons to study islands and archipelagos: for what they are in themselves; for what they may tell us about other places; for what they suggest about other, metaphorical islands; and for what they reveal about us or help us constitute in new ways. This appreciation for the study of singular and collective islands is exemplified in significant numbers of new publications, academic titles, journals, conferences, and other activities, driven by educational institutions, nongovernment organizations, and government authorities.

Notwithstanding, we contend that missing so far from all that welcome activity is a text that offers a thoughtful and measured reflection on *how* and *why* islands and archipelagos get studied. Our ambition is that this book will serve as a comprehensive collection of chapters engaged with specific methodological foundations, challenges, strategies, tactics, and opportunities offered by the study of islands, islanders, and island life and by diverse other assemblages that co-constitute them—from mainlands and continents to ocean floors and riverine shores. Here, we hope, is a timely and handy work for those scholars, educators, students, policy makers, and practitioners working on, with, and for islands and their integral human and more-than-human communities.

DISTINCT DIRECTIONS

We now introduce the subject of this book in a more structured manner by deploying work by Edward De Bono, born in Malta, a small island state. His ideas model commitment to methodological diversity in ways that are also reflected in our collective decision to be visible in this book both separately and together. We realize that we will end up with varied results and takes on islands because a commitment to particular perspectives of inquiry will be accompanied by equally particular data, technologies of observation, and apparata of inscription (Latour & Woolgar, 1986).

Hereunder, then, we refer to six hats that represent distinct modes of disciplined thinking as conceived by De Bono (2017). With respect to very small European islands, those thinking hats have already been tested in a popular, applied, and illustrated text entitled *How to read an island*. In that text, Pleijel (2015) starts with facts about islands (white hat thinking) and then adopts first an optimistic view (yellow hat thinking) and then a pessimistic view (black hat thinking). He turns to feelings and values (red hat thinking), then to creativity (green hat thinking), and ends by considering action-orientation (blue hat thinking). Each mode of thinking—each methodology—privileges an aspect of island life, as well as specific approaches, data, information, and knowledge about how to engage with such life.

A similar approach is adopted here as a starting point from which significant developments are made in subsequent chapters. We start with the factual. The *white hat* invites questions such as *how many islands are there*? For such an answer to be feasible we need to establish a minimum size for the category island—and inevitably that results in the construction of subcategories such as islets and rocky outcrops as well as confounding categories such as peninsulas. If, arbitrarily, we were to settle on a rock with a surface area of 0.1 square meter (or 1 square foot), just large enough for a bird or child to sit on, we could mathematically predict 680 billion such micro-islands. We could also mathematically predict some 370,000 islets ranging in size from one to 10 hectares (that is, from 10,000 square meters to 100,000 square meters). These would include Liberty Island in New York Harbor, United States (4.9 hectares or 0.049 square kilometers), Filfla in Malta (6 hectares or 0.06 square kilometers), and Bau Island in Fiji (8 hectares or 0.08 square kilometers). At the other end of the scale, the world's largest islands are assemblages of its continents: Eur–Asia–Africa (although the Suez Canal has notionally cut off Africa since 1867); America (although the Panama Canal has also notionally split this continent since 1914); and Australia. Antarctica and Greenland are mainly thick ice caps; so, (how) should they be counted and what methodological decisions would their inclusion or exclusion reflect? Or, as asked by Jennifer Mason (2018, p. 55), "the act of focusing through sampling is likely to be as strategic as it is practical . . . [and] the work you are asking of your sample is to help you generate the data which you will need to address your research questions." Of course, that observation invites clarity about what to ask, and that involves a sense of optimism about discovery and the research imagination.

De Bono's *yellow hat* signifies ways of knowing and thinking that involve optimism. Those pondering how, why, or indeed whether to rethink island methodologies might, for example, consider (small) islands. They might reflect on the ways in which small islands are viewed as alluring places to visit or escape to, and on which one might deliberately or accidentally succumb to their implicit promises to cleanse body, mind, and soul (Péron, 2004). Little wonder islands are central to contemporary tourism. And little wonder that tendencies in that industry to enroll islands in optimistic capital ventures at several scales also inform island methodology and critique (for instance, Kapstein, 2017). No wonder, too, that in a post-pandemic scenario, small islands are again subject to heightened mobility, attracting new waves of residents seeking the comparative comfort of quarantine or isolated conditions and flexible work arrangements without accounting for what isolation might also signify, not least for children, families, and vulnerable peoples (Agius et al., 2022; Freeman et al., 2021; Tsavdaroglou & Kaika, 2022).

How to study such dynamics both in real time and over time? How to design methodological approaches that perhaps both consider and, optimistically, seek to advocate for novel approaches to working from home while supporting families in safe and attractive locations yet remaining in global networks and high-paying jobs? Or how to provide innovative research methodologies to creatively support small island states as they design attractive visa schemes for those who may wish to work remotely and may not require jobs on islands where they relocate. From Ireland to Croatia, after many decades of population decline, there is evidence that "splendid isolation" may provide a renaissance to island living (Baldacchino & Starc, 2021). Among other optimistic outcomes involved in rethinking distance, both before and after the pandemic, are notable initiatives in reducing island carbon footprints and expanding island marine protected areas, showcasing themselves as beacons of sustainability (Fabinyi, 2008; Vourdoubas, 2021). Arguably, all such efforts implicate ways of thinking about how to do island studies—explicitly because they are founded in research and implicitly because they change how we understand island places and peoples.

In sharp contrast, *black hat* thinking might be used to expose the dark underbelly of island life and invites careful consideration of how (and indeed why) its trauma-scapes might be studied. Although Gail Adams-Hutcheson's (2017) work is on the trauma geographies of the skin, she aptly points out that trauma is always spatialized—always bounded, contained, and yet leaking. So how to design methodological approaches to consider the ways in which islands and islanders have long been subjected to deep distress? Formal and populist literatures, film and television, art, and music—all these and more are replete with dystopian narratives of things gone horribly wrong: islands become settings for our descent into violence, malevolence, treachery, and deceit (McMillan, 2019; Perera & Pugliese, 2021). Those settings are not simply fictional and on islands there are many instances of corruption, abuse, and codes to silence that render truth claims absent from prevailing cultural scripts (Fletcher, 2008; see Schröter & Taylor (2018) on methodological aspects of studying silence and absence).

To the credit of small island developing states, gripping contemporary narratives of small (and especially low-lying coralline) islands also concern the impact of climate change, global warming, and sea level rise (Richardson, 2018). For atoll states and other small island territories the future seems bleak: on the basis of current greenhouse gas emission rates, many islands may become uninhabitable because of frequent damage to their coastal infrastructure and the inability of their freshwater aquifers to recover between overwash events driven by sea waves (Storlazzi et al., 2018). Either way, at least two questions remain. First, how to study such contexts in ways that do not reduce island to backdrop or some kind of environmentally deterministic effect? Second, in a world characterized by increasing pandemic risks, how to uphold a defining method in many, though not all, studies of island and archipelagos—namely, the value of field work (Reed, 2021)?

De Bono's *red hat* invites people to provide emotional maps of island life. A sound place to start is with the rich and deep feelings that are engendered about being an islander, feeling bounded and protected, yet threatened by surrounding waters that offer not only sustenance but also danger. It is impossible to ignore water's awesome power and the ways in which it shapes island identity and character—including in lacustrine or riverine contexts (Baruah, 2022; Hay, 2013; Kane, 2018). In some such instances, it is hard to avoid island-mainland juxtapositions, which may lead to invocations of island essentialism and proto-ethnic sentiments that, when heightened, can evolve into secessionist or independence movements (Hepburn & Baldacchino, 2013).

For one exemplar with a raw emotional outburst, consider Alistair MacLeod's essay *The return*, a vivid rendition of one islander's view of Cape Breton, Canada. In this extract, witness his returning "from away" to his island home:

> It is an evening during the summer that I am ten years old, and I am on a train with my parents as it rushes towards the end of Eastern Nova Scotia. "You'll be able to see it any minute now, Alex," says my father excitedly, "look out the window, any minute now" . . . "There it is," shouts my father triumphantly. "Look Alex, there's Cape Breton!" He takes his left hand down from the baggage rack and points across us to the blueness that is the Strait of Canso, with the gulls hanging almost stationary above the tiny fishing boats and the dark green of the spruce and fir mountains rising out of the water and trailing white wisps of mist about them like discarded ribbons hanging about a newly opened package. (MacLeod, 1989, pp. 72–73)

Strong and vivid emotions can surface when dealing with critical social distinctions in island communities such that between those born onshore and those who arrive. "Natives" may have a sense of entitlement and assumed privilege based on prior claims; "settlers" may come across as iconoclasts, too eager to push alien agendas framed in contexts that do not resonate with island places or peoples (Baldacchino, 2012b; Houbert, 1985; Marshall, 2008). In some instances, such tensions sometimes seem powerfully and extensively to inscribe complete sociospatial milieux. In Australia, for example, they typify aggressions that span from beaches at Cronulla in Sydney (Perera, 2009) to the borderscapes of the entire nation (Stratford et al., 2011b) to contested ideas about what is insular and what is continental in the national imaginary (McMahon, 2010). A challenge remains finding research methodologies that enable emplaced, displaced, or mobile island emotions and affects while not obscuring difference. Rather, we should allow and encourage ourselves to be "drawn into thinking about other people's constructions of place, other people's ways of reading their cultural landscapes—even when they are in the landscapes that we live in ourselves" (Howitt & Stevens, 2005, p. 41). Creating new research methodologies is more testing, but possible, with innovations evident in "linear models, mixed methods, systems frameworks, machine learning, and new approaches to fieldwork" (Druckman & Donahue, 2020, p. 16).

As it happens, innovation is central to *green hat thinking* as framed by De Bono. Those living on islands wear many hats—in the sense of needing to take on several roles or innovate—and arguably this trend is most pronounced in small islands or islands with small populations. Through the life course, that need to experiment, fail, experiment, and succeed, continuously and simultaneously, is often peppered by juggling stints both at home and abroad. Often, when islanders have been away and can return home, they do (Easthope & Gabriel, 2008); when they cannot, what can island methodologies contribute to supporting opportunities for ongoing connection? And how can residents who "blow in" from mainlands make meaningful contributions to island life in ways that avoid the aforesaid traps of iconoclasm? In at least one case, Kangaroo Island, in South Australia, two "blow-in" academics have taken up that challenge. Focusing on ecological, educational, and historical projects of benefit to their island community, they used "journaling and record keeping, observation, social networking, narrative and art, interviews, documentary analysis, and more" to share insights about islanders with islanders (Teasdale & Teasdale, 2022, n.p.).

Likewise, as if they were surfers of high ocean waves, islanders nurture skill sets and mechanisms that allow them strategically to exploit the benefits, and/or minimize the losses, of episodic economic lurches (Baldacchino, 2011b). Some act as norm entrepreneurs, promoting new ways of doing old things; they can defy, escape, or circumvent convention often on the basis of size (Prasad, 2004). Some act as social entrepreneurs (Island Innovation, 2022) and seek cutting-edge approaches to island challenges and opportunities. That search invites appropriate *island* methodologies and infrastructures if ideas are to move from the drawing board to actualization. After all, when one is on the edge, where mainstream ideas, orthodoxies, and paradigms may be faint, the ground is laid for fueling alternatives to the status quo (Baldacchino, 2007b).

At the same time, innovation in island places is often conceptualized in terms of lack, and that, too, needs to be unsettled in methodological approaches to creative endeavors. For example, To et al. (2021, p. 1100) write of innovation agendas for energy resilience in Pacific Island Countries and Territories (PICTs) in what seem to be deficit terms:

> The lack of data and modelling tools for planning has been identified by stakeholders as a key barrier to improved planning . . . while the changing dynamics of both challenges and possible options for delivering energy services require

process-driven planning trajectories, not one-off plans. This requires research and innovation for improving field data, demand modelling and planning tools for energy.

But to be fair, they also then explore what a strength-based alterative might look like:

> PICTs have unique strengths in tackling the challenges of energy resilience. With excellent renewable energy resources and a strong fiscal motivation to reduce reliance on imported fossil fuels, PICTs have already made energy resilience and sustainable energy a core part of their policy agenda. Existing regional organizations can help to further coordinate efforts, and communities have existing customs, practices and local knowledge that can enhance resilience in the energy sector. (p. 1102)

So, what is asked of researchers in methodological terms for more such strength-based and solutions-focused language to typify our work? How can we account for "affect, hope and inventive methodologies" that enrich both the present and consideration of the future (Coleman, 2017, p. 525)? Such questions are crucial because, in the words of former UN Secretary-General Kofi Annan, islands are "front line zones" where many problems associated with the environment and development are unfolding and unraveling (United Nations, 1999). They are also spaces in which innovations—not least in the use of networks and assemblages—are in evidence, including, for example, in relation to organic farming in the Pacific (Carter & Hollinsworth, 2022) or health responses to COVID-19 in Aotearoa/New Zealand (Kearns, 2021).

Islands are spaces we need to think *with* (Gillis, 2012): they are the iconic and emblematic spaces of the Anthropocene, central tropes where entanglements between the human and more-than-human come to the fore, and where their consequences are most starkly exposed (Chandler & Pugh, 2020a, 2020b; DeLoughrey, 2019a). Thinking is a form of action; hence, we end with De Bono's *blue hat*, which invites ongoing labors to engage in methodological refinements that lead to tangible outcomes—changed views, new approaches, novel insights, reconfigured and original practices. At the same time, caution is warranted in relation to arguments about research impact and the diverse politics that inform them. Nevertheless, research with demonstrable (positive) impacts is crucial, not least in the field where "it is not a foregone conclusion that working on islands has a decided edge" (Terrell, 2020, p. 1).

Either way—but not without dilemmas—islanders are rising to multiple challenges of climate change, proposing decarbonized futures by sunsetting coal- and oil-based energy systems, and replacing them by clean sustainable ones based on renewables that draw from geothermal, wind, tide, and solar power (Kallis et al., 2021). Island states and territories have unilaterally carved out huge tracts of ocean as marine protected areas, minimizing commercial activity and extending a lifeline to marine species threatened by extinction from overfishing. Small island developing states have worked to press the international community to be bolder in its climate action targets. They succeeded in securing a reference to a mean temperature rise of 1.5°C beyond preindustrial levels as an aspirational upper goal in the final document of the UNFCCC Paris Summit in 2015 (Benjamin & Thomas, 2016). But by COP 26, Jackson (2021) was reporting that Pacific delegates had condemned the meeting as a monumental failure, leaving their islands and people in peril; COP27 has made only minor gains, and failed many. It seems possible to ignore islanders even though one in every 10 people lives on an island and one in every five countries is an island or an archipelago—and that enumeration may not fully account for all those living on subnational island jurisdictions of large continental nations, such as the United States (Stratford, 2017). Hence the need for action—and that also means acting to innovate in methodological approach and especially in ways of being in relation.

So, when all these points are considered, the burning question to ask is perhaps not why do people study islands at all but, rather, why is there so *little* focus on islands, given their ubiquity and their significant presence in the world's community of states? And, for our purpose, an equal and perhaps more important question is: why is there so little explicit focus on debating whether, how, to what extent, and with what effects *island methodologies* are possible? The balance of this book seeks to address those very questions.

Chapter 2

Valuing

Why Should We Study Islands and Archipelagos?

Godfrey Baldacchino

Axiology: The theory of value. (OED)
To rethink island methodologies is to rethink the
value of studying islands and archipelagos. What
is gained by labors to consider islands from diverse
disciplinary perspectives. In short, why bother?

One could start this chapter by declaring the obvious: we should study islands and their assemblages
because they are there. Period. The disarmingly
simple and stock definition of an *island* as a piece
of land surrounded by water, larger than a rock,
but smaller than a continent, which remains visible
even at high tide, makes the task of justification
sound even more ridiculous and useless. Not so.
The challenge is real and should not carelessly be
dismissed. One comes across statements where it is
emphatically declared that there are islands everywhere or that the characteristics attributed to pieces
of land surrounded by water can be validly and
profitably extended to other enisled objects, societies, or circumstances. Think of city ghettos, oases
in a desert, taiga surrounded by tundra, mountain
top communities, even exoplanets. Then, there are
statements provocatively arguing that a profound
remapping and a reconceptualization are necessary: the planet's only real "islands" are its tectonic
plates, shifting and colliding over geological time

Source: Jean-Yves Vigneau.

21

(Okihiro, 2010). Still other statements suggest that *only islanders*—a category that may itself be just as hard to pin down—can and should legitimately pursue the study of islands (Hay, 2006). Some contend that islands do not constitute a legitimate field of scholarly inquiry, in which case island studies would be yet another example of the "illegitimate extension of biological categories to social relationships" (Selwyn, 1980, p. 950).

These respectively maximalist and minimalist views need to be recognized. So should other positions between them. Conventions and other legal texts may clearly define what an island is or is *not*, because formally acknowledged status may confer particular advantages or condone preferential treatments. Consider the definition of an "island" applied by EuroStat (2021), the statistical agency of the European Union, and which excludes those islands connected by fixed links to mainlands:

> Islands are territories having (a) a minimum land surface area of 1 km²; (b) a minimum distance between the island and the mainland of 1 km; (c) a permanent resident population of at least 50 inhabitants; and (d) no fixed link—for example, a bridge, a tunnel, or a causeway/dyke—between the island and the mainland.

There is also a definition of islands applied by the United Nations Convention on the Law of the Sea (UNCLOS), which, since 1994, allows coastal and island governments to claim a territorial sea, a contiguous zone, an exclusive economic zone, and a continental shelf (United Nations, 2021):

1. An island is a naturally formed area of land, surrounded by water, which is above water at high tide.
2. Except as provided for in paragraph 3, the territorial sea, the contiguous zone, the exclusive economic zone, and the continental shelf of an island are determined in accordance with the provisions of this convention applicable to other land territory.
3. Rocks that cannot sustain human habitation or economic life of their own shall have no exclusive economic zone or continental shelf.

These are some of the definitional nuances concerning islands; there are others. Each has adherents and detractors. The arguments used to buttress or vilify them may be fielded in many settings where island studies is considered. (Those embarking on island studies topics ought to prepare themselves to face, parry with, and handle such perspectives when they arise as respectful, if pointed questions during conference paper presentations.) In and of themselves, these positions represent the expansive epistemological minefield that bedevils the study of islands, and which we hope to grapple with here.

MAKING A CASE FOR THE VALUE OF ISLAND STUDIES

In 2001, the University of Prince Edward Island (UPEI) in Canada's smallest province short-listed my application for one of its five new Canada Research Chairs, when the Chrétien's federal government decided to finance 2,000 such prestigious positions across the country (Government of Canada, 2021). I was recruited after UPEI agreed to dedicate one chair to island studies—a burgeoning field, as I then described it and, later, a world of islands (Baldacchino, 2007a).

Over two decades later, I can safely admit that this phrase was camouflage for a high-risk but high-returns adventure. And academic members of the Social Sciences and Humanities Research Council adjudicating UPEI's bid were probably aware of that. One senior academic on the reviewing panel was indeed skeptical and not readily convinced of the merit of the proposal. Some conversations later, the proposal was accepted. But it was clear that broader recognition of island studies as a legitimate field of scholarly inquiry would be one of my main objectives as the new Canada Research Chair in island studies.

Today, island studies has its fair share of regular conferences, handbooks, textbooks, professorial chair appointments, and journals. Explicit courses and seminars in island studies and archipelagic studies have been and continue to be offered at undergraduate and postgraduate levels in higher education institutions around the world. Some of them are strengthened by deliberate, careful connection to processes to Indigenize and decolonize the curriculum (McLennan et al., 2022; Williams et al., 2022). But such was not the case 20 years ago. And, given the extent to which island studies features in curricula, it is still impossible to consider the field as mainstream. Two decades ago, it was equally self-evident that, even though islands were *there*, and found all over the planet, their systematic study was scant, a marginal pursuit, without a proper pedigree or champions. After all, is undertaking island research a euphemism when, islands "equate holidays, relaxation and having a nice time; not serious scholarship" (King, 2009, p. 55, tongue-in-cheek)?

It is for similar reasons that, in the inaugural issue of *Island Studies Journal* in May 2006, the editorial introduction was a *cri de coeur* and a passionate appeal for people to accept the valid and valuable pursuit of island studies (Baldacchino, 2006a). It is worth reflecting on the dot-point list that appeared in that introduction of what is now the flagship journal in the field, and which comprised the rationale and *apologia* for the study of islands. Note that practically all the statements below are factual and couched in scientific and positivist terms. They were written because they were deemed important to make the reader aware of the significant role that islands, and their island-ers, should play by their sheer quantity, their vital contributions to multiple disciplines and fields of inquiry, and by a possible, special island effect that begged further research. To be honest, this rationalist approach was insight-fully critiqued at that time for failing to appreciate the just-as-powerful role that islands play in literature and fiction (Fletcher, 2011), not least in the book series of which this volume is a part.

To the content of the original list, which is here updated: In 2006, there were 550 million people living on islands: around 10% of the world's total population; now there may be as many as 730 million. Around 180,000 islands occupied under 2% of the Earth's surface area, but 106 of 812 UNESCO's World Heritage Sites were on islands or else are islands *in toto* (see UNESCO, 2022). At least 43 (22%) of the world's sovereign states were exclusively island states; and many states have one or more island regions or subnational jurisdictions (CIA, 2021). In 2006, it was also noted that many former colonies have rejected political independence outright (Baldacchino, 2006b; Bonner, 2006; Watts, 2000). Innovative forms of sovereignty have characterized island geopolitics and those arrangements on small islands in particular. Many innovative forms of environmental management have involved or been based on islands (Crosby, 1986; Grove, 1995; Landes, 1998): their separateness, distinctiveness, and more manageable size render islands obvious starting points for designing sustainable ecotourism pro-grams via biosphere reserves, national parks, and other diversity-rich areas (Di Castri & Balaji, 2002). Likewise, islands as diverse as Iceland, Mafia, Pingelap, and Tristan da Cunha, feature prominently in epidemiological research. Advances in evolutionary biology, ecology, and biogeography have been founded on pioneering field research on islands with high levels of endemism—and many examples of gigantism and dwarfism—and of extinc-tion (Carlquist, 1974). Indeed, the "incidence of endangered or extinct spe-cies is greater on islands than on continents. More endemic species have been created on islands, but more have perished there" (Young, 1999, p. 253).

Anthropologists and cultural geographers have also been drawn to island settings. Forays by Alfred Radcliffe-Brown (1922) in the Andaman Islands, Bronisław Malinowski (1922) among the Trobriand (or Kiriwina) Islanders of Papua New Guinea, Margaret Mead (1928/2001; 1934/2002) in Samoa and the Admiralty Islands, and Raymond Firth (1936/1983) in Tikopia led to the birth of ethnography and social anthropology's consolidation as a dis-crete social science with its own methodological rigor (Baldacchino, 2004; DeLoughrey, 2001). Social network theory has developed from research contexts afforded by small island environments (Barnes, 1954; Boissevain, 1974). Islands are platforms for the emergence of national identity and/or affirmation of cultural specificities: these are crucial resources in the face of globalization and threats to local cultures and languages, and they foreground the special qualities of locality (Appadurai, 1996; Mühlhäusler & Stratford, 1999). Islands or island archipelagos with small populations have been among those with the highest gross national income per capita levels of conventionally estimated economic development (The Economist, 2003; The World Bank, 2020).

NOT-SO-MAINSTREAM ISLAND STUDIES

All the observations I made in 2006, listed and updated above, remain relevant. New items can be added to them: accelerated interest in artificial islands (Alessio & Renfro, 2021; Mawyer, 2021); ideas about COVID-free islands or islands as COVID carceral spaces (Connell, 2021; Tsavdaroglou & Kaika, 2022); and ideas about islands as emblematic geographies of hope in the face of climate change or pandemics (Farbotko et al., 2018; Ratuva, 2021). Either way, the question remains: given such a powerful clutch of justifications, why is island studies still not yet as mainstream a pursuit as some might think it should be? Why, in axiological or value terms, does it remain at the periphery? As Ginoza et al. (2020) ask, how can a critical island studies flourish?

Explanations about value I

Overall, two sets of axiological explanations are moot. The first set is *ontological* insofar as engaging with questions of being is sometimes underplayed or undervalued in the social sciences. In sociology, and thanks especially to radical feminist scholarship, the long obsession with the analytic primacy of social class has been lambasted as one that systematically privileges white males in place-specific industrial economies. That said, when one's best example of manufacturing capacity is a local brewery (Baldacchino, 2010a), those on small islands can find it hard to fit in with expectations implicit in such classical sociological tenets. Geographical theories of space and place have displaced the primacy and legitimacy of rational scientific doctrines about space as a "container" and the world as a given, stand-alone, and externalized reality—and replaced them with relational and subjectivist renditions of space as reflexively constituted via embodied interactions (Heath, 2000). In those renditions, space is socially and experientially established; it exists and takes on meaning as a result of the actions and interactions of varied human and more-than-human actors. Thus, places have shifted away from being (conceived as) features and backdrops in dwellers' narratives to becoming narratives in their own right (Rodman, 1992) or, as Charles Withers (2011) would have it, they have become subject to spatial modes of thinking—geographies—that involve writing and reading; mapping and depicting; exploring and trusting; experimenting; and gesturing and conversing.

Such shifts in how and what is valued arguably were necessary to foreground the vital role of subjects in shaping their world via its interpretation. Moreover, and helpfully, they were also debunking much older, uncorroborated, and pseudo-scientific interpretations of how, deterministically, environmental features even "caused" certain behavioral traits, leading to *a priori* predictions of the presumed qualities of islanders (Brunhes, 1920; Semple, 1911). The same can perhaps be said today of the assumption that small island folk are hardy, resilient, and adaptable. A corollary is that islanders can therefore be expected to cope with the impact of climate change, including sea level rise and land-based changes, can avoid the need for emigration, or comprise happy and harmonious communities (Argent, 2021; Baldacchino, 2012b; Srebrnik, 2004). Glib and simplistic classificatory premises at the heart of many arguments in the social sciences are to be rejected (Barth, 1969).

Some adherents to a post-material turn have dismissed the potential benefits of critically understanding how material spaces and places—including islands—can somehow contour or influence human behavior, or their perception, or both. The business of lived spatiality became a significant *problématique* in academia at a time when area studies was emerging from a deep epistemological slumber (Goss & Wesley-Smith, 2010). And also palpable for some time now are (re)turns to materialist and other concerns related to hybrid geographies, "naturecultures," and object-oriented ontologies that also inform island thinking (Jackson, 2013; Pugh, 2020; Whatmore, 2006). Welcome are both a return to and reengagement with the realm of the material as comprising "narratives of lived practice and engagement" (Anderson & Wylie, 2009, p. 325; see also Arnall, 2022). Thus, we must acknowledge that there is a keen "awhereness" in play everywhere (Thrift, 2011, p. 9). Context matters. Things take place and they do so on the move—including for academics seeking to connect worlds of ideas and islands. As Mimi Sheller (2022, pp. 53–54) reflects:

> As I sit here at my home in Philadelphia on a rainy day, nine months into the pandemic (during which I have mostly not travelled at all), my Facebook page keeps sending me photos of "memories" that I posted long ago . . . here I am on a beautiful turquoise shore on Rottnest Island, off Perth, Australia, in 2017. These travel memories (all arising from academic work-related trips) precipitate from "the cloud" as reminders of a time before COVID-19 halted travel. But

they are also reminders of what seems like a past age of academic travel. If reducing CO_2 emissions in the face of climate change were not enough to get academics to reduce their mobility, perhaps these grim epidemiological and economic realities will force change upon us. As we look towards institutions of higher education facing constrained budgets, cutbacks on research funding and staff reductions, will we hold onto the necessity to limit academic travel?

Admittedly, then, the status of place in a globalizing world where there is no rest needs to be carefully critiqued. So, any work presenting an island as (just) a steadfast piece of land is a trick of a limited temporality and a slight fueled by a place-based and romanced nationalism. There is a stubborn, visceral materiality in what we do (Baldacchino, 2010b; Baldacchino & Clark, 2013).

Explanations about value II

The second set of axiological explanations is *epistemological*. If islandness is about knowing the nature of being (on) an island, relieved of any emotional or moral baggage, then privileging it would distract academics, students, and policy makers from what are presumably more powerful, better established, and more significant explanatory variables. Instead of seeing the world through particular lenses—some of which would have stood the test of time, amassed their own literary corpus, or developed their own theories and observational methods—the suggestion is that much can be made instead from the fertile and creative space of an island imagination (Baldacchino, 2018a; Gillis, 2004; Marland, 2022). New fields of study—island and archipelagic studies, specifically—are not going to find an easy path—and that is all the more so when considered in light of two critical dimensions in Caribbean and Pacific scholarship in particular. These two regions are important, because they are home to the world's largest assemblages of sovereign small island states and subnational island jurisdictions.

Especially in Anglophone, but also Francophone jurisdictions, the dominant academic discourse in the Caribbean has been driven by a structuralist-radical interpretation of the social order, where race and class are salient categories. The almost total eradication of Indigenous peoples, the atrocious and violent impact of colonialism, a long history of slavery, the struggle for political emancipation, and postcolonial social inequalities that are almost aligned on race and ethnic lines: all that has brought about a hegemonic assessment of the social, economic, and political situation of the region in such stark terms.

The University of the West Indies (UWI) has been, and remains by far, the largest higher education institution in the English-speaking Caribbean, and a long shadow has been cast by academics in social science and political science departments on its main campuses—Mona in Jamaica; St. Augustine in Trinidad & Tobago; and Cave Hill in Barbados. Their value sets and ideas continue to dominate and frame social science debates in racial and postcolonial terms; and their narratives have been disseminated through and by the many graduates who have passed through their classrooms and ended up in senior government positions, among the political class, or as the next generation of academics. A sense of reparatory justice continues to pervade the region: in recent times, the UWI vice-chancellor leads a lobby urging the United Kingdom and Europe to "take responsibility for the living legacies of slavery and colonisation" (Caricom Today, 2020, n.p.). In the face of this position, island studies can come across as a ploy to deflect attention from what is fundamental, to neuter or depoliticize social science in the region, and to devalue the region in axiological terms. Moreover, islands in the Caribbean tend to align as separate and distinct sovereign states—the first being Jamaica, which secured independence in 1960—and as nonsovereign but autonomous territories that are products of European colonialism. And many Caribbean academics shy away from an island studies approach grounded in a fragmentation they denounce as a colonial legacy—but noting some exceptions (for example, Benítez-Rojo, 1996; Lewis, 1974).

The situation is different in the Pacific. The islands in the world's largest ocean were in the last major theater to experience the late advance of European colonial imperialism. There were two significant and interrelated consequences of this: the impact appeared to be less tragic than in the Caribbean; Indigenous peoples were decimated, mainly by disease, but were not summarily extirpated (Fischer, 2013). Consequently, the colonial experience was not just shorter in time by about a half that in the Caribbean; it also witnessed an enduring juxtaposition of colonial and Indigenous systems. By the time these former imperial territories gained independence—starting with Western Samoa, now Samoa, in 1962—South Pacific Indigenous peoples were being prepared to take control of senior government, teach at campuses of the University of the South Pacific (USP), and set up and run their own national universities and governments along hybrid or traditional lines. For decades, a "native versus settler" binarism has gripped the region's political discourse and was mainstream in the region's three, late-arriving, colonial administrators: Australia, Aotearoa/New Zealand, and the United States. But this binarism now appears to be changing: a steady stream of decolonial thinking and writing, and associated research methodologies, is routinely resisting the former mainstream discourse—even if the reframing is, so far, largely rhetorical (Howitt, 2022; Nadarajah & Grydehøj, 2016). Again, in the Pacific, island studies seems not to register; is sometimes deemed to promote a belittling, colonial mindset; and is critiqued for downplaying Pacific islanders' vision of themselves as proud citizens of an exceptionally large Oceania, where land and water are imbricated as one (Hau'ofa, 1998). Island studies now mainly thrives in this region when it becomes a channel and repository to articulate and appeal for Indigenous and climate justice (Farbotko et al., 2018).

Echoing I-Kiribati poet and scholar Teresia Teaiwa (2014), one cannot and should not paint either the Caribbean or the Pacific with the same, broad brush (Husband, 2015). And those in island studies must also acknowledge and value the rich diversity of and among islands and island peoples and the myriad ways in which islands' and islanders' connections to their surrounding waters play out. Nevertheless, we should agree that the "isolation-connection" or "roots/routes" nexus is a critical feature when studying islands (Bonnemaison, 1994; DeLoughrey, 2009). As sketched in *Omeros*, Derek Walcott's (2014) dramatic epic, an island's geography speaks isolation and insularity, but the sea speaks contact.

WHAT TO VALUE AND INCLUDE?

The coming of age of island studies thrust islands into new debates (Baldacchino, 2004). Those debates and consequential writing and discussion have provided new justifications for the study of islands and introduced a new range of diverse professionals into the nissological mix (McCall, 1996), among them climatologists, structural engineers, architectural designers, and brand developers. Below, I focus on six debates to ponder their value propositions and my own thinking on certain of their methodological challenges. The list is by no means exhaustive; rather, it is illustrative and invites the reader to consider other debates and consciously reflect on the value propositions that undergird them.

First are debates about the inclusion of artificial islands as a basic category of island typologies (see Randall, 2021). In the current age of so-called technological solutionism, what had historically been a state of nature can now be conceived as a puzzle to be solved or an ambitious but doable engineering project ripe for funding (Morozov, 2013). Roads are ascendant as a dominant infrastructure of transportation, and artificial or constructed islands are a "getaway" flipside to the urge to connect via the sorts of fixed links noted earlier, bridges perhaps most obvious among them (figure 2.1). Connectivity to islands that accompanied and, in turn, has been facilitated by globalization has also made a modern virtue of the search for isolation. And where no such islands already exist in desirable locations, then they can be built. Hence the international airports in Osaka, Japan (KIX), and Hong Kong, China (HKG). Or various anxious spaces and cultural icons on constructed islands in Dubai (Jackson & Della Dora, 2009). Or work pumping sand onto

Figure 2.1.   Isle of Skye Bridge. *Source*: Wikimedia Commons | Macieklew.

coral reefs by the Chinese to build artificial islands in the South China Sea (Alessio & Renfro, 2021) or to expand the Belt and Road approach to Pacific geoeconomics (Szadziewski, 2021). How do research methodologies that are grounded in diverse, sometimes divergent ideas about space and place contend with, adapt to, and take on board such artificial and engineered island constructions?

Second are debates about tourism. Prior to the coronavirus pandemic, international tourism numbers had continued to grow, and their "personality" had morphed beyond the basic "triple S" or sun, sea, and sand model into various market niches, including in relation to diving and cruise-ship products. Islands continue to be "discovered" and advertised as the latest paradises to explore and continue to be subjected to sudden spurts of tourist visitations that exacerbate concern among local publics, leading to appeals against overtourism and calls for a more sustainable industry. After all, the smaller the island, the stronger and deeper the impact of a tourism spike and the stronger and deeper tourism's economic, but also environmental, effects (Dodds & Butler, 2019; Moscovici, 2017). The specificities of island and archipelago tourism are increasingly recognized and critiqued (Baldacchino, 2012a, 2016a; Carlsen & Butler, 2011). Island branding is a recognized branch of place branding that has its work cut out (Baldacchino & Khamis, 2018; Grydehøj, 2008). Those involved in studying island tourism must grapple in axiological and not simply empirical terms with the specificities of any island under study, including its finite entry and exit points, transport monopolies, and the typical absence of economies of scale. Certainly, any excitement of visiting a (relatively and allegedly underexplored) island may have been overtaken—probably temporarily—by a search for safe and secure holiday spaces in the post-pandemic age. The middle classes, with money to spare and desperate to finally head out somewhere on vacation, nevertheless remain concerned about health and security issues for themselves and their families. No wonder then that this pent-up but conditional demand has been met by attempts to capitalize on and by particular island spaces: from the quasi-private island of Mustique, in St Vincent and the Grenadines, to "Covid-free" islands in Greece and Italy—or a whole island for yourself in the Maldives. Are we back to the alluring iconography of the island paradise, refreshed and reframed post-pandemic, and what new island methodologies are invited by that possibility?

Third are debates about a reverse phenomenon whereby some island states and territories have locked themselves down to avoid the pandemic—not just to tourists but also to undocumented migrants and asylum claimants. Some of the latter were held on quarantine ships (or floating islands) (Baldacchino, 2021a). So, too, various enforcement archipelagos (Mountz, 2011) have been configured in recent years, with island bases or entire islands excised from national territories to park undocumented migrants, sometimes indefinitely. Research methodologies need to be sensitive to such and similar practices of differentiated access that operate along "axes of structural inequality" (Simpson, 2020, n.p.)—notably class, race, gender, and citizenship—and shield some while exposing others to bodily harm, trauma, and even death.

Fourth are debates about public and public–private engagements on islands. Think of aid donors, who have followed scientists and rushed to small islands because there they can see rapid results of projects and whose effects can also be contained should they go awry. Think of work in the nineteenth century in the Galápagos (part of modern-day Ecuador) by Charles Darwin (1809–1882) and in the Aru Islands (part of modern-day Indonesia) by Alfred Russel Wallace (1823–1913) and in the twentieth century on nuclear experiments in Bikini, Eniwetok, and Mururoa: all have been followed in the twenty-first century by a plethora of green initiatives that grab media headlines while requiring relatively low amounts of funding. They also engender their own versions of island tourism, because they often lead to pilgrims and neophytes mobilizing to see what is going on and determining what good practices can be copied and adapted elsewhere. Posterchildren of island sustainability include: Samsø in Denmark and El Hierro in Spain, as pioneer renewable energy island jurisdictions (Iglesias & Carballo, 2011; Sperling, 2017), and Astypalea in Greece, as an island targeted for the exclusive use of 100% electric vehicles (Reichenbach, 2020). There are also both small island states that—following UNCLOS—are effectively large ocean states and sub-national island jurisdictions that have enacted large marine protected areas (MPAs) within the huge expanses of ocean within their jurisdiction (Chan, 2018). These initiatives are commendable in principle. However, they have been criticized for putting publicity and quick results ahead of sustainability considerations; for marginalizing fishers from local Indigenous and coastal communities; for disregarding how powerful nongovernment organizations threaten to effectively take over monitoring and running of MPAs, especially where small island developing states (SIDS) are involved; and for neglecting the reality that the cost *per capita* of such projects is actually often higher on small islands than in other, larger places (Grydehøj & Kelman, 2017).

Fifth are debates about the idea of islands as microcosms, "canaries in the coal mine" and geographical harbingers of hope (or despair), which are easy to peddle and hard to resist. The fallacy of regarding islands as small-scale models of the wider world has a long pedigree. Jean Brunhes (1920, p. 499) has argued that islands are comprehensive "little worlds of humanity" that would lead the way in regional studies, eventually leading to larger-scale studies of less-definable mainland territories. But Harold Brookfield (1990, p. 31) has countered: "the common trap with island studies [is] of assuming that all islands are in some way a microcosm of the larger world. They are not." Today, it is easier to understand and argue that a policy decision and implementation in a small jurisdiction is not simply a scaled-down version of what happens in larger places because of idiosyncrasies associated with small size and scale (see Briguglio et al., 2020). A small-scale syndrome, charac-teristic of small islands, speaks to the ubiquity of government and politics; the stifling social intimacy and low thresholds of privacy; and the disposition toward natural monopolies or oligopolies in the economic sphere (Baldac-chino, 1997). In methodological terms, how exactly does one plausibly "scale up" small island research and its outcomes to meet the ambitions and goals of those interested in larger places? And is such a valid extrapolation at all possible?

Sixth are debates about what has perhaps been the greatest policy impact of and by islands in recent years achieved by a small but powerful subset: that of small island states. Their hallmark has been a steadfast lobbying in favor of a future for SIDS, and particularly those whose very survival is compromised by even modest sea level rise, one of the visible consequences of climate change and global warming. The SIDS caucus at the UN General Assembly has been vocal and organized; and the sustained efforts of the Alliance of Small Island States (AOSIS) has led to the agreement by the international community that mean temperatures on Earth should not just fall short of 2°C above preindustrial levels—but ideally not even above 1.5°C. The Paris Climate Summit of 2015 codified this (Carter, 2020). (At the time of writing, these mean temperatures have already risen by 1.2°C.) Measures toward climate change adaptation or mitigation now constitute a significant component of bilateral or multilateral aid addressed to SIDS, even as global aid finance levels have been in decline. Small island states have danced to this modern tune—even if climate change issues are not necessarily their policy priorities (Baldacchino, 2018b). The methodological implications here are becoming quite clear: international organizations neglect the concerns of small island states at their peril. Indeed, the very legitimacy of their operations may increasingly depend on acknowledging and addressing the concerns of this constituency that seems to have found its voice on the global stage (Corbett et al., 2021).

By way of closure, in a recent paper, Nadarajah et al. (2022, p. 7) have argued:

> Island studies risks producing knowledge that has little or no connection to how people living on or relating to islands experience their worlds—or that takes for granted a few distinct modes of island life and reproduces these in diverse contexts. It risks performing research that is irrelevant and (not always, but often) inaccessible, disconnected, and meaningless. Such island studies scholarship is likely to be nonreciprocal, abstracted; a piece of writing that turns on itself to seek its reviews and justifications.

The values and value judgments that drive island studies cannot be taken for granted. They are often held and pedaled by scholars in well-funded Western universities. Island methodologies are called upon to expose the "social situatedness of knowledge production and the different realities that are produced and experienced" as a result (Nadarajah et al., 2022, p. 4). The burgeoning sites of inquiry that island studies is now engaging with—including border studies, civil engineering, climate action, quarantine stations, and excised spaces—need to be complemented by a wider resort to critical and decolonial reflexivity. The production of knowledge in island studies, as with all areas of knowledge, is not only useful but also virtuous when the positioning of the researcher is known and humbly embraced.

Chapter 3

Being

What Is the Nature of Islands and Archipelagos as Entities and Relations?

Elizabeth McMahon

Ontology: The science or study of being; that branch
of metaphysics concerned with the nature or essence of
being or existence. (OED)

Work that focuses on the nature of being, the relations
that being entails, and the entities involved in being: "At
last, islands not written about but writing themselves!"
(Walcott, 1992, n.p.)

A little while ago, visiting the Aran Islands (*Oileáin Árann*)
off the west coast of Ireland, I experienced one of those
rare, unsolicited senses of profound interconnection with
the world; that deep sense of presence from being-in-place.
On that occasion I felt a sense of familiarity—even
nostalgia—with this place that is not my home; I live
very happily on the other side of the planet. Also, by the
time of my Aran epiphany, I had written screeds about
the romanticization of islands in art, culture, and history, including their symbolic function as the primordial
homeplace. So, I had an armory of theory to critique the
experience and myself in it. I could separate the experience of place (phenomenology) from its material, ide-
ational, and imaginary realities of being (its ontologies).
Nonetheless, there I was, sitting on a pile of ancient
stones on an island at the westernmost point of Europe
caught up or caught out by the islands.

Because such intense experiences are rare, my Aran
experience recalled a similar event from decades before,

Source: Jean-Yves
Vigneau.

35

which had the effect of directing my academic research to island studies. In 1997, I moved from mainland Australia to the island of lutruwita/Tasmania and found myself subject to a kind of slow-release, visceral response to its islandness. This prehension was, in part, the conventional reaction to the bios and geos of a new place; and Tasmania is an exceptionally beautiful place with a very painful history. It is full of emotive charge. For me, however, the sense of being-in-place that it roused was an inaugural recognition of the relationality of bios and geos *per se*. I know now that this is a shared experience of islands. It is thought to be a result of the ways the specificity of islandness, the distillation and compression of elements and topographies, also produces wider and paradigmatic contemplation (Hay, 2006). This effect could also be described as combining both a personal and highly impersonal consciousness—in Deleuzian terms, an "event" in which "life magnifies and extends matter and matter in turn intensifies and transforms life" (Grosz, 2007, p. 299, see also Beck & Gleyzon, 2016; Deleuze & Guattari, 1987). It was also the sense of wonder, a systole of the heart, the cognitive passion, which Albertus Magnus (d. 1280) famously identified as the origin of philosophy (see Lochrie, 2006). That is to say, it led to elemental questions arising from both body and mind about being and space and their interrelationship (Führer, 2020).

The questions prompted for me by these islands at two ends of the world relate to being-in-the-world, to being alive to your *living* self in place and time in a personal and impersonal sense, which islands have long promoted. The articulation of elemental questions about being-in-the-island concerns the *nature* of islands and archipelagos not only as entities but also as sets of relations. They also include queries about how islands tell us about entities of the Earth and their relations more generally. In the case of Aran, they included a jumble of questions about what it might be to live in this place among these rocks and ruins, these fields, the vertiginous cliffs of the coastline, surrounded by the vastness of the Atlantic Ocean, visible from every point on land, speaking this language, navigating these waters, doing this daily work? How do the three islands and islanders relate to one another, to the mainland, to the worlds beyond that? What is the relationship, if any, between the *awareness* of being-in-the-world I experienced—along with millennia of others—and the lived place of the islanders themselves? How does living on this small island compare with living on other islands in the world? What kinds of worlds are they? These are all questions about ways of *being* in the world of islands, or what we also call island ontologies.

ONTOLOGY IN PHILOSOPHY

In philosophy, the study of being in the world, ontology, is a branch of metaphysics that is concerned with the fundamental nature of reality, first principles, and the relationship between material and immaterial realities (van Inwagen & Sullivan, 2021). Within the large scope of metaphysics, ontology addresses the fundamental nature of *being*, as distinct from the fundamental nature of *knowing, identity, time, and space*. Along with many thinkers before us, we may debate and argue about the distinctions between these five categories. Suffice to say that in the twenty-first century we commonly accept the inevitable overlaps among them but retain the utility of their distinctive emphases and their capacity to help us to organize thought, research projects, findings, and solutions to questions and problems.

For researchers in island and archipelagic studies the most striking overlaps that characterize these fundamental realities may be between the nature of *being* and of *space*. In regard to spaces inhabited by humans, this connection invokes what Martin Heidegger named *Dasein*. Translated from the German as *there to be* or in English *being there*, *Dasein* is a term that connects space and existence, and through which the human condition is understood as one of being-in-the-world. Importantly, *Dasein* does not refer to one person or one consciousness but, like a language, it is a "distinctive *way of life*" shared by "members of some community" (Haugeland, 2005, p. 423; Heidegger, 1927/2010). It is a social group's *shared* premises about the nature of reality. Drawing from Heidegger and also offering a more direct consideration of being and space, Edward Casey (1997, p. ix) writes that to "be at all—to exist in any way—is to be somewhere and to be somewhere is to be in some kind of place . . . Nothing we do is unplaced." These ontological foundations frame my approach to the relationship between islands and islanders in the context and objectives of island studies (International Small Islands Studies Association, 2022). On that basis, later in the chapter I turn to ontologies that disrupt the centrality of the human in these formations. First, however, I consider broader disciplinary or domain ontologies.

DISCIPLINARY OR DOMAIN ONTOLOGIES

In the context of research methodologies, ontology has two major, connected applications: the first principles or metaphysics of our respective disciplines; and the nature of the objects of study—in our case, islands and archipelagos. These are the *a priori* aspects of our disciplines and the objects we study—that which comes before, that shape our disciplines and domains, and that come before our research.

In the context of disciplines or domains, ontologies are "a set of concepts and categories in a subject area or domain that shows their properties and the relations between them" (OED). That is to say that every discipline has its metaphysics—*a priori* assumptions and structures that enable and limit our findings and enable their classification and assessment. And if these assumptions sound like structures of knowledge or epistemologies, they should. For there is an ongoing chicken-or-egg (or etiological) tension between ontology and epistemology regarding how first principles are derived, which relates in large part to the evolving history of Western philosophy since its origins in antiquity. Conversely, there is an argument that any acceptance of first principles at all is essentialist; that is, such acceptance supports a belief in realities independent of knowledge systems. There is a deal of scholarship tracing these histories and debates within respective disciplines such as, for example, anthropology (de Castro, 2015; Holbraad & Pedersen, 2017); geography (Tambassi, 2021); and geology (Garcia et al., 2020).

Without rehearsing these complex arguments here but informed by their insights, I proceed with a definition of disciplinary or domain ontology that understands the respective "essences" of each discipline to have been derived through knowledges, and that they are stable entities but are also subject to change (Heywood, 2017). All the while, I keep open enough space to capture elements and residues that resist classification in this way. So, I understand that the "*consensus* of a disciplinary matrix" is a fundamental quality of "mature fields of knowledge" (Kuhn, 1962/1970, pp. 38–40; emphasis added). Such consensus is primarily achieved by "agreement on paradigms-as-exemplars" (see also Bird, 2002). Consensus and agreement are key words here because academic disciplines change when new evidence alters a paradigm to produce a paradigm shift. For example, since the formal establishment of island studies through the International Small Islands Studies Association (ISISA) in 1992, those in the field have articulated its project of effecting a paradigm shift in the conceptualization of islands and their place in the world. Coincidentally (or not?) Derek Walcott acclaimed that same aim that same year in his acceptance speech as the 1992 Nobel laureate for literature. Toward the end of Walcott's address, which identifies the brutalities of slavery and colonialism in the Antilles, he celebrates the current patchwork of Caribbean ontologies, communities who are finding their way beyond colonialism.

Reflection on the first principles of our disciplines is neither navel gazing; nor is it reinventing the wheel. On the contrary, it is necessary for every project. Doreen Massey (2011, p. 6) argues for this process in her own field of geography and refers to the discipline's ontologies as its "spatio-temporal imaginary"—that is, what geography imagines itself *to be*:

> The *imagination* of the field is thus a significant element in the articulation of the relationship between the anthropologist and the peoples being studied. It *substantially affects*, recursively, the nature of the encounter. It is for this reason that addressing the spatio-temporal imaginary within which "the field" is placed is an important part of doing research. (emphasis added)

As Massey argues, the process of reflection is an ongoing and essential practice of research that shapes what we can see and what we find. Indeed, critical reflexivity more specifically is warranted and requires "that researchers understand that they are active participants in the research process and that their identities, commitments, histories, and approaches are part of the production of knowledge . . . [and do so] as if it were something you were studying" (Catungal & Dowling, 2021, p. 25).

Critical reflexivity is crucial to engage in as we start to be and then become more experienced researchers lest the premises of our disciplines are *naturalized* and then unquestioned, even as our skills and knowledge increase. The specific premises of disciplinary foundations enable us to meet our objectives to increase knowledge and identify solutions to questions and problems. But the specific and fundamental principles of each discipline also mean we will always only have a partial view of the reality we are examining because *a priori* assumptions and paradigms shape *what* we can see, *where* we locate our observations in the field, and *how* we assess their significance. These *a priori* aspects of research will necessarily differ from discipline to discipline and, most importantly in relation to islands, they may differ from the *ontologies of islands and islanders themselves.*

It is salutary to identify the first principles of our disciplines to make explicit the trajectories and limitations of our approaches and ambitions. The *a priori* aspects of my own discipline of literary studies, for example, include agreement that written and oral literatures are the most complex form of meaning-making in language, itself the basis of human cultures, and are deep reservoirs of human cultures and their creativity. As Marilynne Robinson (2016) suggests, literature allows us to hear the voices of the long dead; has capacity to summon both the conscious and unconscious minds and create profound understandings of self, others, and world; and envisions and invents new worlds that present novel possibilities for social and cultural development. Many new worlds are imagined as islands.

Based on these principles, research methodologies for literary studies include: multidisciplinary archival research; textual analysis using a range of critical and theoretical lenses; conceptual analysis that deploys philosophical research and method; and forms of comparative (or *synoptic*) analysis that measure the relative development of ideas across disciplines (see da Sousa & Owens, 2009; Galvan & Galvan, 2017).

The *a priori* foundations for literary studies, as for all disciplines, have their own internal logics and functions. They also present different opportunities in the interdisciplinary space of island studies, where a key question concerns the relationship between the *material and immaterial realities of islands.* This relationship is especially significant in island studies because of the position islands occupy in many cultures' imaginaries. To add to that complexity, islands have become a way to represent the Anthropocene itself (Beer, 1989; Derrida, 2010; McMahon, 2016; Pugh & Chandler, 2021). Islands have become a "master" trope—a dominant motif by which we think through the conditions of the planet. How do island imaginaries and this trope relate to actual islands and islanders as they live on the planet and how might we study that? The answer inevitably produces a spectrum of connections and disconnections full of possibilities and illusions, respectively. What we know from history is that islands' conceptual and imaginary forces can have very real effects. On a grand scale, belief in legends about islands that did not exist nevertheless assisted Christopher Columbus (1451–1506) in his voyages across the Atlantic to the Americas (Flint, 2017). They also motivate a contemporary tourist trade to mini-worlds, the primordial homes that islands represent, as I experienced on Aran. In this respect, and to counter both dominant cultures' ontological projections onto islands and their use of islands within those ontologies, part of the project of island studies is, I think, to address islanders' own imaginaries and conceptual ontologies. Doing so is, I suggest, enabled by various critical turns worth further elaboration.

A SERIES OF CRITICAL TURNS: CULTURAL, MATERIAL, ONTOLOGICAL, ONTO-RELATIONAL

Over the last 30 years, researchers and scholars have been exercised by debates about *materiality* in ways that directly affect island studies. In the main, these debates may be traced from shifts in European humanities and social sciences in the period after the Second World War. A basic understanding of these key issues is instructive for analyzing existing research in the field and formulating new research projects. Understanding such developments is important because it assists scholars contextualize work published over the last 60 years and recognize island studies' interventions into those fields. It alerts us to a fundamental issue that the *properties* of what *is*—ontologies— constantly shift along with what *is* as such. It is also vital to understandings of how and why materiality and ontology resonate now including specifically in relation to islands and archipelagos.

In this respect, insights from post-structuralist theory direct us to question the presumption that it is possible to have direct access to the material world (Hurst, 2017). While it may seem self-evident that an object we experience through our senses is real and has substance, that object is always processed for us in and through language and the structures of knowledge and culture. Thus, a word such as *island* does not refer to a single idea but rather provides a range of images and abstract possibilities that depend on cultural understanding and historical and personal experience. The various disciplines and approaches that have constituted this intellectual moment have been grouped together as the *cultural turn*, which marks a shift in understanding and attention focused on cultural and semiotic systems. This reappraisal, which is ongoing, has directed research across many disciplines to investigate the ways the ideologies and structures of cultures affected the nature of what they found (Alexander, 1988; Jameson, 1998; Yusoff, 2015). In this understanding, culture and the semiotic systems precede nature. For example, Pierre Bourdieu (1991) examines the way that language organizes and maintains structures of social power. Michel Foucault (1969/2002) theorizes the ways both the material entities and abstractions we experience only make sense to us when they are organized within structures of knowledge, called epistemes and discourses. These two may be formally organized structures such as geology or anthropology and may also include broader cultural structures such as politics, sexuality, religion, fashion, and so on (Barthes, 1990).

In the genealogy of intellectual thought, the turn to these questions in the latter half of the twentieth century foregrounded how we *know* (epistemology) and raised doubts about existing assumptions about how things *are* (ontology). This *epistemological turn* constituted a paradigm shift, and its profound insights remain crucial. As often occurs, for a period of time the effects of a paradigm shift in one field overshadow other theoretical inquiries there and elsewhere because the perspectival changes the shift brings about require reconstitutive labors—we have to rethink what we are doing.

In time, and over the last two decades in particular, *reframed* attention to ontological and material concerns has emerged and redressed the dominance of epistemological frameworks. Theorists and researchers have found new ways to reconsider ontologies—the material and immaterial realities of the world (Harman, 2018; Jackson, 2000; Lees, 2002). These shifts are known as the *material turn* and the *ontological turn*, and different disciplines have accounted for the impact and implications of this shift in their specific approaches to research (Abadia & Porr, 2021; Levinson, 2008; Heywood, 2017; Holbraad & Pedersen, 2017). A connected development of this reappraisal of ontology and materiality is a new emphasis on the *relationality, multiplicity, and interconnectedness* of all sentient and nonsentient subjects and objects. I understand, for instance, that there are multiple and dynamic ontologies in play in every environment and culture and that these are in a ceaseless process of arrangement and rearrangement. The two conventional approaches most commonly deployed as the bases for analysis in this mode of thinking are Deleuze and Guattari's (1987) theory of assemblages and Latour's (2005) actor-network theory. Both approaches emphasize the relationality and dynamism of the animate and inanimate world, although they differ in their conceptions of those relations (Harman, 2009, 2018; Müller & Schurr, 2016).

It is not coincidental that the turn to materiality and ontology in the twenty-first century corresponds with increasing recognition and experience of climate change effects and enforced recognition of planetary interrelationships.

Islands are affected in shared and specific ways by global warming and rising oceans, including by inundation. Intimately connected to climate change are the operations and networks of global capitalism, which also affect islands and islanders in specific ways, including demographic shifts such as depopulation and economic vulnerability. Little wonder islanders have been among the most vocal critics of the nexus between globalization and climate change and have emphasized its material effects (Jetñil-Kijiñer, 2016; Nuttall, 2009; Pala, 2020).

RETHINKING ISLAND ONTOLOGIES THROUGH CRITICAL TURNS

Many island-specific implications of critical theoretical turns inform research topics, frameworks, and methodologies. One conceptual shift concerns the recognition of multiple and relational ontologies, which has prompted the productive reconceptualization of islands away from perceptions of them as isolated and static objects to others of them as connected and dynamic entities (Baldacchino, 2008; Depraetere, 2008; Stratford et al., 2011a). The shift in ontological understanding from bordered, self-contained identities and objects occupying space-as-container to a *spatialized relationality* comprising multiple ontologies is crucial because they are not isolated, bounded, and unchanging. In that limiting imaginary, both land and sea are receptacles of fantasies—some of which are compelling but ontologically worldless: without actual world. A second major shift is the increased recognition of wet ontologies (Steinberg & Peters, 2015; Peters & Steinberg, 2019). This approach to aquatic entities and environments seeks to understand them on their own terms rather than as the empty spaces between lands. A third fascinating and problematic consideration is that islands have become a symbol for the ontological turn itself. Given the significance of these ontological shifts, below I map out some of the ways in which these new frameworks have shaped research methodologies in island studies to show their radical differences. In so doing, I stress the persistence of older ways of thinking and their copresence with the new.

Land and water

Much conceptual work in island studies to date has drawn on the radical insight and potential of relational ontologies that overturn Western binaries that have shaped the perception of islands and their histories, economies, well-being, and survival. They have complicated the seemingly self-evident *a priori* aspects of island insularity and stasis. Island studies scholars continue this rethinking of island ontologies. In one provocation, Godfrey Baldacchino (2005) includes three free-form drawings of an island on a page produced by his students. As he points out, the image of the island always fits within the limits of the page—how could part of an island be out of sight when, apparently, it is completely surrounded by the "empty space" of water? It may seem self-evident to suggest that an island is a piece of land surrounded by water, but that "fact" depends on what one understands land and water to be and how one then thinks about their interrelation. Why, for instance, do we not characterize lakes as water surrounded by land, which is also a fact (see Starc, 2020a)? When Herodotus (c. 484 BCE–425 BCE) referred to the Saharan oases as archipelagos, was he wrong?

In Western thought and imaginaries, structured as they are by binary oppositions such as good and evil or masculine and feminine, the meeting of land and sea has long been perceived in term of "reality and fantasy, utopia and dystopia, or isolation and connection" (McMahon & André, 2018, p. 297). It also points to an elemental contest in planetary cycles of creation and destruction in which islands inspire awe as a material form of compressed signification of the volatility and scale of ceaseless transformations. The small island that constantly locates us in the littoral zone where water meets land is another such compressed and intensified form (Beer, 1989; Deleuze, 2004; see also one application by Bradshaw & Williams, 2002). Of course, with all binaries one side is accorded a value higher than the other and for most cultures land has a higher value than water. Robert Pogue Harrison (2010, p. 4) writes that within Western thought and imagination the "sea offers no . . . foothold for human worldhood." He quotes John from the Bible's Book of Revelation, who describes a time when the world would be perfected as a "new earth" and a "new heaven" when "the sea was no more." Scholars in the borderlands of science, geography, and the blue humanities have done much to reconceptualize ideas about aquatic realms as empty spaces between lands to new understandings of wet ontologies (Cohen, 2021; Gillis, 2013; Hessler, 2018; Perez, 2020; Peters & Steinberg, 2019; Steinberg & Peters, 2015).

From well before the move to privilege relational ontologies, those in many island cultures conceptualized the relationship between land and water in ways less oppositional and more complex than land/and/water, and much of the critique of that conventional binarism has come from island writers. Numerous critical interventions into contemporary discourses have disrupted the fundamental bases of the opposition and its inherent hierarchy. Epeli Hau'ofa's (1993) essay, "Our sea of islands," remains a landmark—or watermark—offering that challenges perceptions of Pacific Islanders as isolates: for him they are, in fact, a community connected by voyaging (see DeLoughrey, 2013; Te Punga Somerville, 2012). Sea-and-land is their cultural home—conceived as being about mobility as much as emplacement but one also compromised by the bordering challenges of modern forms of sovereignty and territory.

From the Caribbean, Kamau Brathwaite's theory of tidalectics offers a thoroughgoing riposte to the opposition of land and water by reframing the relationship as the ongoing to-and-fro of tidal and cyclical flows. Instead of colliding forces, land and sea are understood as flux and continuity (Brathwaite, 1975; see also DeLoughrey & Flores, 2020; Hessler, 2018; Perez, 2020; Peters & Steinberg, 2019). In turn, Teresa Teaiwa (2007, p. 514) proposes a grammatical solution to the ways in which islands are imagined as static objects surrounded by water: "Shall we make island a verb? As a noun, it's so vulnerable to impinging forces. . . . Let us also make island a verb. It is a way of living that could save our lives." Likewise, both Elaine Stratford (2017) and Brian Roberts (2021) center on upsetting the binarism of islands and continents by which the continents are accorded power. Both seek to decontinentalize the United States by charting its recent claims to oceanic space, which border 21 countries and which reconstitute the country as an archipelago rather than a continent.

Morphology and scale

Islands are imagined as round in shape—even, and perhaps especially those we construct (figure 3.1). The Swedes write Ö for an island, and the Croatian word *otok* comprises *o* (meaning around) and *tok* (meaning flow) (Starc, 2020a). This discrepancy alerts us to the issue of scale. For it is small islands that are rounded in our imaginations, islands where we can see and hold the whole island within our gaze. As D. H. Lawrence (1928, p. 239) wrote, with irony: "An island, if it is big enough, is no better than a continent. It has to be really quite small, before it *feels like* an island; and this story will show how tiny it has to be, before you can presume to fill it with your own personality" (original emphasis). The circle is the ideogram (a linguistic character that symbolizes an idea of a thing) of belonging and inclusion, of homeplace. Like the Swedish Ö, it is the egg of new birth (Deleuze, 2004). It is the *uroboros* (the snake biting its own tail) that symbolizes cyclic renewal. It represents completeness, the complementarity of yin and yang, and the fantasy of self-unity and control, and we know these meanings consciously and unconsciously in multiple ways, including from the rudiments of languages such as Swedish or Croatian.

Moreover, we know that the connection between islands and ownership and control propelled Europe's project of global colonization where islands were ideal colonies (Connell, 2003). We know of that connection from narratives of castaways and tropical paradises and from tourist brochures that promise a temporary alternative world. In the Western imagination, the

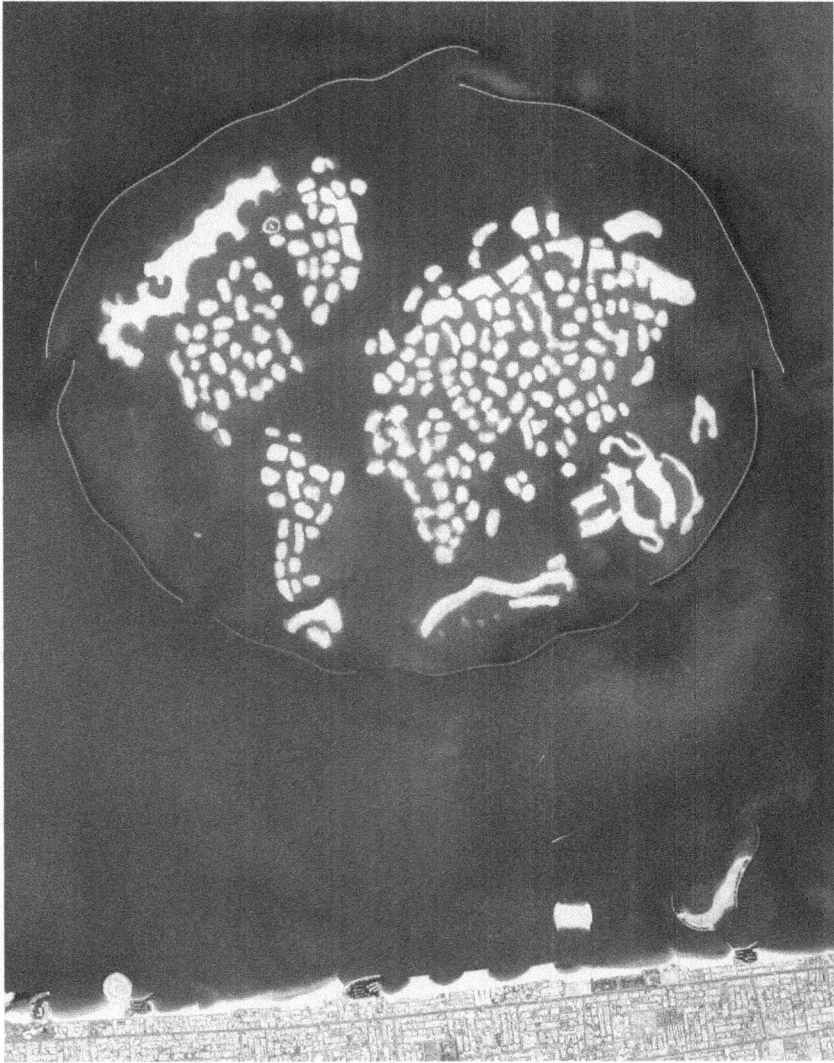

Figure 3.1. Artificial archipelagos, Dubai, United Arab Emirates. *Source*: NASA.

island is also a correlative or external symbol of the self. Gilles Deleuze (2004) argues that islands do not so much represent the egg of birth but that of *re*-birth, a place where we (Western subjects, at least) imagine we can make ourselves anew. He writes that islands are spaces where we imagine it might be possible for geography and the imagination to be unified—which is to say, where a person identifies with the island *itself* and perceives it as a geographical mirror of self. For all these reasons, the island feels like the primordial home. It is a homecoming to oneself. The anecdote of my own experience on the Aran Islands replays this web of geography and fantasy. These imaginaries are powerful and beautiful. But what do they tell us about the island and the islander given they imply stasis, singularity, isolation, and homogeneity and an absence of topological flows and dynamism where time itself stands still? In viewing the island as a static snapshot, we risk the illusion that we can comprehend it—*comprehend* in both senses of believing it is *already* understood before we even begin our research. That is a significant risk. In such a schema, the island is, in fact, *emptied* of ontologies but crammed full of projections. Fixing on such imaginaries, or failing to critique them once noticed, means that little or nothing is revealed about the nature of islands and archipelagos as entities and sets of relations and it shows the extent to which inquiry can be eclipsed by unconscious, naturalized assumptions.

One of the most effective revisions in the project to break down islands' perceived isolation and stasis has been that dealing with their archipelagic relationality—that is, their island-to-island relations (McMahon, 2013b). Efforts have been made to break down two dominant relations foundational to this persistent and limiting oppositionality of land and water and the scalar imbalances implied by island and continent (McMahon, 2010; Stratford et al., 2011a). Island-to-island relationality disallows skewed dynamics of power and ownership, for it speaks from *within* islandness *to* other islands. The ontologies of archipelagos include material and semiotic mobilities, then. They celebrate difference within the category of the single island, but this is a connected singularity that imagines movement and change and is thus also a network or assemblage. It is premised on an understanding of a world in process: "isolated and floating relations, islands and straits, immobile points and sinuous lines" (Deleuze, 1997, p. 86).

Internal difference/where the meanings are

The empty island described above is immediately complicated both when we begin to consider specificity and diversity—including the many divergent factors within categories of islands and archipelagos—and when we peer under the surface of land and water. Key geographical and cultural differences make this complication clear if one considers the six main types of continental, tidal, barrier, oceanic, coral, and artificial island where each category contains many subsets and sets of relations with aquatic environments, other landforms, climates, and ecosystems, including cultures.

Continental islands are unsubmerged parts of the continental shelf that are entirely surrounded by water. These are the largest islands and include the planet's five largest islands: Greenland, New Guinea, Borneo, Madagascar, and Baffin Island. Oceanic islands include volcanic islands such as Hawai'i and Hunga Tonga-Hunga Ha'apai in the Pacific and Réunion and Mauritius in the Indian Ocean (Nunn, 1994). Atolls form when corals build colonies around relatively shallow waters of both oceanic and continental islands (Richmond, 1993; Smithers & Hopley, 2011). Barrier islands are narrow islands that lie parallel to the coastline of a mainland. They are most commonly depositional landforms including spits, drowned dune ridges, or sand bars, which are formed by wave and tidal action (Davis, 2003; Pilkey et al., 2009; Wang & Roberts Briggs, 2015). Importantly, barrier islands usually occur in chains; the longest chain occurs in Brazil and comprises 54 islands and extends for 570 kilometers. There are areas that include combinations of these formations: the Caribbean, for instance, mostly consists of oceanic islands with some continental islands and atolls (Iturralde-Vinent et al., 2016). Of these islands, atolls are the most vulnerable in the wake of climate change, rising oceans, and bleaching (figure 3.2). But imagine if we habitually mapped the world of atolls or just islands (recall figure 1.5).

Figure 3.2.   Bleached staghorn coral, Great Barrier Reef, Australia. *Source*: Wikimedia Commons | Matt Kieffer.

In fact, imagine if we mapped all the islands, which scale usually prohibits! How would this shift conceptions of islands' isolation? How might this decontinentalize our perceptions (Roberts, 2021; Stratford, 2017)? Imagine, too, if the map we produced included tidal flows and if, in three-dimensional simulation, we could see the submarine connections. For, as Brathwaite (1975, p. 1) writes of his Barbadian homeplace: "The unity is submarine breathing air, our problem is how to study the fragments/whole."

Similar categorizations of difference between islands and archipelagos can be made according to other criteria including size, climate, location and access, population, history and colonization, economies, political status, and language. From these basic categorizations of internal differences and diversities within the category of island, research on any involves identifying the specifics of one place, understood in its multiple ontologies. Tim Robinson's decades-long cartographic project to map one island is a case in point. His two-volume study, *The stones of Aran*, focuses on one island Árainn or Inis Mór, of the Aran archipelago, which has an area of 31 square kilometers (12 square miles) and a population of about 840 people. In *Pilgrimage* (1986) he walks the coastline, and in *Labyrinth* (1995) he focuses on the interior. Together, the volumes are 1,000 pages long. In their detailing of phenomena and relationships, they illustrate the limitless complexity of one small island.

Near and Far

What properties are shared by all islands, and what are their points of distinction? *The Notion of Near Islands*, a collection on the Croatian archipelago, defines the quality of "nearness" according to both the physical proximity of the islands to the mainland and their socioeconomic fusion with mainland areas (Starc, 2020b). These factors are not always in alignment: an island close to a mainland may nonetheless be distant in terms of access and involvement and vice versa. It seems that residents of the world's remotest inhabited island, Tristan da Cunha, a British overseas territory, value cultural connection in spite of great physical distance. It can only be reached via a six-day boat trip from Cape Town, South Africa, and is over 10,000 kilometers (6,213 miles) away from Britain. The Tristanians are nonetheless deeply identified with British culture (Royle, 2002). For example, in mid-2022 the *Tristan da Cunha Community News* reported the island's celebration of the platinum jubilee for Her Majesty Queen Elizabeth II, which included lighting a beacon on the site of the island's 1961 volcanic eruption. The beacon would create a direct link to Britain and be "one of over 2,022 lit by charities, communities and faith groups all over the UK" (Jaumotte, 2022).

INTERDISCIPLINARY AND TRANSDISCIPLINARY RESEARCH

The disciplinary range of researchers working in island studies comprises sections of the biophysical sciences, the social sciences, arts, and humanities. Each discipline occupies a position along the spectrum of relative concentration on material and immaterial ontologies. As a scholar in literary studies, my research is primarily concerned with abstract or immaterial realities. Literary criticism and literary theory are inherently interdisciplinary in that they are what Cesare Casarino (2002, p. xiii) terms a *philopoesis*, which he defines as a "certain discontinuous and refractive interference between philosophy [philo] and literature [poesis]." My work has drawn deeply on the discipline of history and on research methodologies from postcolonialism, new historicism, and cultural materialism, all of which involve reading literature as both a product and an agent of history (McMahon, 2013a; see also Faire & Gunn, 2012).

Island studies encourages me further to connect these thought structures and imaginaries to history and culture, the facticity of the real and the material Earth. This thinking was to the fore as I began writing this chapter on the day after the January 15, 2022, eruption of the Hunga Tonga-Hunga Ha'apai volcano, a submarine volcano in the Kermadec-Tonga Ridge in the South Pacific. The explosion generated by the eruption was as powerful as approximately 4–18 megatons of TNT, or 100 atom bombs (Bates, 2022). The eruption plume soared to a height of at least 30 kilometers (18 miles), well into the upper atmosphere or stratosphere (Witze, 2022). Only seven years after a prior eruption joined the two neighboring islands into one landmass, the mid-section, including the volcanic caldera, disappeared in the explosion. The two remaining islands have also been diminished in size. The blast, ash, and subsequent tsunami not only affected its nearest neighbors in the islands of Tonga but also reached as far as the west coast of the Americas and Japan.

The Hunga Tonga-Hunga Ha'apai event raises questions about the formation of oceanic islands. It has "challenged ideas about the physics of eruptions" and generates questions about why the "volcano sent a cloud to such heights yet emitted less ash than would be expected for an eruption of such magnitude [and about why] the shock waves that rippled through the atmosphere and oceans are unlike anything seen in the modern scientific era" (Witze, 2022, n.p.). But thinking about island ontologies in the wake of Hunga Tonga-Hunga Ha'apai also underscores questions about how islands are fundamental to the ways in which we experience and understand the materiality of the Earth and the universe (Bates, 2022). They enable researchers to generalize from the smallest island to a distant planet: from the most specific instance of the planet to the application of knowledges, islands teach us about material creation—and annihilation. And all the while we must still balance that capacity to generalize with the need to greet island each on its own terms.

Arguably, island studies was formally constituted in 1992 with the formation of ISISA. The same year, at the United Nations' Earth Summit national governments acknowledged–in part via Agenda 21–that small island developing states are a "special case both for environment and development . . . [and] are considered extremely vulnerable to global warming and sea level rise" and two years later vowed to "comprehensively [address] the economic, environmental, and social developmental vulnerabilities facing islands" in what became known as the Barbados Program of Action (United Nations, 1994a, 1994b). These three components and the relations among them foreground material ontologies of islands and include an ethical imperative to address material hardship and precarity, which is especially urgent because of climate change but which has been urgent in a range of ways for hundreds of years.

ISISA's foundational terms and objectives prioritize the material conditions of islands and islanders in their specific circumstances and in varied collective conditions and experiences (International Small Islands Studies Association, 2022). For scholars in the humanities, like me, these priorities may seem to discount research in our fields. That is not the case. For islands are defined not just by material but also by immaterial elements—ideologies, beliefs, or social contracts. To deny this point would be to deny what binds cultures and ecosystems. Material and immaterial ontologies are indissoluble.

On that understanding, there is great benefit in interdisciplinary research in the collective project to rethinking island methodologies. Such research enables people to pool disciplinary ontologies and methods and engage in synoptic (comparative) analysis across fields. It can be a highly effective way to introduce ontologies from a given discipline to other research contexts. Without doubt, island studies has extended my interdisciplinary engagement via collaborations with geographers and sociologists and in research across a wide range of disciplines.

In short, work in island studies has led my research—based as it has been largely in *immaterial* ontologies—to more significant engagements with those in other disciplines and with the *material* island ontologies and analytical vocabularies. I am not a geographer, geologist, or sociologist but I have now read enough in those fields to position my research on islands in broader contexts. The disciplinary ontologies remain mostly distinctive but there are points of overlap. So, too, a broader perspective allows the conscious location of research as one set of data among many. Identifying shared and discrete ontological principles is fundamental to constructing collaborative, cross-disciplinary research projects with the capacity to produce new knowledges and provide original solutions to problems that individual domains cannot furnish alone. Crucially, for my inherently abstract research, this practice of engagement allows me to connect imaginary and abstract realities with the material conditions experienced on islands and by islanders and to work with theorists whose positions and considerations differ from those I would otherwise encounter. In exchange, I can contribute structures and vocabularies that shed light on interactions between domains. Together, these placements and interactions help realize the first principle of island studies, which is to investigate islands on their own terms rather than by using the inherited terms of globalized modernity in which islands, and especially small islands, have been rendered invisible or the projections of continental fantasies.

MULTIPLE ONTOLOGIES AND THE DECOLONIZATION OF ISLAND RESEARCH

We are increasingly aware of the problematics of collection and extraction by which data are removed and analyzed according to researchers' cultural and disciplinary ontologies. This need for self-placement in any given research project recalls Donna Haraway's (1988) conception of situated knowledges. Her work invites us to acknowledge that our perceptions and interpretations of data are necessarily shaped by our embodied positions at particular times in history, in place, and even on the move (Sheller, 2022). To produce accurate and meaningful research, then, we need to make explicit our naturalized ontologies and understand the research relationship as a meeting of *ontological subjects*. That need includes the biophysical sciences, where the objects of study are still parts of ecosystems, economies, and cultures (Gugganig & Klimburg-Witjes, 2021). There is a difference, for instance, between research that seeks to exploit natural resources and research that seeks to preserve or rehabilitate them (Povinelli, 1995; Yusoff, 2015, 2019). This approach also allows for us to include *multifocal* and *dynamic* realities and accommodate both their complexity and disagreement.

In the process of doing research on, with, or about islands and islanders, then, it is important to construct conversations among the ontologies of our discipline; the ontologies of the interdisciplinary field of island studies, both of which shape all aspects of our research; and the ontologies of islands and islanders. Connecting these three elements is fundamental to a basic objective of island studies to redress how the ontologies of islands and islanders have been lost in research—even when they are identified as the subject of study. Historically, islands have been overlooked in the continental power of modernity (Gillis, 2013). In the process, a monological course of inquiry on islands has been promoted by perceptions that islands are natural laboratories or control sites with defined and manageable limits—and at scales that correspond with research projects that assume researchers are collecting, extracting, and analyzing objective data to locate within disciplinary paradigms.

Alternatively, island researchers recognize that islands and islanders have their own ontologies and the term *nissology* was coined to reflect the practice of studying islands on their own terms (McCall, 1994; see also Baldacchino, 2008; Depraetere, 2008). This practice requires that islanders be included. For example, in *Atolls of the Maldives*, geographers and other social scientists and ecologists detail their negotiation of Western knowledge systems with the traditional knowledges of the Maldivian peoples, from whose language, *Dhivehi*, the word atoll derives (Malatesta et al., 2021). As this connection suggests, atolls are more than a space for the Maldivians. In fact, the two parts of the Maldivian word for environment, *thimaa-veshi*, inextricably link self (*thimaa*) and the surrounding world (*veshi*) (p. 4). This kind of ontology is increasingly recognized as a necessary shift for planetary survival but nonetheless is at odds with structures informing Western knowledge systems and, indeed, with the logic of the Anthropocene. For instance, in an essay that reflects on brokering these disconnections in research Carol Farbotko and colleagues (2022) describe how the members of their initial research team, all white female geographers, revisited the fundamental terms of their project because it replicated colonizing practices in the study of islands. Their solution was to reform the research team to include an Indigenous Tuvaluan male and adopt as a principle of their approach and methodology the concept of *Fale Pili*—to treat a neighbor's problem as your own.

Inevitably, there will be instances of significant difference between researchers' and islanders' ontologies and of situations for which Jean-François Lyotard (1988) coined the term the *differend*—that is, fundamentally irreconcilable ontologies and approaches. For him, these are "occasion(s) of the least linkage" between (at least) two parties and for which there are "no shared rules that enable judgment" to guide assessment or decisions (Lyotard, 1988, p. 9). Lyotard formed his thesis in response to the devastation and barbarism of the Second World War. This collision of absolute differences has also been a focus of postcolonial analysis. Now, it additionally describes radical discontinuities identified by those working with the category of the Anthropocene and by First Nations' critiques: how do Western cultures and traditional Indigenous cultures meet when their ontologies are irreconcilable? How are Indigenous storybook methodologies informing research (Archibald, 2008)?

Several maneuvers are available to researchers confronting such dilemmas. All require those who operate in conventional disciplines to restructure their approaches and give ground. The first move, revisiting Lyotard's *differend*, is to frame research as a dialogic process that presumes *disconnection* rather than the loss of an apparent common ground, which is so often the assumption of higher ground. For common ground is more common for one party than another; realizing this inequity may help researchers more often to decenter and denaturalize Western research ontologies and approaches and reposition them. The second move, as Farbotko et al. (2022) expound in rethinking their research project, is to commit to re/forming research projects from their conception to include islanders and their approaches as equal parties in research or be willing to re/start projects if that has not happened. Related to this point is an imperative to build in time for a project to engage with islanders' ontologies across a range of resources—but only and always first with their permission or instigation. Such work needs to consume time and space in research; otherwise, it is tokenistic.

Finally, as Marshallese poet and activist, Kathy Jetñil-Kijiñer, insists, the shared planetary crisis of climate change creates applicable rules of judgment by which to assess and legislate the shared interests of ecological survival. Nonislander researchers and islanders have this common ground that enables judgment. In her address to the 2016 United Nations Climate Summit, Jetñil-Kijiñer performed this common purpose. The perceived disparities of scale between one woman from the Marshall Islands speaking to representatives of the "world" and to globalized capitalism do not minimize the mutual applicability of the rules of judgment. Indeed, that is the point.

THE LAST THAT SHOULD BE FIRST: INDIGENOUS ONTOLOGIES, COSMOLOGIES, AND ISLANDS

The idea of human "mastery" has licensed processes of relentless extraction of resources and value from the environment. Among other characteristics they possess, these processes were—and remain—racialized, meaning that ontologies of mastery have only been available to certain peoples and have been exercised over others (Yusoff, 2019). In fact, the "failure" of Indigenous cultures to "exploit" the environment in such ways has been an accepted rationale to dispossess them of their lands and waters (McMahon, 2016). So, it is both meaningful and ironic that the most profound critique of these ontologies comes from First Nations peoples, many of them islanders who have been profoundly subject to them, and from those long perceived as less than human, such as slaves, as we see in works by Hau'ofa and Brathwaite. The turn to Indigenous ontologies and return to other, traditional ontologies is coincident—but not coincident*al*—with global ethical movements led by

First Nations and colonized peoples seeking recognition and justice for geno-cide, dispossession, slavery, and environmental degradation across the span of the Anthropocene (Minter, 2015; Todd, 2016).

An extended example is useful at this point. In their island-to-island collaboration, *Rise: From One Island to Another*, Jetñil-Kijiñer and Ana Niviâna (2018) reassert traditional ontologies from the Marshall Islands and Greenland, respectively. Jetñil-Kijiñer has travelled to Greenland, establish-ing their performance as a mobile relational network between islands. The performance is structured as a ceremonial dialogue of greeting and welcome from one island home to another. The dialogue between speakers and home-places constructs a relationship of reflexivity in both senses of a mirror; it shows likeness and a reversed image. For one is the largest island on Earth, a continental island in the Arctic Circle; the other more water than land, a Pacific archipelago comprising thousands of islands and islets and spanning nearly 2 million square kilometers (772,204 square miles) of the ocean. In their exchange, the two speakers detail the effects of climate change on their respective homelands. These details are acutely specific, even oppositional, yet experiences and subject positions are shared between them. The two are also linked by their relational cosmologies and by their sympathy with ele-ments of the Earth disrespected because of ongoing environmental destruc-tion. One of the most powerful elements of *Rise* is the way the two speakers declare their affinity and sympathy with the disrespected Earth and direct their fear and rage towards the human agents who continue this disrespect.

Numerous scholars have documented the varied ways in which contem-porary Western scholarship has instrumentalized Indigenous ontologies—or cosmologies—as a solution or antidote to the ecological crisis of the twenty-first century. For two, this is the "key trope of 'becoming Indigenous': indi-geneity as the imaginary of a speculative future after modernity" (Chandler & Reid, 2019; p. 6). First Nations scholars and commentators have raised many objections to the placement of their ontologies within Western periodiza-tions. For example, Zoe Todd (2016, p. 6) alerts us to many "Indigenous thinkers who have been writing about Indigenous legal theory, human-animal relations and multiple epistemologies/ontologies for decades" but who still receive little or no recognition. Thus, assuming a critical position that recog-nizes appropriation as a fundamental misunderstanding of difference, West-ern scholars must sit with incommensurability, asymmetry, and disruption of other systems. Those in island and archipelagic studies have significant contributions to make in this respect.

Chapter 4

Knowing

What Constitutes Knowing in the Study of Islands and Archipelagos?

Elaine Stratford

Epistemology: The theory of knowledge and understanding . . . and the distinction between justified belief and opinion. (OED)

The study of islands and archipelagos invites those trying to crack what constitutes knowing to be comfortable with enigmas. How do we know what we know?

I *know* that I live on an island: lutruwita/Tasmania. But I was not born t/here. My *knowing* that the place in which I live *is* an island predates my *being* on that island. In November 1996, I boarded an overnight ocean ferry, the *Spirit of Tasmania*, and crossed the 256 kilometer (159 mile) stretch of water known as the Bass Strait with my partner, our first born, and a second tucked safely in utero. Even so, my knowledge that the place in which I continue to live is an island did not flow from that crossing because I had known for years that lutruwita/Tasmania is the island state of the island continent of Australia.

It is t/here, on the island, that I have forged a life and career, and, on that basis, what follows is partly self-referential and intended to model methodological debts to autobiographical and autoethnographical methods of approach (Moss, 2011; Pithouse-Morgan et al., 2021). Interestingly, it was not until 1999 that the impact of my new home's island status hit me in consciously epistemic terms. That year, the department in which I work at the University of Tasmania

Source: Jean-Yves Vigneau.

55

was visited by Harry Baglole (d. 2018), a champion of island studies affiliated with the University of Prince Edward Island, Canada's smallest and only fully island province. Baglole's visit loosely coincided with two signature developments: the election in 1998 of the Australian Labor Party to government in Tasmania and a subsequent decision, in 1999, by Premier Jim Bacon (1950–2004) to innovate in two ways. One was to constitute *Tasmania Together*, modeled on community engagement work then thriving in Oregon in the United States (Oregon Progress Board, 1989, 1997); the other was to instigate the *Ten Days on the Island* international festival, which was launched in 2001 (Stratford, 2006b). Baglole's visit helped refuel among academics, activists, artists, and political and economic commentators a vibrant, sometimes sharp-edged, and enduring conversation about what it means to live in island settings and to be (or seek to become) an islander (Brinklow, 2022; Stratford & Jaskolski, 2004; Stratford, 2008; Stratford & Langridge, 2012; Stratford & Low, 2013).

It was only at that point, in 1999, that I began to see lutruwita/Tasmania not just as a subnational jurisdiction of a federation but also as an island distinctly different from other jurisdictions on what I was now calling the mainland of Australia—a term laden with its own epistemic baggage (Baldacchino, 2020; Stratford, 2006a). What followed included regular trips to island studies conferences, starting with Prince Edward Island in 2002, and a research agenda and associated supervision and teaching innovations that are ongoing (Armstrong & Stratford, 2009; Farbotko et al., 2022; Stratford, 2016; Stratford et al., 2003).

Throughout that entire period, I have frequently been challenged by colleagues—not least in lutruwita/Tasmania—to describe, explain, and justify why I think islands merit their own form of study, island studies, rather than being absorbed into place, region, or other such apparently superordinate or area studies (Baldacchino, 2006a; McMahon, 2010; SICRI, 2022). In the process, new studies about the archipelago and aquapelago have emerged and been characterized by useful debate (Hay, 2013; Hayward, 2012; Stratford, 2015a, Stratford, 2020; Stratford et al., 2011a). At its heart, such a challenge is about what constitutes knowledge (a noun), the knowledgeable (an adjective), and knowing (a verb). It forms the basis for the rest of this chapter.

WHAT CONSTITUTES KNOWING
(WHAT AN ISLAND IS)?

On the face of it, to have knowledge is to draw from experience or from data, information, interpretations, and understandings provided before (*a priori*) or after (*a posteriori*) "the fact." But one must also be *aware* that one has the knowledge and can gauge its significance, either for oneself alone or in relation. With a nod to René Descartes (1596–1650), such *knowing* is a condition of *being*, by which one apprehends a "truth" and then engages in reasoning or thinking about it; is cognizant or mindful of it.

Were matters actually so straightforward! However, they are not, for alongside metaphysics, logic, and ethics, *epistemology*—the theory of knowledge—invites deep inquiry about the origins, characteristics, and boundaries of knowledge. Thus, supported by a working definition, I may know that an island is an area of land smaller than a continent and surrounded by water (even if only at high tide). On that understanding, lutruwita/Tasmania is an island. Yet, my understanding is quickly muddied by knowing that the island is joined to the Australian continent by "land" currently submerged under Bass Strait. Moreover, Tasmania as a formal state so named within the Commonwealth of Australia is actually an archipelago of some 300-plus islands perched on the continental shelf along with some oceanic islands, as with Macquarie Island far to the south.

That knowledge enjoins me to qualify my working definition by referring to the influence of time or the spatial features of islandness, which, itself, is an ontological term. So, I could extend the parameters of my working definition by reference to Diamond Island, just off the northeast coast of lutruwita/Tasmania, which *is* an island at high tide *but* a peninsula at other times. I could speculate about how time and space give effect to *how* I know that Diamond Island and lutruwita/Tasmania both manifest the spatial characteristics of islands, at least some of the time—be that diurnal or geological, over a day or many millennia.

While the physicality of the island status is unlikely to change rapidly—in the way that Diamond Island's does—Tasmanians and others are ready enough to change how they deploy island status t/here and abroad. Sometimes it is celebrated, but at other times it is tucked away, and the same characteristics of apparent isolation, quietude, and separation have been touted as blessings and impediments (Stratford, 2008). Two examples follow to illustrate this ambivalence about what constitutes lutruwita/Tasmania (and thus a knowingness of it). First, consider how, at a tourism conference in Geneva, Premier Bacon (2003) noted:

Tasmania, Australia's only island state, is in fact an archipelago of more than 300 small islands of which the island of Tasmania itself is the largest. It is located at 40 degrees south, on the edge of the Southern Ocean, with a population fewer than 500,000 people. We are islands of tremendous resourcefulness and innovation, creatively connected to a diverse and spectacular landscape blessed with the world's cleanest air and freshest water. As a state of islands, we are especially connected to other islands of the globe. We have an affinity with all who, like us, have experienced a painful past, and we are building a new connection with those blessed with a creative culture that nurtures our future. Human beings have lived in Tasmania [*sic*] for 50,000 years, and it physically separated from mainland Australia 10,000 years ago. It was not until the 17th and 18th centuries that Dutch, French and British navigators charted the islands of Tasmania. The first permanent settlement was established some 200 years ago. Tasmania is a place that was settled [*sic*] by Europeans in adversity.

In that conference paper, Bacon deploys many of the key epistemological terms that demarcate how one might know what constitutes an island. He describes Tasmania, one of several subnational jurisdictions in the federation of Australia, as the nation's *only* island state, invoking a singularity. But, equally, he renders Tasmania's jurisdictional prowess larger than it might otherwise be construed: as an archipelago it numbers over 300 islands. It is on the edge in its maritime location and in terms of its low population density. And, of note, Bacon uses figures of speech to great effect when he refers to Tasmanians as islands and as a state of islands rather than islanders. It is as if people have syphoned from these geographical formations their abiding strength, resilience, and capacity to cope with invasion, carceral histories, and economic marginalization. In just 200 words, Bacon constitutes Tasmania's islandness as a powerful ontology and, in doing so, seeks to shape its origin stories, comprehensible characteristics, and boundaries. In short, his labors are profoundly epistemological, and they had significant influence both on how Tasmanians have subsequently viewed themselves and been viewed by others.

As a second example, consider essays in the Australian journal, *Griffith Review*, entitled *Tasmania: The Tipping Point*. In one essay on "obstacles to progress," West (2013) refers just three times to "island" in relation to gourmet products; in an aside about an apparent tendency among parents to discourage children's higher education aspirations lest their progeny depart the island; and in passing comments about a divide between the northern and southern halves of the island that has existed since European invasion and colonization in 1803/4. In contrast, West refers to "Tasmania" 79 times and uses the term "state" nine times to describe Tasmania: its wilderness; its position at the bottom of various measures of "economic, social, and cultural performance" (n.p.) relative to other Australian states; its dual existence as both a state and region (that is, not a metropole); a reliance on state-owned and resource-extractive economic entities; and a history of outmigration to other states with more robust developmental outlooks.

Like Bacon before him, West uses synecdoche, collapsing generations of individuals and communities into a singular identity: Tasmania. But it is a characterization as far removed as one could get from Bacon's optimistic knowing of the same place. Not once does West invoke epistemologically foundational *tropes* such as isolation, edge, periphery, marginalization, insularity, boundary, or resourcefulness. Rather, in ways that remove any geographical specificity and somehow render the island/s placeless, he writes:

> The underlying problem is simple but intractable: Tasmania has developed a way of life, a mode of doing things, a demographic, a culture and associated economy that reproduces under-achievement generation after generation. (n.p.)

Paradoxically, and like Bacon's rhetoric, this monolithic epistemic frame has stood the test of time despite, for example, the development of the internationally innovative private Museum of Old and New Art (MONA) in Tasmania's capital, Hobart (Rentschler et al., 2018), or a significant upswing in real estate prices t/here. The reasons for the resilience of West's ways of knowing are clear: MONA has spatial effects that underscore existing disadvantages (Booth et al., 2021). In addition, exponential increases in the sale price of houses and excessively expensive and very scarce rental accommodation have led to housing shortages and exacerbated disadvantage (de Vries et al., 2021).

Clearly, one need not invest in either Bacon's or West's ways of knowing what constitutes Tasmania, or states, or islands; and nor is an appeal from me for the reader to do so implicit in the comparative exercise above. Rather, from a straightforward assertion that one might know what an island is by dint of experience and by reasoning, it becomes clear that any number of complications arise in why, how, and what one knows and in where that knowing applies and for whom at any given point in time, space, or place.

So, there is a need to push deeper into *ambiguity* in order to have a hope of being able to engage effectively with questions about how one knows what one does about islands and archipelagos. Kinks in *truth-telling* are among the ambiguities that characterize ways of knowing. Those earnest about epistemology may be compelled to descriptive accuracy, the apprehension of incongruities, explanatory reach, reasoned and defensible argument based on evidence, graceful refutation and reformation, and the creation of encompassing theories. Yet, it is rash to assume such compulsion is universal; both the inconvenience of *fallibility* and the challenges of *relativity* work to confound what we know and how we know it.

There are many instances of deliberate manipulations of the "truth" or, alternatively, of its disguise, silence, or partial or full erasure. People have long used such practices to ensure that they have the competitive edge on extracting island resources or exploiting or severing their connections to other islands. Consider the tactics used by colonial traders, as Daniel Clayton (1999, p. 86) has in work on the imperial epistemologies of northwestern North America; assuredly, at least some of the traders who plied that archipelagic coastline:

did not connect questions of representation to issues of scientific observation and epistemology to the extent that explorers did [and the latter were not always committed to verisimilitude, in any case] . . . The mode of enunciation of the maritime fur trade was private, competitive and vitriolic.

Indeed, it would take decades before scientific and bureaucratic scopic regimes and cartographic efforts revealed that same coastline.

Or consider how the epistemological frameworks deployed to understand islands and archipelagos are equally malleable. On Favignana, a tourist destination off Sicily, residents produce different versions of maps as a fencing strategy to steer tourists to particular places and, by implication, away from others they themselves favor and wish to preserve (Cassinelli, 2012; Stratford, 2012). Thus, much that might be assumed about the "truth" of islands or archipelagos is questionable at some level.

Other epistemological ambiguities affect *sense-making*. As Clayton's and Eleonora Cassinelli's different works imply, for traders recently arrived on the northwest coast of eighteenth-century North America or for a twenty-first-century tourist just landed on Favignana, it would be challenging to make sense of the (external) world using maps or other forms of representation characterized by silences and absences. So, experiences count. And yet, it also matters how one makes sense of the world experientially. Thus, in terms of knowing, I have also long been intrigued by how to better acknowledge children's and young people's voices (Stratford, 2015b; Stratford 2015c).

I may know I live on an island, but if it is a large island such as (mainland) Tasmania, and I live in an *inland* mining settlement such as Queenstown, then my capacity to make sense of the islandness of the place may be dulled or dimmed by that framing and my orientation is to the *interior* (figure 4.1). At the same time, if I live on a smaller island such as King Island in the Bass Strait, with an area of 1,098 square kilometers or 682 square miles (figure 4.2), then I may struggle with the idea that Saskatoon, on the prairies of Canada, is 972 miles or 1,565 kilometers from the British Columbian coast of which Clayton writes. Because I can see the boundaries of the island on which I live, my sense-making would be redolent of what constitutes those boundaries.

Whether experiential or empirical or based in *a priori* or *a posteriori* theorizing, sense-making has been described as "a way station on the road to a consensually constructed, coordinated system of action" (Taylor & Van

Figure 4.1.   The interiority of Queenstown, Tasmania; not a shore in sight. *Source*: Wikimedia Commons | Emin Başar ÖZDEMİR.

Figure 4.2.   **King Island student's collage of Tasmania. Note the proliferation of references to islandness. In the colour original, blue seas are filled with green kelp; penguins, seals, seashells abound; branded produce is included.** *Source*: **Elaine Stratford.**

Every, 2000, p. 275). Note, however, the contestability of what is meant by the terms "consensual," "coordinated," and "action." There is general consensus that lutruwita/Tasmania is indeed an island and an archipelago; but agreement ends there, including in relation to whether, how, and to what extent the islandness of that specific place matters epistemologically. Little wonder that strident debate typifies views about how Tasmanians can forge ahead—whether under the optimistic energies of, say, Bacon's vision, the pessimism promulgated by West, or via other ways of knowing.

The systems of action to which James Taylor and Elizabeth Van Every (2000) refer are perilous for anyone thinking about what it means to know what constitutes *knowing* what an island *is*. If actions are crucial for shaping how meanings surface or materialize and then, themselves, influence how we know and are in the world via our text, talk, and practice (Hajer, 2006), then it is almost certain that islands and archipelagos are talked into existence as speech-*acts*. As such, what we know about islands and archipelagos depends on effective appeals to stories that have *plausibility*.

> Plausible stories animate and gain their validity from subsequent activity. The language of sensemaking captures the realities of agency, flow, equivocality, transience, reaccomplishment, unfolding, and emergence, realities that are often obscured by the language of variables, nouns, quantities, and structures. Students of sensemaking understand that [in this example] the order in organizational life comes just as much from the subtle, the small, the relational, the oral, the particular, and the momentary as it does from the conspicuous, the large, the substantive, the written, the general, and the sustained. To work with the idea of sensemaking is to appreciate that smallness does not equate with insignificance. Small structures and short moments can have large consequences. (Weick et al., 2005, p. 410)

Described also as credibility or believability, plausibility is central to how one makes *sense* and *meaning*. Consider, for instance, the space that is Oceania, then recall my earlier reference to the submerged land bridge that connects Australia to lutruwita/Tasmania, and then think of the compelling reasonableness of the following argument:

> Do people in most of Oceania live in tiny, confined spaces? The answer is "yes" if one believes in what certain social scientists are saying. But the idea of smallness is relative . . . [and] if we look at the myths, legends and oral traditions, and the cosmologies of the peoples of Oceania, it will become evident that they did not conceive of their world in such microscopic proportions. Their university comprised not only land surfaces, but the surrounding ocean as far as they could traverse and exploit it, the underworld with its fire-controlling and earth-shaking denizens, and the heavens above with their hierarchies of powerful gods and

named stars and constellations that people could count on to guide their ways across the seas. Their world was anything but tiny. . . . There is a gulf of difference between viewing the Pacific as "islands in a far sea" and as "a sea of islands." (Hau'ofa, 1993, pp. 6–7)

Or contemplate how Elizabeth DeLoughrey (2019a, p. 3) speaks into existence views of the Anthropocene as "an ecological crisis that is understood as local and planetary, as historical and anticipatory." She does that work by critically evaluating and unsettling the plausibility of certain knowledge claims. Among such claims are the reduction of "complex archipelagos into isolated islands, the denial of the history of modernity for island subjects, and the perceived threat of Indigenous cosmopolitanism associated with the 'travelling native'" (p. 170). Noting that the island has become a figure of spatial and temporal reckoning, DeLoughrey calls for diverse, typically marginalized voices and the collection of "geostories" to try and understand what the Anthropocene might mean, not least by reference to islands, archipelagos, and the aquatic imaginary (p. 32). Crucially, at no time does she seek to constitute *the* truth; her appeal is for an epistemologically eclectic approach. Such an appeal resonates with other, more general assertions made by Karl Weick and colleagues (2005) about sense-making and attempts to organize flux, notice, bracket, label, systematize, look back or forward, be present, communicate, and act—knowing that there is never one story.

Thus far, I have suggested that knowing what constitutes knowing what an island is may be shaped by truth claims, counterclaims, manipulations, silences, absences, erasures, ambiguities, labors to iron out those ambiguities, and efforts to make sense and make meaning via *a priori*, experiential, and *a posteriori* modes of engagement. Other complications arise in knowing what an island (or indeed an archipelago) is when attention turns to questions of *identity* and, increasingly, to questions of the *intersectional complexities* that always attend or are associated with being sexed, gendered, racialized, classed, or otherwise "located" (see Hopkins, 2019). In this vein, I note in passing that 79% of the 172 authors of papers published in *Island Studies Journal* between 2006 and 2015 hailed from Europe or North America (Stratford, 2015a, p. 144).

In focusing on islands, identity, and the literary imagination, Elizabeth McMahon (2016, p. 5) has already undertaken significant work on knowing islands and knowing oneself; she argues that our enchantment with islands "has created a kind of island ideogram in the collective psyche, one that connects identity, space and desire," not least for control—of context, other, self, or life itself (Donne, 1624/2001). McMahon rightly underscores the immense power of abstraction in Western conceptualizations of island-self.

As a corollary of that emphasis, she works to unsettle its pall by reference to Hau'ofa's archipelagic labors and to Suvendrini Perera's (2009) efforts to destabilize the overwhelming white continentalism of modern Australia (Stratford et al., 2011a). In the process, McMahon (2016) reaffirms the point that not all forms of knowing are atomistic, closed, and isolated. After all, islands also "operate in the spatial metaphorics of self and world, from womb and shelter to cosmos, planet and ego" (p. 13).

Little wonder that identity has become a high-stakes concern in efforts to decolonize both knowledge and epistemological approaches to it—both within and outside island and archipelagic studies. Not without coincidence, some such efforts are linked to militarism and security (Grydehøj et al., 2021) and the Anthropocene and climate crisis (Chandler & Pugh, 2020a, 2020b; DeLoughrey, 2017; Farbotko et al., 2016). Either way, as Craig Santos Perez (2021, p. 432) notes, it is crucial to "develop a critical agenda . . . [and be] critical of reductionist representations . . . [while] highlighting the complexities, agencies, and diversities of Pacific [and other] island experiences and subjectivities."

Perez's comments prioritize Indigenous agendas, and understandably so. The aforementioned Tasmanian premier Jim Bacon—a staunch supporter of Aboriginal land rights—was focused on a different decolonizing agenda. Recall his use in the Geneva tourism conference speech quoted above of tropes by which he inferred Tasmani*ans* were an island. In doing so, Bacon was making identity claims based on his understanding and resentment of Tasmania's marginalized status in the Australian federation and seeking paradiplomatic overtures to other regional and island economies and polities. In effect, he was leapfrogging the sovereign state to secure international relevance and purchase and rewrite how Tasmania and Tasmanians were seen elsewhere. His strategies and tactics were successful at least in relation to "'progressive politics' . . . [and] directly delivered government-funded projects like the Ten Days on the Island arts festival, initiatives that drew on and opened up *deeper wells of expression of Tasmanian identity*" (Cica, 2005, p. 10, emphasis added; contra, see Flanagan, 2004).

Just how does one know what constitutes a Tasmanian identity? Bacon claimed that Tasmanians are an island—a singularity—and much the same is implied by Natasha Cica's phrasing (and see also Cica, 2013). Neither might have actually thought of the island's populace as a homogeneous totality; the politics are too excoriating for that but, at the same time, the discursive temptations too great to resist. So, what is curious here—as it is in other, frequent claims about any kind of "people"—are the epistemological stakes at play. For, "who we think we are (identity) . . . shapes what we enact and how we interpret, which affects what outsiders think we are (image) and how they treat us, which stabilizes or destabilizes our identity" (Weick et al.

2005, p. 416). Hau'ofa and Perez note that the peoples of the Pacific have rightly seized every opportunity to claim and reclaim forms of identity that sever and/or deeply problematize colonial and imperial insults. But here, one might suggest that similar forms of resistance, reclamation, and innovation exist across the ex-colonial territories of the globe. What epistemological labors are done by "shared" understandings or "conventions," by the institutionalization of thought and action, and by the evolution of diverse forms of resistance to these same things (Scott, 1987)? As Sharon Bessell (2021) has shown in biographical narrative work on childhood identities and sense of belonging in Tasmanian coastal communities, these labors start early. They are also powerfully shaped by generational influences, a strong sense of place, and by ideas, such as those captured by novelist Christopher Koch (1958) and also cited by Bessell, that a small island sense of place is more intimate than elsewhere (shorthand, one assumes, for continental sites including, perhaps, their coastlines; and see also Conkling, 2007).

And what labors are performed by virtue of the lack of shared understanding or *conventions*, or by lack of resistance and the entrenchment of institutionalized forms of thinking? So, then, is it that *believing X makes it so*? Are island and archipelagic peoples different—and what, if any, internal differences are there on any one island among Indigenous, native-born non-Indigenous, and migrant residents? How specific need X be to dismiss the possibility that identity formation and politics in "landlocked" places such as Chad, Paraguay, or Nepal simply could not be comparable with those processes in the Maldives or Malta? Either way, the crucial point is that there is no single answer, no universal truth.

Hence, the perpetual need for epistemological work and vigilance in how we think—and how we think about how we think—lest we become unintelligible. And for lay people such as myself, thank goodness for resources such as *Britannica* and *Stanford Encyclopedia of Philosophy*, both of which have influenced the shape of this chapter (see Martinich and Stroll, n.d.; Steup & Neta, 2020).

As it happens, much epistemological work has been oriented to semantic and pragmatic debates about whether all apparently contrasting propositions related to "knowing-wh" (who, what, where, and when) can be reduced to the "generalised intellectualism" of "knowing that" (Parent, 2014). I do not enter into those debates here. What I do is state that I know that I live on an island (a where and, indeed, a what) and I know, despite being here for 25 years (a when), that I am not Tasmanian (a who).

Yet, *propositional knowledge* such as that captured by these few short statements is far from straightforward. If I lived on Diamond Island off Tasmania's northeast coast, I would only live on an island at the whim of tides. At other times, in that very same place, I would live on a peninsula, which could present all kinds of quandaries, not least those related to universal and specific claims about what is and what can be known and how. In fact, no one lives on Diamond Island, which is a nature reserve; although, of course, many nature reserves have human resident populations. Since I have lived in Tasmania for a long time and gave birth to a Tasmanian, I have a certain standing t/here in terms of identity claims; no longer a blow in; nevertheless, I am sometimes told, if only indirectly, that I am *in* but not *of* this/that place.

Be that as it may. If Plato is correct and knowledge requires transcending experience and using reasoning to pinpoint universals—or at very least, constants—then, as part of my constitution of identity and self-knowing, I may decide to claim that I am an islander because I reside on an island. I may also decide to claim I am an islander because I was born in the middle of Canada, where such formations "are not essential properties of space but instead are fluid cultural processes dependent on changing conditions of articulation or connection" (Vannini et al., 2009, p. 124). Or, if Aristotle (384 BCE–322 BCE) is correct, and reasoning (nous) is a power of the soul (psyche/intellect), I may claim I am a resident of Earth, a relational archipelago. As John Terrell (2020, p. 4) notes, "We need to accept that people and places exist down here on Earth *because* they are connected. In short, we need to stop thinking about islands (or populations) categorically and start thinking about them relationally" (emphasis added). In that way, my knowing is a form of consciousness.

Inevitably, complexities arise in how we know about how we know. Knowledge might be *necessary or contingent*. So, I may assert that all islands are always smaller than continents, which would be a necessary proposition. But, equally, any assertion I make that all islands are always surrounded entirely by water is contingent (and usually *a posteriori*), for clearly that is not the case, as islands connected by bridges or tunnels to mainlands remind us (Baldacchino, 2007a).

In addition, knowledge might be *analytic or synthetic*. The assertion that all islands are always smaller than continents is analytic because embedded in the term island is the state of being of a (particular) scale (Greenland/Diamond Island/unnamed rocky outcrop). Propositions are synthetic and *a posteriori* when such conditions do not hold, as with islands that can be surrounded by water but need not be so.

And knowledge might also be *tautological* or *significant*. For instance, according to John Scott (2014, n.p.), "the statement that 'Britain is an island and surrounded by water' is a tautology, since islands are by definition so described. Tautological explanations are similarly true by definition, or circular, and therefore unfalsifiable." However, if the term "surrounded" means that an island (not Britain) is inundated and submerged and its state of being in relation to water was not just about being encircled but being enveloped, then that knowledge would be significant in philosophical, geopolitical, legal, economic, and cultural terms (see Yamamoto & Esteban, 2010). In other words, such knowing would have existential importance.

Logic and fact also shape our epistemological labors. The proposition that all islands are smaller than continents is like the proposition that, if something is a landmass and it is smaller than something declared a continent, it is an island. Factually, North America is a continent, but it is also, in fact, an archipelago in both literal terms (because islands are located on the continental shelf) and political and metaphorical terms (because some islands claimed by the national governments comprising the North American continent are oceanic islands far from the continental shelf but identified as part of national territory) (Stratford, 2017). Thus, these nominations and designations are geographical conventions.

Knowledge might also draw much on *description* and *justification* as key parts of the work of "knowing that" or "knowing-wh." Description is crucial for accurately depicting features and characteristics of the world, including the mind, and for deciding what constitutes knowledge. The more normative work of justification is equally vital for figuring out what can be rationally justified, and it is intimately connected to ethical questions and questions of conduct. I might describe myself as an islander, but can I justify that claim if I do not understand or refuse to comply with the conventions of what islander means on this island or that island or another? Now, arguably, behavioral, social, and cultural conventions of the sort to which I allude exist anywhere and everywhere; but there is a substantial literature on these matters as they relate to islands, chiefly because of other claims that islands amplify both dysfunctional and the ideal (see Fletcher, 2008; More, 1516).

Moreover, all such labors require a range of corporeal, affective, and cognitive capacities. *Perception* is one such capacity—that is, to know by sensing. However, it may be that I spend considerable amounts of time inside the massively multiplayer online role-playing game known as *World of Warcraft* inhabiting the world, Azeroth. My perceptions may be so powerful that, as someone drawn to islands, I am persuaded that I really do come and go from one of the three major archipelagos in the Great Sea: the Broken Isles, Zandalar, or Kul Tiras (figure 4.3). Some commentators might then suggest that I am exhibiting dissociative behaviors (Guglielmucci et al., 2019). What I sense and perceive directly and indirectly and what those terms even mean become contested.

Introspection is another such capacity of knowing. If I think about it, I may realize that my persuasions about Azeroth are questionable and that time away from the game is useful. Or, switching to a different example, I may realize that, in island places, degrees of separation may be less than six, and I may need to inspect my own views and perceptions about the relational

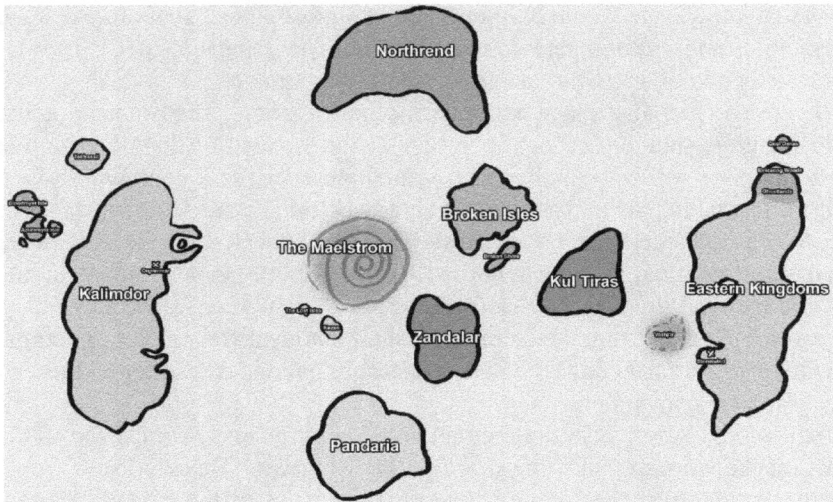

Figure 4.3.   Azeroth in *World of Warcraft*. *Source*: Wikimedia Commons | EdoAug.

dynamics of highly connected groups. For example, I recall having been in Tasmania only a matter of months when a colleague asked how it was all going. I said everything was fine and that I was establishing some interesting research but finding it really testing getting used to the ethical protocols the university then had in place. I happened to mention that I thought the person in the ethics office was giving me a difficult run and, to my chagrin, my colleague said, "Yes, she can be like that at home, too." He grinned, and then said, "Remember you live on an island now." That object lesson in diplomacy was also one about how introspection can aid one's thinking and help avoid varied pitfalls related to feeling infallible. The evaluative power of introspection is one to be harnessed, then.

We also have the ability to perceive, internalize, and think, associate what we are perceiving and understanding with what we already know, draw on memory, and then learn afresh. *Assimilation, association, accommodation, and memory* are, then, key capacities of knowing, for example, that the ghosts of Alcatraz, Ellis Island, Robben Island remain in the stories, artefacts, and infrastructures of those places (Drozdzewski & Birdsall, 2019; Maddern, 2008; Strange & Kempa, 2003). The same can be observed of mobile elements of island life such as the South Korean Sewol ferry disaster (Shin & Jin, 2021). Simultaneously, such capacities cannot be taken for granted. Remembering Ellis Island because one was there in, say, 1892 is different from remembering it reliably 50 years later in eyewitness testimony (see Głomb, 2021). Remembering that one was quarantined on Swinburne Island in Lower New York Bay is different from having been quarantined on Hoffman Island to the north (see Poole, 1937).

The past is not what it seems; neither is the present, nor the future. Little wonder that additional capacities to *reason* are important, even if they are also contingent on and affected by cultural influences such as gender, race, and class politics and dynamics. I might think I know how one should govern an island outpost because I have been trained in political science and can reason what works. But, without some other forms of knowing *in place*, literally and metaphorically, I will not know (as in understand) the relations that pertain there. I might even go and govern on-island and still have no sense of association or empathy and might therefore do what so many have done before and willfully or unwittingly disrupt fully functional cultural contexts.

Is it any wonder that knowing is so very difficult? For in the final analysis, were one considering islands and archipelagos or any other phenomena at all, there would be the sorts of navigations that have characterized this chapter. It would be so simple to know that I live on an island . . . and I do. But that knowing is, I now recognize, forged by a heady mix of *a priori* and *a posteriori* conceptions, stirred by ethical frameworks, particular logics, and theories. It is swirled through definitions and speculations, experiences and perceptions, diverse languages from spoken to haptic—diverse intelligences I may or may not be fully conscious of. And my knowing that I live on an island—and all that may entail—is also underwritten and overarched by truth-making and sense-making . . . my own and others. It is shaped by conventions and propositions over which I may or may not have influence, but that I can still subject to analysis, synthesis, and introspection. I would speculate that all such labors are handy, but that comes next.

Chapter 5

Speculating

What Approaches Are Used to Know in the Study of Islands and Archipelagos?

Godfrey Baldacchino

Speculate: To observe or view mentally; to consider, examine, or reflect upon with close attention; to contemplate; to theorize upon. (OED)

To speculate about islands and archipelagos is to theorize or conjecture—whether boldly or with a tentative demeanor—to stretch insights and possibilities.

The island is a proving ground for that which awaits discovery. Many narratives involve living things being or finding themselves isolated on islands, often against their will or purpose. And that is where the narrative tends to start: first, with the isolate "transforming" the island or adapting to its environment and—if given enough time—evolving into its own endemic and distinctive species. And then with the isolate facing and reeling from the inevitability of contact, there is discovery and incorporation into the larger world, for better or for worse (Getty, 2021). In the case of the Mauritian dodo (Quammen, 2012) or William Shakespeare's Caliban (*The tempest*; first performed 1611), the external agent gets the upper hand; for the island species, this spells extinction and slavery, respectively. In the case of *Robinson Crusoe*, the isolate gets the better of nature and culture, becoming the effective authority of

Source: **Jean-Yves Vigneau.**

71

his island, and complete with his own subjects: well, goats, mainly (Defoe, 1719). For those like Crusoe, who succeed and emerge stronger from the engagement with the outside world, this ambition to control and lord over island space and species may be pathological: "Can one be but a Governor on one's own island" (Redfield, 2000, p. 12; see also Weaver-Hightower, 2007)?

Figure 5.1. Thomas More's Utopia (1516, More: 1478–1535). *Source*: Wikimedia Commons | Public Domain.

A (small) island is an invitation to embrace, a thing that is beguilingly easy to hold, to own, to manipulate (Baldacchino, 2005). Might this quality not explain why so many islands are also self-governing jurisdictions, antecedents to the territorial sovereign state (Steinberg, 2005); and might it not also explain why *only 10* populated islands in the world are shared between more than one country (Baldacchino, 2013)? No wonder *Robinson Crusoe* is a paean to invasive colonialism (Hymer, 1971; Kinane 2016) and read critically in relation to "male-hero-human, on the side of the subject; and female-obstacle-boundary-space, on the other" (De Lauretis, 1984, p. 121).

The isolation-connection nexus is a critical feature of all islands. It is embodied in every island map, sketch, or diagram: first, a self-defined territorial landmass, totally surrounded by water, and thus separated physically from the mainland, or other islands. Then, at a different scale, wells up a realization that there may be an airstrip (and an airport), along with a seaport, a ferry, a container or cruise ship terminal, a jetty, a yacht marina, all the latter preferably located in sheltered bays and harbors. Already in Thomas More's *Utopiae insulae figura* (1516), these two characteristics are evident (figure 5.1).

Moreover, Utopia had been a peninsula, but King Utopus had transformed the territory into an island through a deliberate act of civil engineering: digging a channel 24 kilometers (15 miles) wide. That act was not simply to improve Utopia's defensibility against attack but to illuminate the point that the perfection of its social and political state would be fittingly matched by its equally special geography.

BEYOND THE ISLAND

Before getting to "the island" *per se*, let us first recognize that an island focus is not compulsory when dealing with islands. The reference to archipelagos, mainstreamed in this book, is testimony that adopting a pluri-island or interisland—as against a single island—frame of reference is also a useful heuristic, conceptual, and analytic stance. Sea-faring, nomadic and foraging communities would conceptualize islands as parts of larger, mental schema, incorporating mainlands (Capistrano, 2010).

Today, various jurisdictions consist of combinations of island and mainland (including coastal) regions, possibly or precisely to thwart the emergence of island-specific, pseudo-ethnic identities. This jurisdictional arrangement is fairly clear in the case of Scotland: out of 32 local council areas, only three—Western Isles, Orkney, and Shetland—are made up only of islands. In spite of being the smallest, it is these three local councils that have successfully lobbied Edinburgh to recognize their particular predicament and development challenges as island units and secure their own £100 million Island Growth

Deal (2022). And then, there may be internal differences that merit recognition on particular islands: as the archaeological record attests, a feature such as a mountain range may separate two communities on the same island—while their closest neighbors, trading partners, or hunting grounds may be on another island, a shorter and easier boat ride away (Gosden & Pavlides, 1994).

KNOWING THE ISLAND

There are multiple ways of knowing an island, and some of these approaches are specific to the island form.

The land-sea dichotomy

First is the land/sea dichotomy, taken for granted when islands are defined as land surrounded by water. One current understanding is that such a dualism, like all dualisms, is crude and not too useful as an explanatory technique. We inhabit a "terraqueous globe" (DeLoughrey, 2019a, p. 171), and we must remind ourselves of how island (and coastal) lives in particular are incorporated and imbricated in and with the sea in multiple ways, across time, space, and scale (Gillis, 2012). Indigenous knowledge is a helpful reminder of how, for example, ocean currents can be more important—and indeed vital—than land features when it comes to island maps (figure 5.2).

The island as graphic object

Second is the topographical technique itself. For example, ask anyone to draw "the island." Not a particular island but a stylized, imaginary island that would have the essential characteristics of an island, any island. Various representations will result: lush green habitats, with palm trees; or dark outcrops, with dormant or active volcanoes; or busy and densely populated settlements. (The isolation-connection nexus described above is likely to feature in all of these.) Islands, after all, reflect diverse urban, suburban, and rural landscapes worldwide but arguably do so in extreme ways: from totally empty or depopulated islands, some protected for scientific study (Aldabra, Surtsey), to the islands with the highest population density on the planet (Ap Lei Chou, Male). But the particular way in which the island is represented is insightful: and two particular techniques are typical (Bonnett, 2020). In the twenty-first century, accustomed as it is to airplane vistas and Google Maps, a top-down rendition of the island is common; and the *whole* island would be represented within the borders of the sheet, screen, or canvas. (This rendering is impossible with a mainland state, unless it is fantastically drawn, shorn of

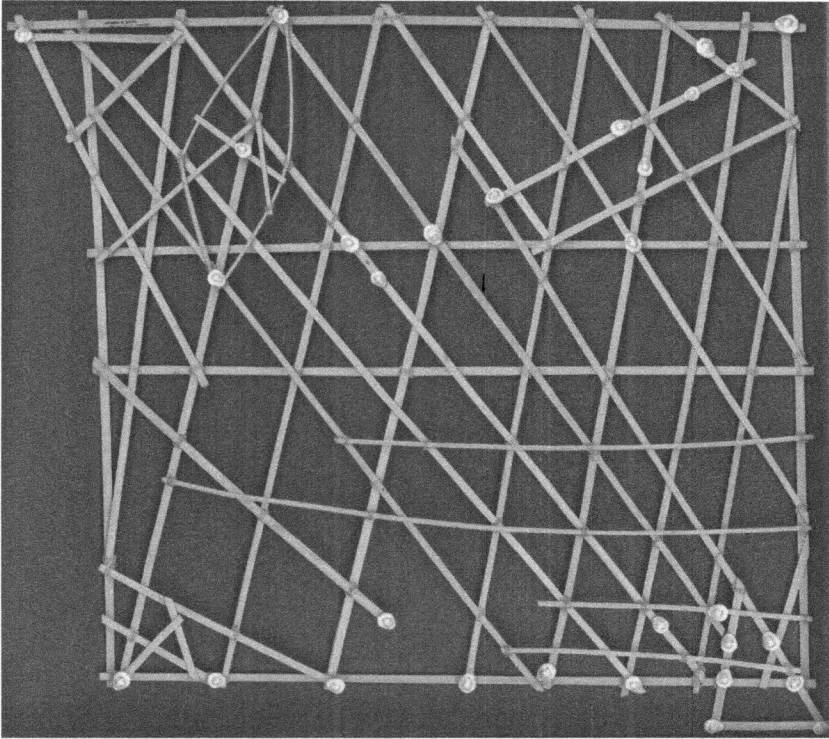

Figure 5.2. Marshall Islands navigation chart, Rebbelib type, made up of shells bound to palm leaf sticks with bast strings (Majuro, 1920?). *Source*: Library of Congress.

its landward neighbors.) Rarely, there is a horizontal, panoramic rendition of the prototypical island, suggesting what it would look like if, say, it is being seen by a passenger on board a ship heading toward, or away from, its main harbor (figures 5.3 and 5.4).

The island as known by others, including scientists

Third is the nature and background of the person undertaking the "knowing" exercise. The "insider-outsider" nexus is another critical binarism in island studies (Randall, 2021). The smaller, poorer, and/or less populated the island, the more likely that its web, textual, and literary content and its own representation are driven and shaped by nonislanders: well-meaning sponsors and benefactors, tourists, travel agencies, property developers, even academics (Baldacchino, 2008, 2010c). Where islanders lose control of the capacity to decide the basis for any lure their islands may have, they (and their locales)

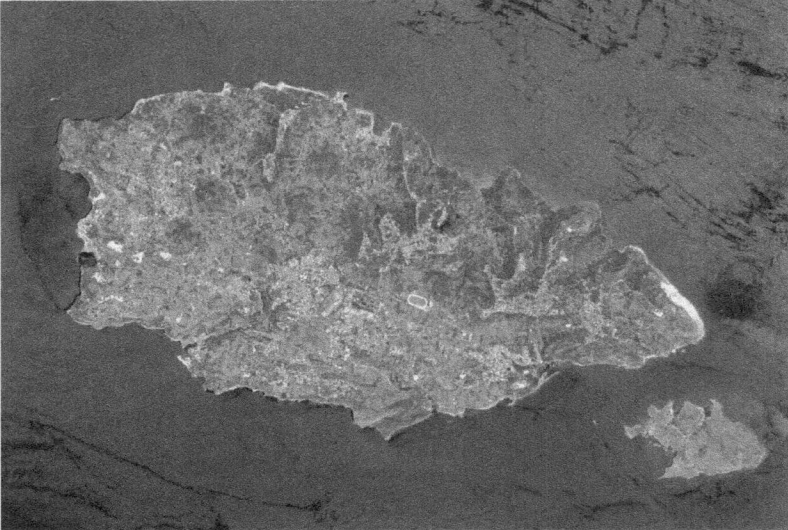

Figure 5.3.   An image of the island of Gozo, part of the European archipelago state of Malta, the world's tenth smallest country by land area. Captured by the Copernicus Sentinel-2B geostationary satellite of the European Space Agency in 2017. Gozo's main harbor, called Mġarr, with its breakwater, is on the bottom right, facing the islet of Comino. *Source*: Contains modified Copernicus Sentinel data.

Figure 5.4.   Approaching Mġarr, the main harbor of Gozo, with the ferry, under good weather conditions. The edge of the breakwater is just visible on the left (image taken in 2019). *Source*: Wikimedia Commons | HH58.

may fall victim to exercises in caricature, stereotyping, and casting that speak to often profit-driven motives and intentions (Baum et al., 2000; King, 1993; Lockhart, 1997; Lockhart et al., 1993). References to hospitable and welcoming people, inviting lifestyles, lush climates, and intriguing landscapes abound—and are not just propagated by "outsiders." Just consider various schemes related to "citizenship by investment" or "remote working" that are peddled from various small island states.

Among the most celebrated "outsiders" visiting islands, and doing so specifically *because* they are islands, are natural scientists. Each of the two pioneering British scientists propounding evolutionary theory adopted their own archipelago to observe and document the evolutionary dynamics that come into play among species on islands, given that the latter are relatively more isolated habitats: Charles Darwin in the Galápagos (Ecuador) and Alfred Russel Wallace in the Aru Islands (Indonesia) (Kutschera, 2003). These forays, initially accidental, have spawned a whole branch of science where island diversity serves to develop a better and more informed understanding of how certain parameters play out—their age, size, location, geology, altitude, climate, degree of isolation from other islands and the closest mainland, and so on. For example, consider the number and type of species one would expect to find; the existence of endemic species and their vulnerability to non-natives; changes in species size (dwarfism, giantism); the effects of invasive species—including human settlements and developments—on "pristine" habitats; the effects of extreme weather events such as hurricanes or volcanic eruptions; and the overall dynamics of species arrivals and extinctions. All these are generously manifest on, and informed by, island exemplars (Kueffer et al., 2016). That is because islands are clearly the most explicit and active natural evolutionary nurseries; they "can serve as large-scale [but small enough to be manageable] laboratories for the investigation of biological processes" (Cliff & Haggett, 1984, p. 10). "They present clear examples of the evolution of unusual forms due to the founder effect, small gene pools and genetic drift, limited predation, inescapability, [and] unique microclimates" (Scott, 2020, p. 1). The understanding of these island dynamics as not simply subject to chance or individual choice and behavior but as liable to modeling and forecasting is often credited to Robert MacArthur and Edward Wilson (1967) and their theory of island biogeography.

Natural scientists deploy the scientific method to develop this knowledge. They get to know what they know by virtue of well-established processes of hypothesis or theory generation, hypothesis testing, and then hypothesis affirmation or refutation. Physical observation of phenomena, in the field or in a laboratory, is standard practice. To proceed on the basis of an objective assessment, scientists also deploy the rigors of transparency, systematicity, and repeatability. They collect evidence, consisting of quantitative and/or qualitative data (which have different tests of validity as aired elsewhere in

Figure 5.5.   A scientist out in the field, collecting data. Mackay Island National Wildlife Refuge, North Carolina, United States. *Source*: NC Wetlands.

this volume), and they seek to logically understand what data tell them in relation to initial questions. That work is done in a way that can be tested, replicated, and confirmed or refuted in varied ways by others (figure 5.5). Many scientists thus may see themselves as positivist researchers, searching for falsifiable generalizations; some embrace the interface with qualitative research (Philip, 1998).

It is valid to ask here whether and how the scientific method is itself nuanced by a small island's geography. When dealing with small islands and fragile populations, for example, scientists' presence can change a finely balanced ecosystem, setting into motion changes leading to habitat change or species extinction. Some places, such as Australia's subantarctic Heard and Macquarie Islands, are highly susceptible to colonization by species introduced by humans and are subject to strict quarantine protocols intent on preventing contamination (Potter, 2007). The Hawthorne effect suggests that the mere act of observing something will change it: this brings in elements of subjectivity, personal bias, and indeterminacy and therefore suggests a fallacy of repeatability to all human science, one predicated on observations (Oswald et al., 2014).

The island is known by others, including fiction writers

Islands are terrifically exciting habitats that have animated fiction and doing so long before they were associated with advances in evolutionary science.

They sometimes impose an isolation that obliges characters to travel in, face the trials of reinventing themselves, and then travel out: changed utterly (if successful); or to lose, succumb, and die (if not). There is a thin line between the island being haven or horror—and its often-accidental inhabitants ending up victors or victims, protagonists or agonists. Consider the travails (and travels) of Ulysses, Lord of Ithaca (including seven long years with the sorceress Calypso on the island of Ogygia); the meditated education of Ibn Yaqzan (Ibn Tufajl, 1180?); the journey of the characters stranded on the "stone raft" of Iberia (Saramago, 1986), to the frightened characters on a small island in Devon, in the United Kingdom, in the world's best-selling mystery novel (Christie, 1939). All these plots fall easily within this utopian/ dystopian mold.

As with most stories, readers are privileged observers, gazing consumers of the saga unfolding under their scrutiny. They know what is going on and at times are equipped with hindsight, have possession of the *denouement* of the narrative, glean the insights of multiple characters, or deploy varied technologies of surveillance. Occasionally, readers are fooled into believing that persons or even objects are actually agentic subjects (Bioy Casares, 1940; Lehane, 2010).

Unlike most stories, however, *island* stories also have their characters somehow also knowing about and coming to terms with their enisled geographies. They climb up to the highest point and circumambulate or circumnavigate their space such that they suffer the stark realization that they are indeed on an island, often uninhabited, with the despair (or perhaps relief) that comes with that discovery.

An enduring (Western) tradition has considered islands as special places of mystery, solace, danger, or worship, first in the Aegean—the world's original archipelago—and then beyond (Gillis, 2004). With the onset of the European age of "discovery," islands started being constructed as outposts of aberrant exoticism, populated by innocent and exuberant natives (Gillis & Lowenthal, 2009; Lowenthal, 1972). Islands are presented as locales of desire, as platforms of paradise, and as habitual sites of fascination, emotional offloading, or religious pilgrimage, hence their intrinsic appeal as tourism destinations across cultures. The geophysical forces that have shaped islands have also created some spectacular landscapes, which have become tourist allures in their own right: consider Bora Bora (French Polynesia), Hạ Long Bay (Vietnam), Big Island, Hawai'i (United States), Santorini (Greece), Soqotra (Yemen), Prince Edward Island (Canada), Yakushima (Japan), the Tasmanian Wilderness (Australia), and part-time island Mont-Saint-Michel (France). Additionally, the manner in which people have sought to conquer or engineer island landscapes has ushered in other exceptional, cultural-cum-natural formations that draw the curious from all over the world: from the islands of Gorée (Senegal), Hashima (Japan), Lindisfarne (United Kingdom),

Skellig Michael (Ireland), Zanzibar stone town (Tanzania), to the megalithic temples in Gozo (Malta). Not surprisingly, all these locations are inscribed as UNESCO's World Heritage Sites. In fact, almost one-sixth of these world heritage sites are on islands or islands *in toto* (Baldacchino, 2021b).

Small islands in particular attract visitors and seem to invite those visitors to come to know them fully and deeply, since they can suggestively be "done" and "taken in" in a day or two, or even over a few hours—for visitors disembarking cruise ships. Such a fast knowing was also practiced in early anthropology. The tantalizingly simple "pattern" of small island life presents "a unique opportunity for authoritative and definitive scholarship by external 'experts.' *Veni, vidi, vici*, in a flash" (Baldacchino, 2004, p. 276). Here is a marketable possibility of claiming an understanding of the totality of a locale as trophy (Baum, 1997). It is relatively common to look at "the island" as synecdoche for larger wholes (the Earth) or as a microcosm—with the false euphoria that results when, by virtue of "knowing" an island, one presumes to know the world (Deschenes & Chertow, 2004; Gugganig & Klimburg-Witjes, 2021). But these metaphors are also pernicious and deserve a critical reckoning.

The island as known by islanders, on their own terms?

Finally, islands are increasingly known *as islands* by their own island residents. That stance is neither automatic nor common-sense: many islanders grow up socialized in worldviews that privilege continental interpretations of reality. By way of example, the imperative of having a manufacturing industry as a prerequisite to development may remain unquestioned—even though that trajectory fitted best the material, financial, and human resources and scales available to those in large jurisdictions. Out of a sense of obligation, those who govern small, often island, states and territories have often toyed with but struggled to set up any productive, manufacturing capacity of note—their failure down to a lack of markets, labor, raw materials, and economies of scale (Kaplinsky, 1983). It has been evident for some time that small island development trajectories may sidestep manufacturing altogether (Bertram & Watters, 1985); the latter only becomes significant if it mainly supports tourist consumption (Baldacchino, 1998). For most small island states, their largest locally based, and often locally owned, manufacturing facility is a brewery (Baldacchino, 2010a). Hence a turn that seeks to understand islands on their own terms. McCall (1994), following Christian Depraetere (1991), coined the term *nissology* to identify how to recenter and reclaim island studies around the visions, needs, and perspectives of islands and islanders themselves. Yaso Nadarajah and Adam Grydehøj (2016) have subsequently made a strong case for island studies as a decolonizing project that is perhaps unfinishable.

That islanders write about their own islands is long overdue. They do so to confront and dispel the heavy layers of paradisiacal myth that have bedeviled their representation over decades, if not longer—even as they struggle to project the appearance of a harmonious community to tourists, since such is deemed implicitly as part of the "package" (Baldacchino, 2008; Grydehøj, 2011). They do so to provide their own interpretations of island life, warts and all, even while the growth of the field of island studies owes much to work by mainlanders or those from the Global North. And they do so to deliver a corpus of scholarship that privileges local and Indigenous voices and stories—including in their own native languages.

These offerings are packaged and transmitted via a whole range of formats and research methodologies: these include both scientific treatises and works of fiction; music, dance, and song; and prose and poetry (Baldacchino, 2011a; Patke, 2018). It helps that almost a quarter of the world's sovereign states are islands or archipelagos, 27 of which have resident populations of less than one million. The United Nations, with its General Assembly where every sovereign state has one vote and voice regardless of size or heft, has been a significant institution in alerting the international community to the predicament of small island developing states and has been supporting specific programs of action since the UN Barbados Conference in 1994. Climate action has also provided a powerful incentive to those in small island jurisdictions to appeal to a global readership and listenership that nowadays seems sensitive to their predicament and may perhaps be galvanized to take resolute action to save the planet. The visible impact of the Alliance of Small Island States (AOSIS) and its moral authority on climate action negotiations at the 2015 Paris Summit (Bolon, 2018) is accompanied and bolstered by some powerful island voices from civil society, such as those of Marshallese poet, performer, and educator Kathy Jetñil-Kijiñer.

INSIDER/OUTSIDER PERSPECTIVES TO "KNOWING THE ISLAND"

Whereas ethnic, racial, ideological, or partisan divides may be significant in the social and political lives of most communities, the insider-outsider division seems especially poignant and relevant to (especially small) island societies (Marshall, 2008). Islands are transnational: as Kenneth Olwig (2003) recognized, a full understanding of "small island life" is not possible without integrating an appreciation of its often extensive and powerful diaspora, now more likely to be nourished by waves and cycles of circular migration. Concurrently, "small island life" is vastly impoverished without acknowledging the influence and contribution of foreign workers, rotating civil servants from central government, second home residents, short-term students, and visiting experts and consultants. Critical battles would be waged over rights to land and property, citizenship and nationality of "settlers" versus "natives," and their overall effects on local gentrification (Clark et al., 2007).

Being identified or self-positioned as either an insider or an outsider is naïve and superficial: many researchers may find themselves somewhere in between, situated in such a way that they would fit within their researched group on at least a number of variables—but not others (Gair, 2012). Each of these two essentialized factions of insiders and outsiders may enjoy or expect privileges with respect to island research and scholarship in general. Two contrasting ways of "knowing" are at play here. Natives may accuse outsiders of the so-called Gulliver effect: of dropping in and peddling advice and opinions without grounded appreciation of the island where they are, and its nested politics; of proposing deductive, cookie-cutter solutions that do not necessarily work for their small and enisled locales; and of being instrumental and predatory with their subjects, treating these as means to an end such as securing data or fulfilling the terms of a paid contract (Higginbottom & Serrant-Green, 2005). Indeed, local subjects may reject opportunities to participate in outsider-driven research because they may feel that their well-being is not the principal focus of the researcher: the latter would take the information required and run, giving nothing back to the community (Randolph et al., 2018).

In their turn, outsiders may dismiss locals as being vain, obsessed, and driven by petty parish pump politics, unable or reluctant to see "the big picture" to learn from past mistakes or from others' practices, and often unwilling and loathe to accept "come from aways" into their inner social circles and networks. At the same time, outsiders may think that they know best; and yet they still have to admit that they are completely reliant on one or a few local, knowledgeable gatekeepers in order to access their research sites or subjects. Without such well-placed resources, one's "efforts and valuable research time will evaporate, without meaningful progress being made" (Kydd-Williams, 2019, p. 426; see also Creswell, 2015).

Françoise Péron (2004) suggests that the different ways in which insiders and outsiders know the same islands is also evident from the manner in which they represent them graphically. Assuming a top-down cartographic rendition of an island space, outsiders are more likely to illustrate island maps with landmarks, locations of cities and towns, and tourist spots, possibly to justify or show off their familiarity with the place. Insiders are more likely to identify places on the map that have meaning to them and may connect with personal experiences. At a 2022 international island studies conference in Croatia, participants were asked to meet at the site of a *former* bus station. Even the manner in which places or directions are referred to would differ: outsiders use a Google Maps-style technocratic paradigm, referring to street names and highway numbers. For example, by car to get from Charlottetown to Summerside, Prince Edward Island, Canada, it would normally take 55 minutes along Route 2 West, the Veterans' Memorial Highway. Not so for locals: to get from Charlottetown to Summerside by car takes about an hour, first on the Malpeque Road, then continuing on the Blueshank Road.

It may appear ideal to undertake research on one's own small island; but, unbeknownst to them or otherwise, insiders doing research in their own small island communities face additional dilemmas. First, it may prove difficult to anonymize respondents or research sites. There may be single examples of businesses and professionals on a small island: to camouflage any such sources would be challenging. Additionally, respondents based on small island would know about this problem and implicitly understand that whatever they may say, even in strict conditions of anonymity and confidentiality, could eventually still be traced to them: this may have consequences, such as reprisals from members of the local community. Thus, truths may go unspoken, counternarratives untapped, and subaltern voices silenced (Matheson et al., 2020). The price for going against the grain and the dominant social code in small communities may be very high and may involve exile/ex-isle: island life can be hell for dissidents (Baldacchino, 2012b; Bongie, 1998). Either way, the discussion is not settled and any decision to erase identities in order to protect them must be weighed against an increasing disposition and ethical expectation to privilege unheard voices and engage with one's research subjects and communities.

Second, for better or for worse, researchers may know, and in turn they may be known by, their subjects. Once again, in such cases it is assumed that a research ethics template developed elsewhere—where respondent anonymity and confidentiality of gathered data can be more readily guaranteed—applies to small island locales. Not so. It may even be impossible to avoid a meaningful relationship with one's research subjects; and both researchers and their participants must weigh the real prospects of meeting again in other circumstances after the interview, as they go through the research encounter. Would they risk local retribution by what they disclose, or would they rather prefer to stay silent or uncommitted? What happens when one's putative respondents would be known directly or indirectly, through friends, relatives, and other contacts, by the investigator? How do respondents massage their replies when they may know juicy details about the background of their interviewers, that not even the latter may be aware of? These may include episodes from those persons' past, including details of their education, transgressions, political sympathies, and former close relationships. Thus, there is a case to be made for privileging researchers who are either insiders or outsiders to the island contexts they may be studying (Baldacchino, 1997; Matheson et al., 2020).

In short, island studies theory is messy and nuanced: by location, by research traditions, by the paradigms of the researcher and the researched. And that is how it should be, as a maturing field of inquiry. It is a timely work in progress that is catching up on the silence, invisibility, and symbolic or physical violence experienced by many island peoples over time. It helps us reflect on old questions about islands and islanders, where these have been posed—but also, to frame new ones.

Chapter 6

Guiding

What Rationales and Rules Typify the Study of Islands and Archipelagos?

Elizabeth McMahon

Guide: [n] One who leads or shows the way, especially to a traveller in a strange country. [v] To act as guide to; to go with or before for the purpose of leading the way. (OED)

A fundamental assumption of research is that it will yield new knowledge that will fill gaps in our understandings and/or shift our accepted conceptions—including in relation to island studies. Filling those gaps involves addressing questions or problems in the field, which may be conceptual or practical or both. This chapter and the next, which focus on research methodologies and research methods respectively, provide the means by which we can achieve the objectives the proposed problem has identified.

This chapter considers particular perspectives on research methodologies, positioning them as the rationales and rules that help us shape research design and construct the frameworks for each research project in which we engage. These rationales and rules are shaped by the ontological and epistemological frameworks of our disciplines and fields, as noted in earlier chapters. Research designs and frameworks govern our decisions regarding the methods we deploy to conduct the research, which are the topic of the following

Source: **Jean-Yves Vigneau.**

85

chapter. Together our research methodologies and methods determine what our research can discover. They set the goals, scope, and the limits of our projects and guide the pathways by which new knowledge is delivered.

Not all research methodologies are equal and a survey of various such methodologies via databases shows they are far more thoroughly documented and more widely deployed in some disciplines and fields than others. The social sciences have the most defined and widely applied practices of delineating methodologies, and this chapter is deeply informed by those models and debates. However, their range has been expanded here to include methodologies from the natural sciences—as they are axiomatic to those disciplines—and the humanities and creative arts—where methodologies are far less explicit. Moving across these fields will enable us to think through some of the challenges and enormous rewards of working at the intersections across and between disciplines and fields to see how we might develop complex methodologies that span them. In all aspects of this endeavor, I am guided by an overriding objective to flesh out how we frame productive research projects that create new knowledge and address problems in island studies.

DECOLONIZING RESEARCH METHODOLOGIES

An objective among island studies scholars to study islands and archipelagos on their own terms is also a call to decolonize research. Decolonized research methodologies acknowledge the primacy of islands and islanders over and above a long history of imposed assumptions that viewed and treated islands as ideal colonies and prisons. Especially significant for researchers is the ongoing objectification of islands and islanders according to durable perceptions of islands as ideal laboratories and ready-made case studies (Blaim, 2020; Darwin, 1859/1997; Fitzhugh & Hunt, 1997; Hennessy, 2018; Mead, 1928/2001; Taitingfong, 2020; Wallace, 1869). The decolonization of research methodologies needs to be considered across all aspects of any research project, including implications for its circulation in accepted knowledge economies such as universities and research institutes and relative to institutional research support. That point is well summarized by scholars from Aotearoa/New Zealand, for whom the study of:

> research methodology in the current political and social context is not free from the influence of western disciplines of knowledge that have defined what counts as research within academic institutions, science organizations, publishers, funding bodies and the media. The knowledge economy, knowledge society, and policy links between knowledge and wealth creation are powerful political drivers for how different forms of knowledge production are viewed, supported, rewarded and legitimated and conversely how other forms are not. (Smith et al., 2016, p. 141)

In studies of islands and archipelagos, the multiple forms of island colonization and devaluation include many First Nations peoples, whose ontologies and cosmologies are integrally interwoven with place (Chiblow, 2021; Taylor-Bragge et al., 2021). In Australia, First Nations peoples talk about being "on Country" as a complete condition of being:

> For Aboriginal people "country" does not just mean the creeks, rock outcrops, hills and waterholes. "country" includes all living things. It incorporates people, plants and animals. It embraces the seasons, stories and creation spirits. "country" is both a place of belonging and a way of believing. (Aboriginal Art, 2022)

This ontology challenges many Western knowledge systems at their core. What might the processes of decolonizing research methodologies entail in these contexts? For Linda Smith (1999, p. 5), "research is probably one of the dirtiest words in the Indigenous world's vocabulary." However, Bagele Chilisa (2019, p. 3) notes that, alongside the enduring colonialism within research ontologies and epistemologies, there is nevertheless a need to bring "Indigenous methodologies into the research arena as a means of addressing the goals of enhanced human rights and social justice." How do we fulfil the directive to study islands on their own terms in this context? What are the implications of this imperative for conceptual and practical research projects? How can they be embedded and mapped throughout the development of our research designs and frameworks? These are questions so profound on so many levels, and we cannot effect a complete transformation in this research guide. However, Marc Higgins and Eun-Ji Amy Kim (2019, p. 113) helpfully suggest that "it is productive for researchers to shift attention from the *ends of* research to its *means*: methodology" (original emphasis).

This focus on methodology alerts us to the need to attend to the very categories, concepts, and structures of research and to their implicit colonial baggage. The focus helps us identify the primary site of decolonized research as one pertaining to methodology rather than solely or predominantly to findings or conclusions. It stresses that non-Indigenous researchers cannot merely state a position against colonial practices and need to enact that objective by disrupting and complicating their methodologies. Those labors may include deploying Indigenous methodologies (Clapham et al., 2021; Smith, 1999). They may involve juxtaposing knowledge systems and accepting their nonalignment (Manathunga et al., 2022). Those labors definitely mean reading and deploying works by First Nations theorists even where that requires rethinking the research team, framework, and project design (Farbotko et al., 2022). In my own field of literary studies, such efforts involve an ethics of intense attention to the modes of the text's meaning-making that respond to aesthetic, political, and philosophical differences. They also require that I make explicit the (known) shortfalls in my (the non-Indigenous reader's) understanding while also bringing to the text the armory of Western literary criticism (and see George et al., 2020). Such attention is an act of respect to acknowledge the text's capacity to commandeer a dual vision and a dual heritage; the text is a surplus, not a deficit.

IMPLICIT, EXPLICIT, AND DIVERSE METHODOLOGIES

Island studies comprises scholars from diverse fields and disciplines who deploy a wide range of research methodologies and methods. It is worth spending time thinking through that diversity before diving into the detail because there are different levels of familiarity with the concept of methodology, let alone its varied practices across the disciplinary spectrum.

To those researchers unconvinced that research methodology applies to your discipline, I urge an open mind. In particular, researchers in the arts and in sections of the humanities may find much of this discussion to be new ground and may think it is not relevant to them. I am an arts and humanities scholar and learned these methodologies through interdisciplinary projects, especially in island studies, and they have proved invaluable in all aspects of my research.

To those from disciplines more used to formalized research paradigms, the more interdisciplinary perspective adopted here will provide a greater literacy for reading across the span of disciplines that comprise island studies and constructing interdisciplinary and transdisciplinary research projects. Importantly, too, it will develop the capacity to develop and adapt conventional research practices to projects that involve island cultures that may not share or value those methodologies.

ASKING QUESTIONS AND IDENTIFYING PROBLEMS

Research projects begin by identifying a problem or proposition. In the research context the word "problem" is not used in the everyday sense to mean something inherently negative or unwelcome but in its older meaning of a riddle or puzzle or a "question proposed for academic discussion or scholastic disputation" (OED). A research problem might address a *practical* issue such as environmental sustainability or economic systems and diasporic patterns that include significant "problems" as they are understood in the everyday sense. But it does not have to do so. Alternatively, a research problem might address a *theoretical* or *conceptual* problem to increase knowledge and understanding related to the paradigms and practices of a given discipline or field. Knowledge gained from investigating theoretical problems may help people develop research projects focused on practical problems by prompting or providing new research methodologies and approaches. Island studies spans a great range of both these types of problems. That the problem presents itself for investigation means that there is a gap in knowledge that needs to be filled; it may be a small gap dealt with incrementally or a large one involving paradigmatic leaps, but all of it is useful.

Remember, scholarly research aims to yield new knowledge by dealing with problems. Implicit in that statement is that research has value and will benefit disciplines, fields, individuals, and societies. How do we measure such value and benefit? How do we maximize the potential of research to achieve those ends? Who are the major beneficiaries of research? The gaps in knowledge we identify provide sound indicators of value. So does the range of relevance and application. Not all our research has to change a paradigm or revolutionize the field, but the question of its relative importance may prompt us to redesign or expand the scope of our questions. On that understanding, it is generally understood that there are five categories of research problems:

1. exploratory research investigates phenomena that are little understood; this research involves identifying and/or discovering new data or variables and generating questions for more research,
2. explanatory research aims to explain phenomena and events including their causes and consequences,
3. descriptive research collects and depicts data without necessarily speculating on causes or consequences,
4. interrogative research seeks to understand processes, relationality, people, and phenomena including cultural products and events, and
5. predictive research forecasts events and behaviors based on phenomena under study. (adapted from Kitchin & Tate, 2000, p. 3)

It is usual for some or all of these categories to overlap and one research project may have more than one objective, but it is beneficial to identify the main one on which to focus research and organize the design of a given project. The examples below examine how several projects in island studies identify and justify their research problems.

Theoretical and conceptual problems and limits

In the abstract for the influential essay "Envisioning the archipelago" (Stratford et al., 2011a), a group of us identified a set of common assumptions about islands that we sought to scrutinize because it was problematic for us in the sense outlined above—a puzzling set of ideas. The essay's mode is predominantly interrogative but it was also an exploratory response to others' calls for definitional shifts in how islands were and are conceived (Baldacchino, 2005, 2007a; Depraetere, 1991, 2008; Hay, 2006; McCall, 1994).

The essay opened with the observation that "*certain limitations* arise from the persistent consideration of two common relations of islands in the humanities and social sciences: land and sea, and island and continent/mainland" (p. 113; emphasis added). In it, we characterized the dominant approach to island ontologies across a range of disciplinary fields as limited and, therefore, as impeding meaningful research. We argued that research on islands was limited by approaching islands according to two sets of oppositions— "land and sea, and island and continent/mainland" (p. 113). And we identified a gap that we sought to fill and gestured to the need to provide alternatives to the habits of binary analysis. Specifically, in the following terms we put forward a model that we hoped would enable islands to be studied on their own terms: "What remains largely absent or silent are ways of being, knowing, and doing—ontologies, epistemologies, and methods—that illuminate island spaces as inter-related, mutually constituted and co-constructed: as island and island" (p. 113). Finally, we proposed the means to address absences and silences via the model of the archipelago. As works by Caribbean and Pacific scholars in particular show, we were not the first to do so, but the work was an important theoretical and conceptual watershed—at least for us and possibly others (see Benítez-Rojo, 1996; Blomgren, 2021; DeLoughrey, 2001; LaFlamme, 1983). In short, therefore, we sought to map out and justify:

> a *research agenda* proposing *robust and comprehensive explorations* of a comparatively neglected nexus of relations. In advancing those aims, the essay's goal was to (re)inscribe the theoretical, metaphorical, real and empirical power and potential of the archipelago: of seas studded with islands; island chains; relations that may embrace equivalence, mutual relation and difference in signification. (Stratford et al., 2011a, p. 113; emphasis added)

In retrospect, we now think it noteworthy that archipelagic thinking has been explored across several disciplines and fields, incorporating domains of abstraction, imagination, history, society, and materiality. For the archipelago is both a material geographical topography and an overarching metaphor, although even that notion has produced debate (Hay, 2013; Hayward, 2012; Stratford, 2020). The interconnection of material and immaterial realities is especially important in island studies because the unique status of islands in the imagination produces potent effects in real terms. Accordingly, the shift being proposed in our 2011 essay could only be effective if the methodology reached across the ontologies, epistemologies, theories, and discourses of multiple disciplines.

Another exemplification of problems and limits is found in the introduction to a collection of essays on the Croatian archipelago; Nens Starc (2020a) identifies another limitation arising from existing definitions of islands, namely that they are overly generic. He questions or *interrogates* both the *scope* of existing definitions of islands (do they cover too much?) and their *utility*

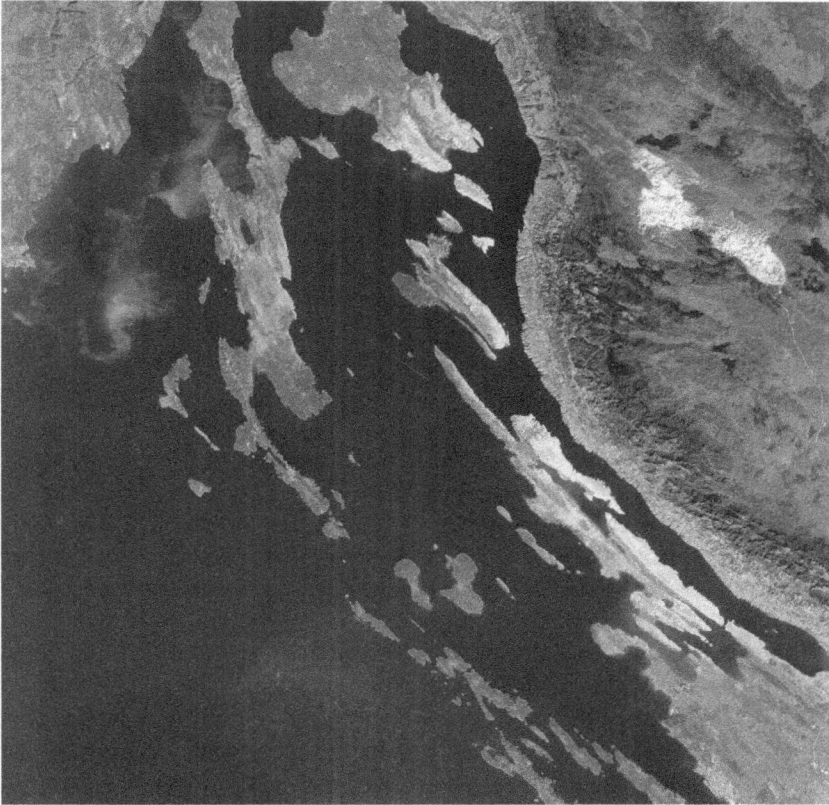

Figure 6.1. Islands off the Croatian coast. *Source*: **NASA.**

(are they "practical" enough?). After detailing several definitions of islands across cultures, scholarship, networks, and federations, Starc proposes a new approach that *narrows the scope* and which, he argues, *increases the utility* of island definitions. Specifically, he proposes the subcategory of near islands, such as the 1,246 that comprise the Croatian archipelago (figure 6.1).

These aims and methodology categorize his project as being *explanatory*. Starc then proposes a second shift in perspective of approach, a reversal of perspective, as he terms it, so that islands become the viewing point rather than the object of observation. In that way, he argues, "the mainland replaces the islands as the secondary term or point of comparison" (p. 3). Such a reversal, he suggests, might enable researchers to question dominant mainland perspectives about insularity and identify, instead, the heterogeneity and specificities of islands on their own terms. His emphasis on heterogeneity and specificities sets up the descriptive function of the essays in the collection and underpins a collective project to record what characterizes the details of particular islands and their interrelationships. Indeed, Starc's *problem* directly connects the proposed shift in perspective to specific historical, social, spatial, and practical problems taken up in the collection. As such, the book as a whole supports the initial problem Starc raises in his introduction. In answer to his question about whether existing definitions of islands cover too much, contributing authors narrow the focus to particular spaces and experiences, hitherto under-represented in research and overlooked in government policy. As Starc notes, the hope is that these smaller, specific case studies will have impact on and influence broader definitional framings of islands and provide power to island peoples.

Practical problems

Some research problems aim both to redress large (or small) gaps in knowledge about places and peoples underrepresented in current debates and thus include them within broader fields of knowledge production. The labors involved in framing and dealing with those research problems have multiple forms of value, not least of which is that new knowledge will necessarily expand and change the fields in question.

Another example is useful at this juncture. In their introduction to the collection *Atolls of the Maldives*, Stefano Malatesta and colleagues (2021) identify their key research problem as ameliorating the indiscernibility of the Maldives beyond its image as a tropical paradise or in its relation to discussions of small island vulnerability (figure 6.2). Their specific aim is to expand and complicate such an amorphous perception in view of the "radical change and hard challenges the country has faced since the 1990s" (p. 10). For them, "cross-thematic analysis and echoes within and between the chapters [among] . . . contributors from different disciplines and cultural backgrounds may help readers to understand Maldives through its complex net of socio-environmental inter-relations, connections and disconnections" (p. 13).

To increase the Maldives' visibility to others elsewhere, the primary objectives of the collection are both descriptive and explanatory. Each chapter addresses a particular component of Maldivians' approaches to radical and rapid change over 30 years to the present including in relation to education, migration, climate change and sea level rise, governance, and the economy, tourism, environmental protection, and ecosystems management. In one chapter, a problem about guest houses bears out the editors' overarching argument about the extent and rapidity of change in the Maldives (Zubair & Bowen, 2021) and revisits an earlier *predictive* research project based on quantitative data to revise those predictions. Specifically, Shahidi Zubair and David Bowen document how they adapted and revised their research problem

Figure 6.2. Maldives. *Source*: Contains modified Copernicus Sentinel data 2020.

in response to a range of volatile forces, among which they identify significant divergence from official plans designed to regulate tourist accommodation in the Maldives, which complicated and compromised the prognostic
veracity of research published earlier (see also Bowen et al., 2017; Brunsdon,
2016). The later chapter reappraises or corrects that work on power relations
and dynamics in the tourism industry in the Maldives.

SITUATING OUR RESEARCH

What comes first?

One issue that can be confusing when thinking through research methodologies is the sequence of tasks: *what comes first* in the design of a research

project? While the abstract, proposal, or problem leads the research, and it is the text the reader first encounters, that proposal is supported by an extensive process of research into the field. It helps me to think of the process like the two plotlines that organize a classic detective novel. One plotline follows detectives as they pursue clues, some of which are productive and others not. By these means the detectives piece together the other plotline, which is the story of the crime itself. One is a story of the process, method, and discovery (like us as the detective), and the other is the story of what happened: the who, what, how, where, and why of the event that is seamlessly narrated at the end (our research findings). At the end of a detective novel the two plotlines finally coincide and the novel ends. The red herrings that led detectives astray are exposed as false and disposed of and we have a clear perspective of both plotlines and their interaction. We researchers may also be led astray by red herrings and blind alleys in our research, which we excise in the documentation of the research unless they are meaningful in some way. As Wendy Belcher (2019) helpfully suggests, we need to think both like a detective and like a lawyer: organize the evidence but be clear that it is not the argument we seek to advance: that comes from our own conceptual labors.

How much is enough?

Another issue in research design is this: *how much is enough?* Making sure we are across relevant work in the field can be time-consuming. For an undergraduate essay, the expectation of how much research is adequate tallies with the assessment design and its value. Undergraduate work should show awareness of and engagement with research discussed in the course and, ideally, demonstrate some independent initiative in following research trails and making sound judgments regarding the relevance and utility of that work. For postgraduate work and beyond, it is expected that researchers will be across all the important work in the area. If we are not, we cannot make new contributions to knowledge. I have found that one gets better at making assessments regarding the relevance, salience, and utility of research once immersed in the process, which also gets easier with experience. More practically, our ontological and epistemological frameworks direct us in this process and establish parameters. It is all very well to see a world in a grain of sand (Blake, 1803?) but we cannot go back to first principles or examine every piece of knowledge every time we do research. The issue of the expanding archive of research also means that we need to consider any project's feasibility, including in terms of its scope. We may want to change the world with our research but, almost inevitably, our individual contributions will be limited. As Starc (2020a) realized for islands and archipelagos, smaller, focused studies will have impact upon and influence the wider field. With that said, it is also possible to be too narrow.

Situating a research project within an existing field or fields has become markedly easier for many but not all of us because of digitized resources. It is usual to locate additional research of relevance as a project develops but we need to be as thorough as possible at the outset, within set parameters, because—alongside research methodologies and research design—those boundaries will help shape a project's validity and topicality. It is crucial that we are up to date with current work in relevant fields if our research is to have purpose. In some fields, if not all, there can be confusion regarding the originality of work. If, for instance, I were to formulate a concept or model and then discover that the formulation has already been addressed in a way similar to that I thought to propose, but the publication in which it appears does not have a wide readership and/or the research has not been cited any-where, am I obliged to consider it? Always. Here again, Belcher's (2019) ideas about significance are helpful: my work can still be useful if I can work through whether I am making claims about its novel subject matter; utility for particular audiences; capacity to address gaps in the literature or shape new practices or change methods; produce new findings or unsettle established ones; influence thinking in a field or discipline; destabilize theory; or influence policy, for instance. All good stuff.

How old is too old?

A third consideration in research design is this: *how old is too old in research?* Assuredly, it is important to use current research in a field because findings from older scholarship may have been superseded—equally, they may remain absolutely central. This observation may seem self-evident in relation to certain disciplines but for others it is more ambiguous. For example, what if someone has published on a subject for which the research framework is no longer accepted even though some of the data are of interest? We know that there is an extent to which data are inextricable from the ontologies and epistemologies by which they were included and we know that there may be some rich theoretical or empirical residue of significance. In such cases, researchers need to set out the logic of such significance. We must always signal our awareness of historical context and justify the terms for a work's inclusion in the present.

Thus, it is important not to use outmoded research structured by super-seded ontologies and epistemologies as a kind of "straw man"—an easy but ineffective foil for your own proposition. According to Ralph Johnson and Anthony Blair (1983, p. 71) the straw man is a category of fallacy that emerges when "you misrepresent your opponent's position, attribute to that person a point of view with a set-up implausibility that you can easily demolish, then proceed to argue against the set-up version as though it were your opponent's." It is important to identify and refute the limitations in flawed work. Just think of how island studies is partly predicated on the urgent need to reconceptualize our approach to islands and archipelagos not least because there is no shortage of sometimes powerful misconceptions about them. They may need refutation.

At the same time, several useful checks can be used to manage the risk of *unproductive* engagement with inferior research. For example, we can check the authority of conventional research publications via peer-reviewed status in reputable publications. I include book reviews here for, relative to journal articles, both books and chapters gain far less exposure and far fewer citations than they merit. The tendency to privilege electronic journal articles assuredly limits people's exposure to the humanities in particular—and even that privilege depends on having access to institutional subscriptions where free online publications are not available. Or, for example, we can examine scholarly practices in disciplines and fields of research, testing the strength of arguments emerging from them and interrogating their relevance to our own works. If a piece of research makes little sense or contains errors of fact, there is little point in engaging with it in any detailed way unless it has had a strong impact in the field for some other reason. My sense is that one should not waste time debunking a straw man to find a gap in knowledge or revise accepted understandings. It is more beneficial to engage with compelling works that meet high standards, even if you also differ with their premises, methodologies, and findings.

There are, of course, several sound reasons to investigate older research works and using their methodologies because they may—and likely often do—contain relevant perspectives, even if those then need recontextualizing. This book, for instance, is filled with references to works that span centuries of thinking about islands and archipelagos as well as different methodological frames. Deference to that which precedes us can also furnish deeper understandings about the evolution of ideas and practices in the present. Research affecting historical paradigm shifts, for instance, remains a vital part of thought in a discipline or field. Historical knowledge of a given field or fields can undergird reevaluations of discarded methodologies that sometimes assume renewed relevance as situations change. Heather Love (2013) traces this experience in her essay on "close reading and thin description," which revisits the practices of observation and description in postwar microsociology and suggests that they provide a model for contemporary practices of reading both literary texts and society. The model of *thin* description that is unadorned and empirical was superseded in the 1960s by *thick* description that is complex and interpretive (see Geertz, 1973). Yet, Love argues that thin description may in fact be helpful as a way to avoid projecting our own values onto the subjects of study and that is a corrective to intrusive practices of interpretation that respect the otherness of different peoples.

Areas of limited scholarship or methodology

Of course, some research projects are located in contexts where there is little or no prior scholarship; of course, this is a golden opportunity for new research but it may mean it is difficult to situate one's project. That is an issue I encounter in all my work in contemporary Australian literary studies because there are few scholars in the field and an ever-expanding body of new literary texts, including a renaissance of writings by First Nations peoples. However, gaps or absences in scholarship do not provide an excuse to bypass secondary research. Rather, they direct researchers to look to related, and sometimes distant, fields in order to weigh other models by which studies' objects and subjects are examined in order to generate new knowledge. It is important to make this more speculative process explicit in research project design and note it is time-consuming and produces uncertainties.

An abstract about adaptation to climate change in Small Island Developing States (SIDS) by Carola Klöck and Patrick Nunn (2019, p. 196) shows how work to identify and characterize limited or inadequate research is intrinsically worthwhile in knowledge production. They write that "research on the nature and efficacy of adaptation across SIDS is fragmentary" and work to "systematically review academic literature" to address several matters related to adaptation among SIDS in relation to climate change. And they find that "evaluation of concrete adaptation interventions is lacking; it thus remains unclear to what extent documented adaptation effectively and sustainably reduces SIDS' vulnerability and increases their resilience." In short, after much work, Klöck and Nunn conclude that limited available scholarship prohibits clear findings. In that instance, the eventual finding is, in fact, a gap in knowledge usually associated with the outset of a project rather than its conclusions. Would they have known that before setting out? Perhaps, and speculation proved sound when backed by evidence and analysis.

I had parallel experience as the result of some initial research I did for one project led to a decision not to proceed; it is important to know what to give up or give over. A couple of decades ago, when I lived in lutruwita/Tasmania, I edited an arts journal called *Siglo* and conceived of an issue on the theme of collections. The curators of several museums and galleries were involved, alongside many amateur collectors who abound there. One topic I sounded out was the status of palawa property and objects still held but not displayed in the Tasmanian Art Gallery and Museum. The group I assembled talked into the night and, in the end, it was decided we should not proceed. In some ways, I was disappointed but it was, in my view, the right decision. Typical of the generosity of the palawa participants, one "filled the gap" with a poetic record about the impasse and the impossibility for us to publish; that statement of impossibility was, I think, the proper evidence of the moment.

Subject Positions

Island studies comprises researchers who are islanders and others who are not. Some islanders now reside on continental mainlands, and some mainlanders are blow-ins to island places; others are peripatetic, even fluid. Island studies also includes researchers undertaking work on islands not now or not ever their own. These various positions may shape the questions that can be asked and the research methodologies that can be deployed. Such considerations relate to what Haraway (1988) terms situated knowledges—that is, awareness of the personal, disciplinary, or institutional relations that undergird our work and the relations of objects and subjects in our studies.

Haraway recognizes that it is nearly impossible and not always desirable to achieve objectivity. Rather than persist with the illusion of subjectivity, she suggests that we identify and clarify the networked relations of any particular project and set out their implications. We need, she asserts, to clarify our own position: what is our physical, cultural, disciplinary, and conceptual relationship to the subjects and objects of study? We then need to identify the position of the subjects and objects in any study we propose. Finally, we need to map all parties' situations to identify what insights they may enable and to determine what limitations they entail. Situational modeling is especially important in island studies because they have long been objectified and once so emplaced lose their agency, if only for a time.

BLIND SPOTS AND INTERDISCIPLINARY OPENINGS

Scholars in the natural and social sciences are far more used to articulating research methodologies than are those in the arts and humanities such as myself. In my own field of literary studies, which is a strong component of island studies, training in methodologies and their application is loose.

Notwithstanding that observation, I have come to see great benefit in articulating research methodologies in order to develop sound and explicit research designs, even if—and in fact *because*—those protocols sit uneasily and in complicated ways with the speculative processes of literary studies. Literary studies scholars have not had the practice, common to other disciplines, of making explicit their methodologies and then relating them to specific methods of investigation. This tendency exists because, in the main, we do not use methods such as large data collection exercises such as questionnaires or interviews and focus groups—although there have been some large data projects in the last two decades formulated through connections between literary studies and sociology. In the humanities more generally, similar observations sometimes apply, noting exceptions such as the very significant database on transportation to Van Diemen's Land (Maxwell-Stewart, 2015, 2016) or work on Aboriginal massacres (Ryan et al. 2022).

Those of us in literary studies and many in the arts and humanities, and those working at the borderlands of these and the social sciences, often need little equipment and few if any laboratories or complex software—unless we partner with those who, for example, are digitizing the world, including islands (Schott, 2015). Nor do literary studies scholars conduct field work in the conventional sense. For most projects, we do not need to travel to far-flung places except to visit library archives. For while literature is one of the greatest forms of transport—indeed the word *metaphor* means *to transport*—this effect is conventionally conceptual, imaginative, and internal. What we do need in large spadefuls is time. We do not "write up" findings *per se* but, rather, make most of our discoveries in and through the process of writing itself. We think in and through writing as a *philopoesis*—a combination of philosophy and poetics. In that sense, writing is both an *object* of study and a *method* of research in very particular ways.

Taking all that into account—and possibly to the surprise of many of its scholars—literary studies *does* have research methodologies that can be quantified. They include multidisciplinary archival research; textual analysis conducted through varied critical and theoretical lenses; conceptual analysis that deploys philosophical research and method; and forms of comparative or *synoptic* analysis that measure the relative development of ideas across disciplines (Ajakaye & Ogunniyi, 2021). In recent times, among the most important shifts to these methodologies that have direct significance to island studies are those related to protocols for engaging with First Nations oral and written literatures, which may require real-time and embodied engagement.

Of course, literary studies is not alone in having blind spots or occulted or occluded knowledges. In relation to geography, for example, Rob Kitchin and Nick Tate (2000, p. 1) observe that "research is rarely just a process of generating data, analysing and interpreting the results. By putting forward answers to research questions you are engaging in the process of debate about what can be known and how things are known. As such, you are engaging with philosophy." It is, then, salutary for each of us to consider these blind spots and question what they suggest about our resistance to elements of the research process and their purposes. Those reflections are especially important in the context of interdisciplinary research and the negotiation of multiple methodologies.

Ultimately, the modern world requires researchers to work together to solve complex problems (Tobi & Kampen, 2018). Without doubt, many contributions to island studies have emerged from interdisciplinary projects. There is even greater potential for interdisciplinary work to address the host of competing urgencies in this field, including in relation to archipelagos and archipelagic studies, and that work requires innovative research across the spectrum of the field. It is not, nor will it always be easy. Researchers across fields will have different training including different ontologies and epistemologies. Collaborative and interdisciplinary research will necessitate "a process of critical inquiry based on a more dynamic open ontology and epistemology that can take account of multiple constructions of knowledge" (Clark et al., 2017, p. 244). Such a process—or, more properly, processes—is replete with tensions. Those are recognized by Lisbeth Frølunde and colleagues (2017, p. 30) in one assessment of a collaborative process with a somewhat ominous aim "to destabilize views on research collaboration that tend to present an idealized celebration of diversity in collaborative processes and methodologies [by showing] . . . how dynamic forces of difference disturb (our own) ideals of collaboration and dialogue." More recently, one of the same team has written of the many benefits of collaborative research, noting that "collaborative analysis, which disturbs and resists mental and institutional frontiers, can create moments of human encounters that question conventional ideas about difference, norms, academic tradition and sense making" (Pedersen, 2021, p. 5). In the process, other innovations emerge, not least among them the doing of research, which is the subject of the next chapter.

Chapter 7

Doing

By What Methods Do We Acquire Knowledge in Studies of Islands and Archipelagos?

Elaine Stratford

> Methodology: the branch of knowledge that deals with method generally or with the methods of a particular discipline or field of study . . . the study of the direction and implications of empirical research, or of the suitability of [its] techniques. (OED)

> Method: A procedure for attaining an object. . . . More generally: a way of doing anything, especially according to a defined and regular plan. (OED)

According to Stacy Carter and Miles Little (2007), epistemological choices are logically linked to and shape choice of research methodologies, and to those choices we add that there is need for explicit commentary upon axiology, ontology, and ethics. In turn, methodological choices justify, guide, and help researchers to evaluate the methods selected for a given study. Those methods are the tools used to collect, analyze, and interpret data and undergird how new knowledge is generated and existing knowledge confirmed, refined, or unsettled (figure 7.1).

For Carter and Little (2007), *methods* of approach to studying the world are bounded by and reveal *methodological* choices made *in advance* of those methods being used in a study. Thus, for them, a hallmark of excellence in research is to have

Source: Jean-Yves Vigneau.

101

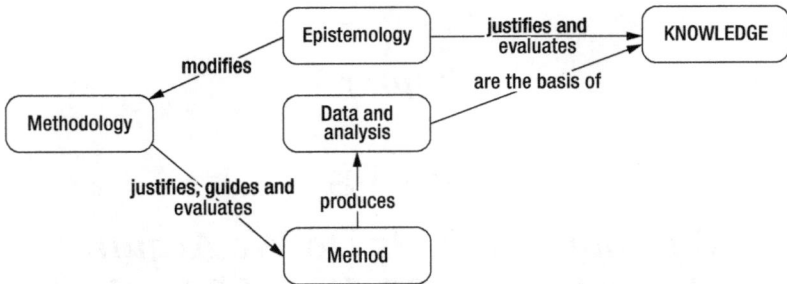

Figure 7.1.   Simple relationship between epistemology, methodology, and method. *Source*: Carter & Little, 2007, p. 1317. © Reprinted by permission of SAGE Publications.

internally consistent practices the characteristics of which are always apparent. I agree with that position, which informs the work in this chapter. In my own reading, this position also affirms work in chapter 6 about defining problems, situating ourselves, and engaging with each other as guides to how to work alone and in company.

This chapter focuses on the distinction between methodologies and methods. In the first of three sections, I address the point that methodologies and methods are not the same and refer to quantitative and qualitative approaches and to mixed and multi-methods. In the second section, I touch on how research design is a framework by which to select methods that enable data collection, analysis and synthesis of information, and inference and the creation of new knowledge or refinement of existing knowledge. I describe my understanding of the field—including knowledge repositories such as archives, museums, and libraries—and refer to the literature review as a product of engagement with such repositories. I also consider other field sites such as literal laboratories and island laboratories, which leads to a brief discussion about research ethics. In the final section, I return to Carter and Little's admonishment that researchers always ensure that our work engages with considerations of quality and excellence. This work is important because researchers need clarity about values and ways of being, knowing, and doing but too often get tangled up when differentiating between two terms that appear alike but are not, in fact, synonymous.

METHODOLOGIES AND METHODS: THE DISTINCTION MATTERS

The words "methodology" and "method" are often used interchangeably but signify different ideas. Methodology refers to the general reasoning we might apply to a study and to the theoretical or speculative viewpoints we might bring to it (Bogdan & Biklen, 2007). There is no one methodology. Rather, methodologies reflect different understandings about valuing, being, and knowing that have been considered in other chapters in several ways drawing on a wealth of examples. Methodologies are also about different disciplinary and interdisciplinary traditions and perspectives that inform how and what we do to speculate, gather evidence, and create new—or add to existing—knowledge.

Perhaps our formal training is based largely in positivism, which assumes that objective accounts of the real world are possible and that from them certain laws are discoverable. Chances are we will default to broadly quantitative approaches and vest significance in replicability, numerical data, statistical analysis, and the representativeness of findings. For example, if we know and value the idea that the world of islands and archipelagos is optimally understood in quantitative terms, our study's aims, objectives, questions, and research design will be influenced accordingly. For example, in foundational work on island biogeography, Robert MacArthur and Edward Wilson (1967, p. 1) argue that islands are inherently appealing because they are the first entity that, in cognitive terms, we:

> can pick out and begin to comprehend. By studying clusters of islands, biologists view a simpler microcosm of the seemingly infinite complexity of continental and oceanic biogeography. . . . By their very multiplicity and variation . . . islands provide the necessary replications in natural "experiments" by which evolutionary hypotheses can be tested.

Work by MacArthur and Wilson has since been both refined and criticized and yet it remains potently illustrative of a broadly quantitative mindset, hence the reference to it here (Losos & Ricklefs, 2010).

But perhaps our tendency is to think that only partially objective accounts are possible, and we may view the world as an interlacing coil between more or less objective observers and phenomena. Our understanding of the world might then be oriented around critical theory or postpositivism. We might want to use qualitative approaches or both quantitative and qualitative methods: Kaya Yilmaz (2013) provides an exemplary comparison of these. We may vest significance in both numerical data and words and deeds—what is said, written, enacted, performed, or conveyed expressively, whether deliberate or not, explicit or not. For instance, when examining occupational accidents' impacts on a small island economy by reference to workers in Mauritius, Ramessur Shalini (2009, p. 974) suggests that:

> quantitative approaches should be backed by the use of qualitative research approaches (including ethnographic interviews, focus groups, population-based surveys and questionnaires, and case studies) in order to calculate the true economic and or social costs of occupational accidents.

Or perhaps we think that the world of islands is a social construction internalized via customs, habits, and values and continually being reconstructed by social actors. We might see social constructions as co-created and contested, such as occurs when island peoples push back against discourses that constitute them and island life as inherently vulnerable (Farbotko et al., 2016, 2018). For example, Adam Grydehøj and colleagues (2021, n.p.) deconstruct particular discourses of development to show how islanders are actively and problematically marginalized by them:

> Discourses of development targeted at former colonies are . . . grounded in the discursive ideal of elevating the "developing" society to metropolitan standards [and] . . . targeted at islanders . . . [they] often simultaneously promote metropolitan strategies while implicitly acknowledging that such strategies are doomed to failure on account of the territory's small land area and/or population size.

Or we might want to emphasize individual subjective understandings and then our work might be based in interpretivism. In that case, we might argue we cannot fully access the world except through subjective and contextual filters and might defend that position by noting that science and quantitative approaches are never, in fact, value-free (Gracio, 2014). If we subscribe to such views, chances are we will select qualitative approaches and vest significance in language and discourse—including music, art, dance, or literature— as well as historical comparative studies, locational comparative studies, or comparisons of individuals' works on creativity (Runco & Albert, 2010).

In general, such studies of creativity can embrace psychometric, experimental, biographical, biological, computational, and contextual perspectives (Mayer, 1999; see also Long, 2014). More specifically, creativity studies also engage island peoples and the ways in which island worlds are constituted via creative endeavors. Among the methods used are comparative poetic analysis (Brinklow, 2021, 2022); narrative analysis of work experience, island life, and creative industries (Stalker & Burnett, 2016); comparative analysis of the constitution of islandness among visual artists (Stratford & Langridge, 2012); and action research with children on climate change arts projects (Stratford & Low, 2015). Or we may be interested in how islands are deployed in literature as the feminized background to masculine conquest and reinforce specific gender politics. Then, as McMahon (2019, p. 170) does, we might point out:

> There is no direct female equivalent to the male Robinsonade mainly because there is no perceived equivalence between the female subject and the island . . . The "female Robinsonade" operates quite differently [from those about males] in that the women are generally not alone, and their stories are commonly framed by romance conventions, which, by definition, involve more than one person.

Crucially, the lines demarcating these various positions are more or less porous, and ideas about methodology *per se* remain strongly influenced by ongoing debates about being, valuing, and knowing. In short, it is important to be heterodoxic or open-minded rather than adhere unswervingly to orthodoxy.

Methods, then, are *not* methodologies but our selection of methods is *always* influenced by choice of methodology and by underpinning values and ways of being and knowing. So, methods refer to specific procedures, techniques, and tools—ways of doing—that enable research (Guba & Lincoln, 1989). Methods allow us to find and/or generate data and information and then examine, explain, integrate, and make meaning from data and information and from others' primary or secondary knowledge.

In simple terms, data are the "raw" elements of our work: which parts of an island's coastline are subject to inundation (Sharples, 2006) or which words in poetry by Kathy Jetñil-Kijiñer (2022) point to the monstrosity of colonial imperialism and rising seas. Information is a term incorporating the cumulatively processed forms of many data. It might include, for example, the island's coastline length + data about which parts of the coastline are rocky or sandy + data about tides and sea level change + human use of the coastline [+/− 3 kilometers/1.8 miles inland and nearshore/offshore] + biogeographical communities + customary land rights, and so on. When analyzed and compared with primary data and information from the past or from other islands and/or with secondary information in the form of others' studies on similar matters, for example, that information leads to knowledge. Among other outcomes, that knowledge informs decisions about how to understand island coastline histories and current and future management strategies.

In many studies, researchers combine different methods but, as Teresa Anguera and colleagues (2018) point out, there is some confusion about whether such an approach involves mixed methods or multi-methods; for some the two are synonymous, but not for all. Anguera and her colleagues suggest that mixed method research combines quantitative and qualitative approaches to bridge the gap between their epistemological and methodological foundations. Noting the amount of debate about whether mixed methods and multi-methods refer to different things, they agree with Burke Johnson and colleagues (2007, p. 119), for whom multi-methods are identifiable because "different approaches or methods are used in parallel or sequence but are not integrated until inferences are being made." Our own understanding accords with that described by Abbas Tashakkori and Charles Teddie (2010): multi-methods combine various quantitative or qualitative approaches; mixed methods combine quantitative and qualitative ones.

Either way, a key insight is that the latter requires an eclectic and tolerant stance, given that researchers are dealing with:

a positivist approach that gives rise to quantitative methods and a constructivist approach that is home to qualitative methods . . . [and their] differences . . . must be . . . reconcilable [which] . . . necessitates an engagement with those who hold that the quantitative/qualitative dichotomy is unbridgeable. (Timans et al., 2019, p. 208)

Such engagement invites reflection on methods and also paradigms—by which we mean patterns, models, precedents, examples, or logical or conceptual structures (Online Etymology Dictionary, 2022). Usefully, Katrina McChesney and Jill Aldridge (2019, p. 225) assert that there are opportunities to work toward the "flexible (but intentional) integration of any research method with any research paradigm." Work by Christian Wennecke et al. (2019, p. 49) strongly exemplifies a methodologically intentional approach because it:

> takes an abductive, mixed methods approach . . . in which insights from field-work and interviews are used to inform the crafting of the survey and, again, after the survey was conducted, to supplement its numerical outcomes with quotes and to revisit and inquire back into our qualitative material.

The authors thus weave together numbers and stories, following Carina Ren and Renuka Mahadevan (2018), whose own work on sustainable tourism describes mixed methods as "valuation devices" to enable them to know the measurable outcomes of a noneconomic event in Nuuk, Greenland, in 2016—an Arctic Winter Games. A similar approach to both methodology and methods has been used for comparable reasons in a study of sustainable tourism on the Isle of Man. In that work, Brendan Canavan (2014, p. 133) has argued that mixed methods were advantageous because the weaknesses of individual approaches were offset by the strengths of others.

In summary, methodologies and methods are different. One term applies to general reasoning that underpins a study, including in relation to axiology, ontology, and epistemology. The other flows from that reasoning and informs the choice of procedures, techniques, and tools drawn on in the execution of the study. That choice informs how we might go about collecting data, processing information, and deriving insights. The two are mutually constitutive in how we create new knowledge and add to existing knowledge.

The balance of this chapter is a metanarrative on doing rather than a catalog of what can be done and how. It presents a scan of the range of important considerations we need to consider when thinking about methods and about doing research, not least in island and archipelagic studies. The scan is limited and partial. For instance, it does not deal with methods to collect and understand species richness data such as those which might apply to island biodiversity research (Baker & Bode, 2021; Kreft et al., 2007); address methods used to determine, for example, the relationship between invasive species and inundation models at different scales (Courchamp et al., 2014); or engage with geographical information systems (Lucieer & van der Werff, 2007). Even so, it is important to note that in preparing this book we went to significant effort to engage with natural science researchers but as one (anonymized) colleague noted in response to our call for expressions of interest in joining us in the book project:

> The tricky thing, as always, is finding common ground between different disciplines—social science in particular with physical and biological sciences. For the biological and physical sciences, there isn't a huge amount to discuss in terms of the relationships between theory, method, and data (you use certain methods to collect data and test theory—very linear and straightforward). And approaches are the same whether we're thinking about islands or continents.

METHODS: THE "DOING" ELEMENT OF RESEARCH IN ISLAND AND ARCHIPELAGIC STUDIES

Research design is a critically important framework that makes explicit the methods to be used in investigative work of all kinds. It helps with transparency, accountability, and other measures of quality in research—which vary by disciplinary tradition and methodological stance—and there are reams or gigabytes written about it. Helpfully, Norman Denzin and Yvonna Lincoln (2005, p. 25) describe it as adaptable guidelines:

> that connect theoretical paradigms first to strategies of inquiry and second to methods for collecting empirical materials. A research design situates the researcher in the empirical world . . . [to] sites, persons, groups, institutions, and bodies of relevant interpretive material, including documents and archives . . . [and addresses] representation and legitimation.

That description informs what follows

It would be reasonable to think that this section might cover field methods and ways of doing literature reviews, but it does not do much such work. Surprisingly, perhaps, a Google Scholar search on variations of "field work on islands" produces under 100 items. Some articles are about how field work in island locations involves challenges such as transportation, equipment issues, labor, and isolation and remoteness (Fitzpatrick et al., 2016). Some refer to a specific method such as field survey but treat it as a given without further explanation (Martin et al., 2019). Some raise interesting questions about trips versus field work, island versus other sites, and specific versus general insights gained but also take the methods used as given (Howkins et al., 2019). In short, in relation to island and archipelagic studies there may be limited numbers of self-reflexive works on the field as such, so a brief attempt to unsettle that is the focus here.

To start, the "field" is a specific but diversely understood idea in research. In the biological sciences, it is generally assumed that field work is done outdoors. The fruits of such work may then be synthesized with material from archives, museums, and libraries, analyzed in laboratories, written up in offices, and disseminated in conference halls or online journals—both of which involve constructed physical and virtual environments. But among biological scientists, those indoor locations are not, themselves, considered field sites. That kind of categorization does not apply to the social sciences and humanities. According to Michel Foucault (1967/1984, p. 7), archives, museums, and libraries are heterotopias. That is, they are diverse discursive, cultural, and institutional spaces that capture the impulse to "enclose in one place all times, all epochs, all forms, all tastes . . . a place of all times that is itself outside of time and inaccessible to its ravages."

And yet, Foucault (1969/2002) also suggests, for example, that the archive is a space of possibility, an idea that constitutes the archive as an ever-present relational field. So, if we understand the archive as a field in that sense, our field work method may involve logging in to the British Library newspaper archive to search for articles on "isle" and "drown" and "flood". There, virtually, we can readily engage now with any of 30,189 items meeting the search terms published between 1700 and 2022 and held in the field as we constitute it. To aid (or confound) our argument, we can then refine our search by including only items that meet explicit criteria— for example, a date or an island, event, individual, or idea. We can then download, read, and analyze the narrative content of many fewer items than that which the full search produces. In the process, we can bring to the present another place of times and read and understand them in new ways, including in relation to material published in more recent times. We have not treated the archive as a static repository but as a dynamic field in the production of knowledge.

At the same time, because it is expected that research will be positioned inside and in relation to existing debates in a published literature, it is useful to see literature reviews as methods and not as mere background to the "real" research. But too often researchers fail to reveal the methodological and technical choices we make in doing those reviews. Those choices are, we suggest, inevitably influenced by ways of valuing, being, and knowing; they should not be done unreflexively, or set to a default mode. The reasons are straightforward: how research is contextualized in larger debates then shapes how knowledge is constituted and understood. Thus, if we subscribe to the idea that archives, museums, and libraries (and their electronic resources) are "just" repositories from which we syphon literature for instrumental or narrow ends, our method fails to account for the biopolitical and geopolitical forces of violent expropriation that underpin collections. Such effects are now subject to redress—not least in island and archipelagic settings (Hummel-Colla, 2019; Voirol, 2019).

An expanded sense of the field is also crucial because constructed environments are archetypical sites of individual and group occupation and engagement and because people are at the center of inquiry in the social sciences and humanities. Like archives, museums, and libraries then, laboratories are field sites and not just workshops for processing *ex situ* field data. Apt here is Jonas Salk's introduction to work done by Bruno Latour and Stephen Woolgar (1986) on laboratory life that outlines Latour's method. As Salk (2013, p. 12) notes, Latour's method was "a kind of anthropological probe to study a scientific 'culture'; to follow in every detail what the scientists do and how and what they think." What Salk is describing is field work in a constructed environment.

Equally, whole islands and groups of islands have been described as living laboratories. As Riley Taitingfong (2020, pp. 5–6) notes in this regard:

> The laboratory is a salient conceptual scheme through which islands are understood as "natural" sites of experimentation, and through which conventional boundaries between "expert" and "lay" knowledges are maintained . . . [but scholarship shows] all knowledge as situated . . . embodied and produced within particular historical and cultural conditions.

As with the repository, much harm has been done by reducing islands to this analogue as if all islands were somehow conceptually the same when their very ontologies insist on more nuanced approaches to singularity, multiplicity, fresh or salty surrounds, inshore or offshore locations, urban or remote settings, and so forth. Being reductive about islands seems, inevitably, to lead to being reductive about islanders, a net effect of which is to constitute them, among others, as experimental objects—as "lab rats" (George et al., 2014, p. e21). Hypervigilance is needed in thinking about how to work with "specific communities in the margins of society . . . Indigenous peoples . . . minorities in territories and states over which they once held sovereignty" (Smith, 2005, p. 86). Methods of approach to empowerment can and often should involve coauthorship, including with Country (Bawaka Country et al., 2019) and others—not least those seeking asylum (McMahon, 2005).

Thus, both field work and reviews of literature drawn from the repository-as-field are complex, relational methods and, in island and archipelagic studies, their deployment should, we suggest, be thoughtful, explicit, and deeply conscious of methodological underpinnings. This exposition is both necessary and insufficient, and we think much more work could be done to unsettle methods of approach to both and to how those destabilizing labors are enacted.

Finally, the foregoing discussion also points to the imperative to undertake work in ways that uphold international standards of ethical best practice in research (National Health and Medical Research Council, 2018; World Health Organization, 2022). Methods of research involving humans in general, specific humans, and the more-than-human world should always be subject to scrutiny by qualified peers if we are to avoid the lab rat outcomes that have typified much work, including in island places. We need to think about and set up appropriate responses to "the risk of harm to participants; informed consent and coercion; privacy, confidentiality and anonymity; as well as issues such as institutional risk and researcher safety" (Mason, 2018, p. 85). But it is not enough to rely blindly on ethics committees, because they "do not have all the answers . . . tend to promote the idea of universal ethics values . . . [and] are not usually well acquainted with ethical issues involving creative methods, for example visual methods" (Mason, 2018, pp. 84–85). Nor does adherence to ethical precepts in the conduct of research relieve researchers from the need to also be vigilant when disseminating findings and working with publishers, editors, and reviewers (Grydehøj, 2018) or when ensuring that data management protocols are adhered to and the efficacy of research itself is monitored and evaluated. Again, there is little in the literature on ethics and island and archipelagic studies.

The foregoing suggests that researchers need to consider research design, existing knowledge repositories as relational fields, literature reviews as dynamic conversations, ethical frameworks, and approaches to dissemination, data management, and self-evaluation *in advance* of methods being used to investigate an intriguing problem. By the time all those crucial matters are clear, what will also be transparent and justifiable are the methods—the procedures, techniques, and tools—by which to collect, analyze, and synthesize information, make inferences, and create new knowledge or refine existing knowledge and then disseminate it.

QUALITY COUNTS

Finally, returning to Carter and Little (2007) and initial observations on the need for excellence in research, it is clear that no matter my methodological stance and choice of research methods, I need to be able to argue my case creatively, constructively, and critically. I must be able to demonstrate that I have accounted for quality criteria. In other words, my work must have rigor (Stratford & Bradshaw, 2021).

A simple and accessible online guide to some such criteria is offered by Janneke Frambach and colleagues (2013, p. 552). In it, they list several quality principles common across research methodologies and note the quantitative (Qt) and qualitative (Ql) expressions of those principles, as follows (my abbreviations):

(a) truth value of the evidence

internal validity (Qt)—the extent to which observed effects can be assigned to a "cause'
credibility (Ql)—the extent to which the findings are trustworthy and plausible or convincing

(b) applicability of the evidence

external validity (Qt)—the extent to which sample results are generalizable to a whole population
transferability (Ql)—the extent to which findings can be transferred to and applied in other settings

(c) consistency of the evidence

reliability (Qt)—the extent to which, if done again, the results are consistent
dependability (Ql)—the extent to which findings are consistent relative to their wider context

(d) neutrality of the evidence

objectivity (Qt)—the extent to which biases are removed and information is value-free
confirmability (Ql)—the extent to which findings come from participants and not (just) researchers

Frambach and her colleagues also provide a comprehensive list of techniques to improve research. Those to enhance quantitative research include rigor in relation to hypotheses, sampling frames and sizes, standardization, internal consistency, and replicability. Those to enhance qualitative research include rigor in relation to triangulating methods and data, researchers, and theories and to case selection, thick description, working until saturation occurs and no new themes emerge, and using iterative approaches. Both approaches also benefit from stringent reviews by others. Sometimes such review is done via double-blind peer review and sometimes by convivial conversations. The latter is what we model next.

Chapter 8

Conversing

What Does It Mean to Share and Stress-Test Ideas about Rethinking Island Methodologies?

Elaine Stratford, Elizabeth McMahon, Godfrey Baldacchino, and Colleagues

Converse: To move about . . . dwell in . . . among people . . . to keep company . . . to be familiar with . . . to inter-change ideas by speech or writing or otherwise . . . to commune with . . . to keep company with . . . to com-municate with. (OED)

For almost a decade, the authors of this book have been working on the *Rethinking the Island* series with Row-man and Littlefield International and aspired to write the last publication in the series. We decided we wanted a conversational chapter in which we asked others to help us stress-test some of the thinking about the question why and how to do island studies.

Elaine: So, let's start with introductions and then turn to questions we have for you.

Godfrey: Hi everyone. I am Godfrey Baldacchino, Profes-sor of Sociology at University of Malta, in Malta. I started studying at the University of Malta and I've never left, I'm still there. I spent some time in Canada at the University of Prince Edward Island as a Canada Research Chair and as a UNESCO Co-Chair in Island Studies. I launched Island Studies Journal in 2006 and I'm currently President of the International Small Islands Studies Association.

Elizabeth: Hello everybody. I'm a Professor of Literary Studies at the University of New South Wales, Australia.

Source: Jean-Yves Vigneau.

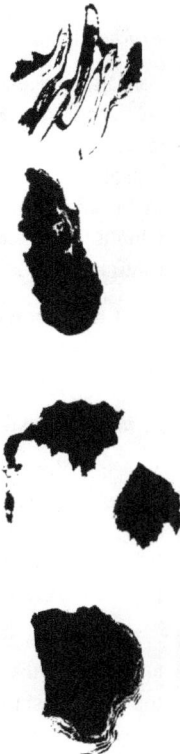

I got into island studies via my past tenure at University of Tasmania and, as Elaine can vouch, you become compelled by that place, and that directed my work in island studies for the last two decades or so. One of my most recent books is *Islands: Identity and the Literary Imagination* and I've also written with Elaine and Godfrey before and at the moment as well. I think that part of my contribution to these kinds of forums is that I am deeply in the humanities and am trying to get the humanities and the social sciences to make some connections. So, that's me.

Elaine: Thanks Liz. Aideen, can I ask you to introduce yourself, please?

Aideen: My name is Aideen Foley; I'm a Senior Lecturer in Environmental Geography at Birkbeck University of London, in the UK, and I came to island studies via climate modelling. My PhD back in Ireland was looking at future climate scenarios for Ireland and I got interested by the mismatches in terms of this great global scale that we produce this information at versus the local scale that decision-making in islands takes place at and got interested in alternative ways of knowing essentially about islands and that's kind of the direction that I've taken since then.

Elaine: Thank you. Jon, are you happy to introduce yourself next?

Jon: I am a Reader in Island Studies at Newcastle University in the UK, and my work over the last 10 years or so has been involved with relational and archipelagic thinking; more recently, that has developed into "Anthropocene Islands," a project considering the figure of the island and how it's become generative in broader Anthropocene thinking and critical theory more generally. I think islands are exceptionally important for different pathways of broader critical thought today.

At the moment, along with David Chandler—with whom I wrote *Anthropocene Islands: Entangled Worlds*—I'm working on a book that looks at how the Caribbean has become generative in broader critical Black studies.

Elaine: Fantastic, thank you. Marina, will you introduce yourself, please?

Marina: Yes, thank you, Elaine. Good day to everybody. I'm Marina Confait, a freelance consultant following recent retirement from the Seychelles public service. I was a career public servant for 44 years. My last two positions were Principal Secretary for the Department of Foreign Affairs, so I was a diplomat. I was also the former Vice-Chancellor of the University of Seychelles.

While I am an islander I have not really done island studies but, coming from an island, I always find myself having to defend being an islander and showing the case of islands and people from small island developing states. Godfrey was in Seychelles recently and we were chatting about our vulnerability and about how islanders should make their voices heard. I'm happy to join the team and I'm really looking forward to learning more and sharing my knowledge and experience from being an islander. So, I look forward to sharing ideas with learned colleagues. Thank you.

Elaine: James, would you like to introduce yourself?

James: Hi everyone, thanks so much for the invitation to be here. For those of you who are not aware I run a social enterprise network called Island Innovation, which leans heavily on sustainable development, although we try and engage with a range of island studies issues and we have a media platform, organize events, and disseminate information. One of our big goals is to disseminate academic research in island studies to a broader audience of policy makers and island-based NGOs and, more broadly still, to islanders. So, I am happy to be here and contribute to this conversation.

Elaine: Thank you, James. Carol, are you happy to introduce yourself?

Carol: Sure. I'm Carol Farbotko, from the University of Melbourne in Australia. I'm not really technically an island studies scholar; I work in more interdisciplinary Pacific Islands, climate studies, and cultural geography. I'm very much focused on the Pacific region, so I guess islands are a big part of my thinking. And I have recently become a Tuvaluan citizen, which was exciting because of my marriage to a Tuvaluan person, so that brings on a whole new range of responsibilities and ethical considerations in addition to being an Australian citizen.

Elaine: That's grand, thank you. Andrew Harwood, can we hear from you now?

Andrew: Thanks, Elaine, and hi everyone. I'm excited to meet you all. I work at the University of Tasmania in Australia, in the School of Geography, Planning, and Spatial Sciences. I did my PhD on the constitution of islandness in the context of Tasmania, which Elaine supervised, and which Godfrey and Liz also were responsible for assessing and thank you both again for your assessment of the PhD all those years ago now.

I teach a third-year geography unit called Geographies of Island Places, which I inherited from Elaine, and I also teach both qualitative research methods to postgrads and first-year geography. I am excited to be involved in these conversations and think these dialogues are important for us all, spread out around the world, so we can hear and learn from different people.

Elaine: Thank you. Mitul, how about you?

Mitul: I'm Mitul Baruah, an Assistant Professor of Sociology/Anthropology and Environmental Studies at Ashoka University, located outside of Delhi, in India. I am trained as a human geographer, although I have moved between various disciplines: environmental studies and history, sociology, and so forth—thus pursuing interdisciplinary scholarship. I'm relatively new to island studies. Thanks to Godfrey—who sent me an email a couple of years ago saying that he came across my PhD dissertation, which was based on a river island—and who invited me to be part of the island studies community. My forthcoming book,

Slow Disaster, Political Ecology of Hazards and Everyday Life in the Brahma-putra Valley, is an ethnographic work on Majuli Island, where I'm from.

Elaine: And Maria Hnaraki, welcome.

Maria: Hi everyone. I am the founding Director of Greek Studies and currently an adjunct professor at Drexel University in the USA. I hold a BS/MA in Music Studies from the National and Kapodistrian University of Athens in Greece, and an MA and a PhD in Folklore and Ethnomusicology from Indiana University, also in the USA. My main activities include publications, instruction, performances, and event organization.

Elaine: Finally, my name's Elaine Stratford. I'm Professor of Geography in the School of Geography, Planning, and Spatial Sciences at the University of Tasmania in Australia. I moved here 25 years ago thinking we might stay for three years, fell in love with the place, realized that it also needed people to be here and love it because it is a wounded place in some respects. Was lucky enough to work with people like Liz and Pete Hay, met Godfrey, have had the privilege of working with PhD candidates like Andrew and Carol and, as a member of the International Small Islands Studies Association, I have been privileged to meet other colleagues like James and Jonathan.

OUR CONVERSATION

Elaine: Carol let's start with a question for you: What are the burning questions we need to ask about island and archipelagic studies?

Carol: Well, thank you for asking me this big question! I think Elaine asked me to speak to this one because I can be controversial, so if that's how it comes out then that's probably just me, not a reflection on the discipline.

I've been to a few island studies conferences, had really wonderful mentorship in island studies, and think the field has come a long way since the mid-2000s when I entered it. So much interdisciplinary, leaning toward the social sciences, but also histories, geographies, cultures, politics, and environments, and so much multifaceted knowledge of diverse islands and ideas about islands and how they shape each other.

There's also powerful decolonial, feminist, and relational island studies work going on and an exciting time. For example, in one recent paper in *Island Studies Journal*, led by Australian-based scholar Yasothara Nadarajah, the authors point out persuasively that there's a lot of work to do for island studies to be truly critically reflexive. They argue quite powerfully that it's time to focus less on what islands are and why they matter and more on who is seeing islands and from where. From that, I take away that it's time to be careful and truly—rather than tokenistically—inclusive of collaborators and to think about audiences in island studies work.

On that basis, I think there's many burning questions: what islands remain invisible despite the many advances of island studies? What island realities might be elusive to current approaches, including cutting-edge approaches? What's still elusive about islands? How much is the "invisibility" of islands the result of insidious—rather than overt—forms of colonial or patriarchal thinking?

Elizabeth: And there are always both insidious and overt forms in colonialism?

Carol: So, given those questions, I start to think would the next step for island studies mean a radical departure from the very term that defines the field? So, what I'm wondering is whether there's going to be some time in the future when the word island itself disappears in the way that the term "the third world" has; you don't see that term being used much anymore. Is that change on the horizon for island studies? So, what would happen to island studies if we no longer studied islands but an alternative, as yet unknown and unnamed set of multiple geographies? What language would we then use? What invisibilities might become visible and, critically, whose perspectives might become central?

Elaine: Thanks Carol. I'm reminded of French philosopher Jacques Derrida's practice of writing a word and then putting a line through it, an elision, but leaving the word with the line through it. ~~Island.~~

Mitul: Carol, thank you so much. This response probably is expected from me, given I am from a river island but, in terms of what is visible or invisible, first I think there is a greater need to engage with river islands in island studies—there is so little of it currently. By river islands, I'm referring specifically to the shoals or sandbars, locally known as chars or chaporis, in the Indus-Ganga-Brahmaputra river systems. Majuli, my field site, is one of those riverine islands but there are many more. These islandscapes are interesting in so many ways: they are hybrid geographies—part water, part land, part sediments; millions of people inhabit these islands; and they are socially and ecologically diverse places. The chars bring the question of sediments to the forefront; thus far, they are inadequately studied. In fact, research on these river islands would perhaps help us reconceptualize the "hydrosocial cycle" by incorporating the element of sediment into the cycle. That work would also broaden our thinking about the question of materiality of islands.

Second, many of the chars in in South Asia have been home to millions of refugees from the partition and wars. Thus, these are politically volatile geographies, which has further intensified in recent years with religious fundamentalism making its way into the mainstream politics in the region. So, if we are to study those islands we are going to get into questions of ethnic and religious conflict, citizenship, transboundary river issues, and so forth. Such scholarship, I would emphasize, will certainly enrich island studies. In a nutshell, I think there's a need to study more river islands.

Marina: As I listen to Carol and Mitul, I can identify with points they raise. But coming from the Seychelles a burning question for me relates to why there are very few locals who write about their own island countries. International or foreign researchers are writing about islands and sometimes they are not clearly representing the island in their methodologies or practices and certain key areas are not considered. Seychelles is a classic example whereby there are few researchers and limited research capacity. Research takes both capacity and interest. So, how do we get locals interested in writing about their own islands—about which they are knowledgeable and can contextualize them to give studies rigor and experience. When Seychellois undertake their PhDs, they often write case studies about the Seychelles, but it ends there. So, one of my concerns is the need to develop capacity and attract experts to write about their islands.

Elizabeth: And capacity is such an important part of what this book is about, and what, we think, island and archipelagic studies are about—including the extent to which local capacity building is part of such considerations and efforts.

Jon: Marina, that's a persistent point, isn't it: the question of how local people get more involved in research or lead research rather than having it imposed on them—whether they're on islands or not.

Marina: In the Seychelles, right now research is internationally driven and sometimes international researchers include a local as a co-author, which is great. So, yes, it is an issue that needs to be addressed to attract more locals to pursue island research.

Elaine: Mitul, does it matter how researchers study islands and archipelagos?

Mitul: Absolutely. It matters a great deal how researchers study islands and archipelagos. In fact, in all disciplines it matters how you study a subject and what methodologies and frameworks you adopt. In 1974, with reference to the population debate, geographer David Harvey argued that the question of methodology is an ideological question and that the conclusions we draw depend on the methods we choose. Challenging the value neutrality of science, Harvey argued that methodologies matter for knowledge production and social justice. Feminist scholars, among others, have dwelled a great deal on the question of objectivity versus subjectivity and argued that knowledge is partial and situated. Great significance is borne by the roles that researchers adopt; how they approach a subject, who they are, and how they address concerns of positionality and reflexivity as they navigate the field.

Island studies has grown impressively in the past few decades, which is largely to do with its methodological pluralism. The archipelagic turn, if you will, has allowed some exciting work in the field as we have seen in *Island Studies Journal* and other journals. Likewise, the focus on decoloniality, although new, is promising. Nonetheless, I would like to highlight three areas that island studies scholars can perhaps pay more attention to:

First, as a framework political ecology can advance island studies. Given that political ecology combines political economy and studies of biophysical nature, islands are uniquely situated for political ecological research. I think nowhere is the materiality of nature felt more acutely than in island geographies. In fact, could political ecology, too, benefit from island studies? Also, island studies could be advanced by political ecology's attention to the questions of scale and power and both benefit from fieldwork. More importantly, a political ecological approach might help us better imagine island futures and sustainability, given island geographies' increased vulnerability in the Anthropocene, particularly with climate change in context. After all, political ecology is also about "doing."

Second, what could a decolonial island studies look like? Is it mainly a methodological question or does it also suggest that we need more work produced by islanders, and, if is so, what does it mean to be an insider-researcher? As researchers, are we ever fully insiders or outsiders or are we always in-between? How do we juggle these multiple identities?

And third, do we need to move beyond what sometimes appears to be self-referencing and to reach out to a much wider audience? Does that mean we should be even more eclectic methodologically or should we reach out to more people? I don't know but I hope these points will open up more conversation.

Elizabeth: Such important insights, Mitul, and ones we will pick up on in refining the book's final draft.

Marina: Yes, as Mitul was speaking and since this conversation is about rethinking island methodologies, I was thinking about longitudinal studies. The tendency is that we do those short-term assessment of a situation in research and I wonder: if we engage more longitudinal studies maybe we can get better understandings?

Elizabeth: One dominant idea is about decolonizing island studies, and I think it is enormously problematic. Obviously, it is utterly necessary, but in my own field of decolonizing literary studies, for instance, I don't think the methodologies have changed. I don't think it has really done its epistemological turn and actually taken hold. So, what does decolonization look like, really?

Godfrey: To add to what Elizabeth is saying: what does decolonization look like on islands without a history before colonization? Because that's an assumption. Take the Pacific, which, of course, has a relatively recent brush with colonization and that has Indigenous populations that have survived to maintain vibrancy and activity and be involved in governance. Compare that area to the Indian Ocean island states, for instance, where places such as Mauritius or the Seychelles don't have any evident history before Europeans arrived.

Elizabeth: I think it requires a lot of thought about what decolonization is in this space; it's one we won't be able to solve but cannot presume about.

Elaine: Andrew, how do you translate these conundrums into your teaching? Can we prepare undergraduate students and doctoral candidates to be methodologically innovative given time constraints and complexity?

Andrew: One key thing I do in the island geographies unit I teach is to get students to think about the interrelationships between some basic philosophical questions central to the practice of methodologies and research. I don't want to hit you with a whole lot of "ologies," but these are ideas around ontology, ideas about what we think can exist; and ideas about epistemology, how we know what we know and as we know it. So, how we think we can know the world and methods to generate data; ideas to do with axiology and politics, about what valuing is implicit when we deploy particular methodologies?

In the intersections across the what, the how, and the why, and the techniques or methods we might use are a whole series of interesting questions that relate to innovation. To be innovative implies that you can refer back to some sort of tradition, so what are the traditions in island studies scholarship? I should say I think island studies is a field not a discipline. I think it's usefully characterized as a field that's drawn in repeated waves on different forms of understanding, different ways of understanding that have come from elsewhere and variously reinvigorated it, challenged it, shifted it. So, openness to different ways to know the world is one key aspect of how we might want to think about both traditions and innovations.

I also think it's useful to think about a point that John Law makes in *After Method,* that current methodologies that may constitute our traditions are good at generating particular sorts of understanding of the world that relate to stable entities, to prediction, to singular understandings of the world. But maybe we need to give more weight to forms of methodologies and of methods that can bring other worlds and other possibilities into existence as well?

For me, that is not just an ontological question but also a deeply political question. So, in my teaching I ask students to try and see interrelationships between what, how, and why and relate them to some real-world issue or experience, some sort of concrete skill or technique they're working with. So, in my island geographies unit, students might start out thinking they're just learning a technique but, as part of that, I get them to think through interrelationships between what, how, and why as well. As part of that, echoing Mitul, I think it's so important to get out of the classroom to into real landscapes talking to people about their experiences and exposing students to other perspectives and possibilities, so they become aware of how they're carrying various sorts of assumptions with them and can find ways to have those assumptions safely challenged as they learn.

But I'd love to hear from others in terms of whether you incorporate those sorts of interrelationships in your teaching and how you might do it in critically reflexive ways. I think it was Carol who talked about the need for more critical reflexivity; and I think it was Mitul who talked about the need for situated knowledge and awareness of the situatedness of knowledge. I think Jon has written around the relationships between knowledge production and different geographies, so it would be great to hear from people.

Maria: My approach in teaching is experiential learning, so I'm doing a study program on the island of Crete. So, the main idea is to invite students to feel what is involved in the self-sufficiency and resiliency that comes from living on an island. Because most, if not all the students come from mainlands, I'm trying to give them a sense of what and how it means to be an islander and ask what really is an island? Does the water surrounding an island give fluidity in life and are islanders more open to change even as we want to preserve our traditions and feel like we need to defend them? We just had the hardest winter on Crete, and I've learned that it's not the beaches or the mountains the students are drawn to; it's people's mentalities, their behaviors, the philosophies informing what it is to be an islander, and material expressions of all those things: products, food, Mediterranean diet that are local but also global and universal—and the students get that.

Elaine: So, on one hand there are important ideas about what, why, how, and also about the political and, on the other hand, there's a different kind of politics and materiality of the island as a form. All those insights invite discussions about changing research practices to address challenges in island studies and facing island peoples. Aideen, given what you've heard so far who should be leading the charge and what are the most pressing challenges?

Aideen: The question of who should be leading the charge comes right back to what Carol and Marina were saying about the need for inclusivity: members of island communities should be leading the charge on many issues and should be central in defining and addressing what the challenges are. But then sometimes we come up against a tendency to romanticize island communities and think they are close-knit and cohesive and that downplays the diverse perspectives in play. When others were talking about invisible islands earlier, I wondered if we need to be more careful about the voices being heard and those that aren't? That's a challenge.

Coming back to my interest in scale, something challenging about working with islands is thinking about and working across the global–local interface. On islands that I'm engaged with, it feels—in both environmental and social terms—that the issues are local and place-specific and also enmeshed in a wider global picture. Sometimes the shift across scales is challenging from the perspective of a research community or from a policy perspective—including in relation to communication. And I think climate change is a really good example of that tension; on one hand, climate change is a global challenge; but, when you get down to climate change as a lived experience on a local scale, you've got local environmental factors and the local social system, and so much of that then shapes experience, doesn't it?

As Mitul was saying, specific environments and ecologies give rise to a set of circumstances and sometimes there's an urge to generate a unified narrative of how climate change affects islands, which might be problematic because, again, that tendency gives rise to invisibility or obscures certain experiences. I think that comes about as a result of difficulties in scale and the fact that we're all dealing with the hyperlocal and global at the same time.

James: I was just thinking that so often conversations about island studies are comparative and awareness about comparisons can vary a lot. So, because I'm so used to this approach, I'll be having a conversation about Shetland and then compare that to Barbados and be given a quizzical look. But to me it's obvious that there are comparisons between these different places but, for others, the comparison might be irrelevant. Even so, comparative work is especially useful but outside the discipline how widely is that understood and how widely is acknowledged?

Thinking about climate change, there's a lot going on in small island developing countries and there are some obvious comparisons but then the conversation about climate change in Tasmania is, I'm sure, different from the conversation in the South Pacific. So, why is that and how do we do comparison; that becomes interesting for me.

When Andrew was talking about how we can prepare undergrads or doctoral students I thought about how we take a lot of people on internships and fellowships and work with students looking for experiences—for example, from the University of Prince Edward Island in Canada or the University of the Highlands and Islands in Scotland. That has been different from working with students from the University of West Indies because of different approaches from different regions. It would be great to see more involvement from the University of the West Indies, but I know island studies is not engaged with in comparable ways in different types of institutions.

Godfrey: I'm reminded of what Carol asked us when she launched the conversation: who is in the middle of island studies? Few of us are in the middle; we're probably approaching a peripheral topic from a peripheral perspective and are often constrained to look at islands through much more established lenses and perspectives. James referred to the Caribbean. Despite our efforts there are no Caribbean scholars in this conversation. One possible reason is that Caribbean scholars are careful about and suspicious of using an island studies' methodology because they think it deflates and detracts from—let me use their words— more serious lenses and epistemologies: class, of course, race and colonialism. If they use a geographical focus, they may think that they are diluting what they should be looking at.

Elaine: Thank you for those insights, everyone. Let me turn to Maria now and ask what are the possibilities for new approaches working with children and young people and the elderly?

Maria: I think if all of us all over the world search deeply within, we may understand and realize that we come from water and islands. In my work with older people on islands, they always want to transmit what they know to younger people and build bridges with younger ones: their wisdom, myths, stories, all have something well respected that should be passed on. Younger people often resist listening to older ones and we have stories from all over the world that show us that. There is a reaction to tradition, to upholding ties to the past; but, in the end, when young ones come close to nature and their search for identity, they also look deeply within and often come to find peace in relation to what their elders say.

So, I think education is the tool that each of us has and there are ways through art, music, and particularly dance, because it's nonverbal and you don't have language barriers that you might come across when you teach traditional history through song. Everybody comes together in a performance and speaks through the body, transforming words into body movements. You step onto the land; you are grounded. You get off the land if the dance is a leaping, jumping one; you are connected to the skies, to the highlands. Metaphorically speaking, these are ideas that speak of what is an island. As I was saying earlier, are we islands? Are we mainlands connected to islands? Are we the ones to bridge one island to another island? I think that there's multidisciplinary and interdisciplinary ways. We can use technology to teach younger and older people or people who are not from islands about sustainability, connection, and ties with the environment. You don't necessarily need to be an islander per definition to do so.

So, teach about resilience, teach about locality, teach about identity, look for your own identity. Here on the island of Crete, we are very well tied to the soil, to the ground. In this endless journey, with all the turbulences and disturbances it may bring, we like going back, nostalgically, to where we initially belong. That has been well defined in poetry and mythology and I'm pretty confident there are similar stories all over the world about those ideas.

Elizabeth: As you were speaking, Maria—and because we're talking about specific issues related to place, island, and scale—I was thinking of the piece by Kathy Jetñil-Kijiñer and Ana Niviâna in which someone from the Marshall Islands goes to Greenland. They are quite different; one is an atoll in the Pacific, and the other is the largest island in the world; different climates; so much difference. But what is extraordinary about this work are the similarities, comparisons in how earth, water, myths, respect, sociality are woven in those places. It's not the same is it, because they're culturally specific? Their performance tells the viewer: yes, there's difference and yet there is this core of imaginative and material culture, and one is coming from the other; they are not separable, and they are connected. So, here are those two issues together that Aideen, Maria, and James were discussing, scale and comparison, and questions about what can you compare? But important in this case is that the work comes from two poets, performers who have done it themselves, and that insight speaks to the issue of involvement that others have raised in this conversation.

Elaine: So, James, arts communities, civil society organizations, and social enterprises are important in island places. How do you see civil society organizations engaging in burning questions about islands?

James: There's a lot of directions I was thinking about going in with this question and my organization uses the quadruple helix in all its work. I'm not sure how familiar people are with that term but it's basically about how nongovernment organizations, private sector organizations, academics, and governments engage with each other. On an island setting, people in those four sectors clearly need to collaborate in some form for any meaningful change to "development," for want of a better term. But then even within the civil society or NGO sector, the role of, let's say, a climate activist in the Pacific is quite different from, I don't know, the role played by someone in a large international NGO. And I think those large international NGOs are just as guilty as anyone else of using island tropes and—to use a term from one of Carol's papers—"wishful sinking" methodologies in order to raise money and fulfil their goals, and that is just like a commercial organization.

So, again, individual activists or those in small local NGOs or international NGOs engage and approach islands differently. Even small local NGOs or activists may be able to use to their advantage some of those tropes in order to raise money or fulfil other goals they have. I think it's interesting to see how islanders in places that are vulnerable to climate change have used certain ideas that may not necessarily be wholly agreed upon locally but fulfil a goal on the world stage. So, my point is that within civil society, there are many ways that these organizations can engage with the big questions, and their methodologies depend on scope.

When it comes to the private sector, I think the same applies. In April 2022, we're running an event called the Island Finance Forum. We set up that event because we found our most significant event, the Virtual Island Summit, did not bring in enough commercial organizations. We wanted to network with banks because ultimately you can have policy makers and innovators and sustainability nerds talking about ideas but if no one's going to pay for them at the end of the day then why are we talking? So, we had to ask: how do we bring banks into these conversations? What came out of that process was that scale and the profit motive meant islanders may have markets that interest a private organization but if the organization can spend all of its market entry costs to go into Mexico, Colombia, or Brazil instead of St Lucia or even Jamaica—which is a relatively large market—it's not worth it for large international banks or other such private sector organizations to do island-based projects.

So, the insights we got were all about scale. To refer back to the Caribbean and Pacific, there have been efforts to create one larger market by harmonizing policies on some level. There have been 50 years of those efforts in the Caribbean, leading to mixed results. One could argue about the extent to which there is a single market in the way that the European Union has a single market. Those integration efforts have been limited but ultimately for there to be opportunity there needs to be harmonization for the private sector. So, there is an interesting tension between island autonomy or independence and the need for harmonization to build big enough markets.

Small island markets are never going to be interesting to a large international bank and the role of local and regional banks in financing projects is especially important. But those banks use a different language and engage in different ways. So, again, when we were setting up the forum we used terms considered passé in large international finance markets related to environmental and social governance, but those terms were not really resonating with some of the local banks. It's not to say that the topics weren't being engaged with; but the language being used was completely different, and so was the vibe between organizations working at different scales in different ways.

Godfrey: That's got me thinking on something else in the case of small islands again, which also has to do with scale and what James and Aideen have said. In some islands, especially if they have jurisdictional capacity, there's politics in everything; everything is political. Even if you don't want an issue to be political, very soon it "rubs shoulders" with somebody in government or in opposition or both; it's unavoidable. However, then the opposite occurs if you have islands that don't have jurisdiction. In those places, you may feel really far away from politics, and you may have to go through some fairly creative engagements to connect and get the ear of any particular Minister, especially if you're just an inconsequential part of a constituency.

James: But there is the idea as well that they may be very inconsequential but by leveraging islandness then they can actually get more attention than might be expected from that population. I'm thinking of huge projects that the UK government invested in the Scilly Isles. The Isles constitute the smallest council area in the UK, just around 2,000 or 3,000 people only; but their development attracts much more attention than would a town or village of that size on the mainland.

Godfrey: True. So, a project becomes more visible when it is dumped on a small community, even though the value added per capita is not as effective as with a large-scale operation.

Elaine: I think this is a segue to a question for Marina, which is how do you see local, regional, and national governments and international instrumentalities in terms of island studies methodologies given your experiences in diplomacy?

Marina: Thank you, Elaine. Just before I answer that question I wanted to add that civil society organizations always have to deal with politics from a place on the periphery. And I think they need to be more central, engaging, and assertive so that they can live up to their promise.

Now, with regard to local, regional, or national governments and international instrumentalities, earlier we talked about who can make and lead change. In my view leaders, policy makers, researchers, and academic institutions can all assist with that and lead change. But at the end of the day, it is about politics; we go back to the politics, and we go back to leaders—those highest in authority. That is especially the case in small island states, and here I'm talking about Seychelles, which has a population of about 98,000—it's just like a village elsewhere.

So, when we ask how local, regional, and national governments can intervene in islands and the study of islands, do we start by sharing best practices?

Locally, it is crucial to involve local researchers and experts. But in a small island state context—where everybody knows each other—if you fall out with somebody, nobody will call you because you are a troublemaker: you've been labelled and can no longer participate. We need to do away with those kinds of attitude and involve everybody—involve the population, involve the experts.

Small island developing states also depend on larger regions, where unity gives strength. So, one method is to collaborate with people from other small island states who are experiencing similar issues. Then, it is easier to effect change and that's why we have groupings such as the Indian Ocean Commission, among others: to strengthen the voice of small island developing states in expressing their views. Networking and bilateral and multilateral relations can help those from such states learn and team up with others from other countries to effect change and influence decisions in favor of small island developing states.

Politics in small island states are such that if you get politicians on board and secure national commitments you generate support to address issues. For example, we started the University of Seychelles in 2009 for a population of only 98,000. Some Seychellois are hesitant to study at their local university! They want to go abroad for the experience. They say, "we don't want to stay here; we want to experience life abroad." So, we're trying to bring in international students for the Seychellois to interact with. We have also been undertaking more research, but unless the government and politicians provide research funds for the university it will be difficult to transition from being just or mainly a teaching university.

Mitul: When I think about riverine islands in South Asia and about the functions of civil society and multiscalar governance, I think involving different states becomes extremely important. The hundreds of small islands dotting the Brahmaputra, for instance, are as much a result of its governance as they are of the river's fluvial dynamics. Therefore, collaborations among the riparian states' collaborations and civil society's involvement in the governance of the river are of great significance. The reality is, however, that there is very little cooperation among India, China, and Bangladesh vis-à-vis the Brahmaputra, a river all three nations share. This lack of collaboration has serious implications. For instance, a large dam upstream can radically transform the river's watercourses and configurations downstream and threaten the existence of some of these islands.

Carol: Tuvalu's population is even smaller than the Seychelles, and its situation captures some issues of scale discussed throughout this conversation. With around 11,000 people in the country, and another 4,000 or so who identify as Tuvaluan living abroad, it's a really small place. When dealing with some of the challenges of climate change the scale can be almost inverted and used to advantage. So, recently the Foreign Minister Simon Kofe was nominated for the Nobel Peace Prize for making a speech to a recent climate conference of parties half submerged in water and using the island trope to his advantage. It was a fairly simple public act and went global, and huge publicity was given to Tuvalu.

If we look at climate change studies or climate change art or climate change activism or climate change leadership in the Pacific it's massive. I have seen it grow from this tiny thing at the beginning of the century to something affecting every field, with amazing graduates coming out of University of the South Pacific's climate change programs and related courses. They're ready to work on climate change challenges. They're talking about it everywhere, working on it in every government department, in every civil society organization, every church, every village. A lot of the narrative is about disappearing islands and damaged islands, but you don't see the same focus on island studies. I don't think there's any Pacific university with an island studies program.

The same can be said of Kiribati and other small islands in the Pacific and the Indian Oceans—you've got the Maldives, as well. Climate change studies and climate change activism are huge and so is climate change innovation but is island studies in there helping that work? I don't know, but I don't think so. I mean yes, there's lots of overlap, but is the island the central focus of the way island climate change academics and activists think through these problems? No. Decolonization is; climate change is. So, what do we do in island studies?

Elaine: Jon, my next question is for you: We have been talking about what we need to do to innovate in island and archipelagic studies, with a focus on methodologies. What risks are involved in opening those conversations and for whom?

Jon: So, we've been talking about local involvement, money, education, decolonization, island studies, and islandness. That's what I've picked up so far.

So, what key risks do those questions raise? I think they're probably twofold. The first one relates to money, decolonization, involvement of local people, and the risk here is that we don't acknowledge the elephant in the room, which is the Western university and how it works.

For many years, I didn't tell my students this story but after a while I got older and a bit more secure in my job, so I didn't need to worry about it so much. So, this story is that, for many years, I worked in the Caribbean with fisherpeople. After a PhD and postdoc, I became good friends with them, and we tried to develop a cross-island network for fisherpeople, developing unions, that kind of thing. Now, I was still relatively young and naïve, and I would say to funding authorities, "why don't we give all the money to the fisherpeople rather than me?" Oh, what a "stupid" thing that was to say within the climate of how academia really works—of course, my contract at my university wasn't renewed.

This point gets right to the crux of why local people don't really get involved in academic work and why they are reduced to "informants" or "participants": the Western university makes its reputation and moves up league tables by getting large grants. What's bizarre is that much of the money from the grant does not actually go to the university itself, because, of course, it goes on the actual project. In many ways the university does not care though, because what "matters" is that the grant is seen to be obtained by the Western university, to go through its bureaucracy, so that the university can say it is doing good research on the poor, or whoever, demonstrating its "impact" and "reputation" because it is spearheading large grants to do so. Today—and I cannot stress this point enough—everything from project design to method and implementation is fundamentally controlled, at a deep psychological and material level, by this kind of target and metric culture. It shapes everything, from how we come up with and frame research questions, to how we undertake and reflect upon what is found from the research and report it. Of course, the power of metric culture is proliferating as universities seek to compete on the open market.

This is one reason why I like organizations such as the International Small Islands Studies Association—the vibe is different, or, at least it acts as a kind of "buffer." So, for example, as a young academic there is a relatively safe space where you're not being judged so much according to metrics; it's about the ideas you're looking at. I cannot overstate how important this vibe is within the broader climate of academia today. That's also why we have a monthly reading group and monthly study group with island scholars from around the world in the Anthropocene Islands initiative too—we try and create a safe space where ideas and discussions, readings, and conversations matter, and not the metrics.

The second risk relating to the key topics we've been discussing today is to think that islands don't matter, when they really do. Now Darwin produced his theory of evolution on islands: there was an islandness to that; it matters. The discipline of anthropology, Margaret Mead's work: developed on islands and by thinking with islanders. I think islandness matters even more today. The whole conversation related to "Anthropocene Islands" is about how islands matter to the generation of broader contemporary Anthropocene thinking; from tropes of "resilience" to recent powerful developments in Black studies. Because of time constraints, I cannot go into those ideas more here, but this key point is drawn out in our book in detail—much Anthropocene thinking is developed today by thinking with islands, islanders, and islandness.

So, Elaine, the risks are that we don't think about those things as much as we should—the power of the Western university and how it really works, the power of "islandness," and how to keep developing "island studies" as a kind of "buffer," a more open and experimental space, against the increasing, constricting pressures of wider academia.

Elaine: Thank you Jon; a good segue to a question for Carol. What are the benefits of asking and answering questions about how we might influence the methods by which we study islands?

Carol: For me there is a need to reignite interest in the on-the-ground reasons why island studies might still be important—or not? I think that question is beneficial for all of us to ask and to keep asking and never take it for granted. And there is a need to reach out beyond the field of island studies. As Jon noted, for those in the Western university it's so important to stay unsettled because there is so much knowledge beyond the university system; to what extent are people in island studies grappling with that? I still think there's a heck of a lot more that we could be doing in terms of that multiple, local, Indigenous alternative knowledges that are still invisible. If we keep asking those questions I think then we will continue to develop the field in decolonial and other ways that we want it to go.

Elizabeth: Can I just say something here? I think institutions can be helpful places by which to institute revolutionary practices and alternative practices as I have experienced editing the journal *Southerly*, Australia's oldest literary journal—so a kind of institution. With First Nations writers, Southerly helped enable the first Indigenous-edited, -published, -content issue some years ago but that was because we were at an institution with some weight behind it. It was meaningful to everybody involved in ways that I don't pretend to understand or it's not my business to understand. We also produced an issue on the incarceration of refugees across Australia's carceral regime, working with hundreds of people in prisons. Negotiations worked because we were at a university—an institution—and we could do this work with authority. We didn't get funded by the government for that issue (surprise, surprise) but we had networks we could use to get the work out. So, I know that institutionalized constraints are a problem, but institutions' influence can be used, can't they?

Elaine: Thanks Liz; an important point about a particular methodological approach. Aideen, you are also at a university.

Aideen: What Jon was saying resonates with me, in that institutional practices of not just universities but funding bodies, publishers, and so on inform how research is done. I was also thinking there's something problematic about the formalization of impact in research. Because that focus comes back to perverse ideas about scale—the bigger the better: the bigger the audience or the effect on national policy. All those "bigger" things are held up as the ultimate measures in terms of research impact, aren't they? That approach creates problems or challenges for island studies because sometimes you are talking about problems that affect a small proportion of people or places. When I'm speaking to people in the Scottish islands, it's a tiny proportion of the UK population. On paper, the impact of research in island communities seems limited, so we try to make broader connections and find overarching frameworks to show broader impact. Comparison isn't always right, though, when you actually want to focus on something unique, however small it is, but it comes about because impact has been formalized as a metric and process. But, really, anytime I speak to colleagues who've had impact from research that they're proud of, the experience has been organic and built over a long period of time from deep interpersonal relationships—so it's not been a formal process at all. I think that gets us into some challenges too.

Elaine: Thank you; such important insights. So, the last question for everyone is this: what else should we be asking about ways to study islands and archipelagos and to whom should those questions be addressed?

Maria: I wonder if we need to rethink morality and ethics in island studies, because everything each one of us has been talking about relates to a sense of islandness. If I were to create courses at universities all over the world, I would definitely include a required course on cultural anthropology in terms of island-ness. Can island studies help us redefine what's moral and what's ethical in all the crises that we are living globally today?

Andrew: I think that's a great question, Maria, and for me it prompts me to think about the ethics of place and the ethics and moralities that attend place. The thrown-togetherness of people in small island settings, which is something that Pete Hay has written about, really means people have to try and engage in dialogue, engage in discussion in order to live together. So, I think there's an interesting set of challenges about ethics and morality that comes to the fore when we think about island places.

Elaine: That really resonates with what Marina was saying too, doesn't it? Marina, when you were talking about the implications of a small community on an island and everything ricochets.

Godfrey: It's also captured in the ABC acronym, articulation by compression, isn't it?

Marina: Right. So, I wanted to add that maybe we need more local champions and should ask the question Elaine just posed to politicians and leaders; they are the ones who can influence change. Without them it will take longer time frame for us to achieve whatever we want to achieve.

Mitul: I would like to add that perhaps we need to start thinking about island studies as praxis: how can island studies be more useful? This question is related to our earlier conversation about ensuring our research has meaning for island-ers and collaborations among researchers, policy makers, activists, and locals. Let me also highlight the importance of documenting oral histories of islands, especially of those ephemeral river islands that I've talked about already. We must capture these histories before islands disappear. Methodologically, this work calls for us to engage more with the elderly in these places. In Majuli, for example, I was enthralled by stories older people told me about both existing and eroded island wetlands. That work led me to develop a map of the wetlands to highlight physical transformations on the island. I think oral history can be a great methodological tool for island studies scholarship.

Jon: Can I just come in on the question related to islands, morals, and ethics and whether islandness should be in the frame? I think the answer is islandness is absolutely being put to work to develop broader morals and ethics today. If you think about concepts like resilience, islands are not just symbols but are productive and generative in masses of contemporary mainstream policymaking and critical thought. I think the way in which islandness is being put to work is reshaping how we think about ethics and morals. People may or may not like how that's taking place, but I think it's undeniable that islands are not on the periphery of how we think about many mainstream concepts today. James will know this: C. S. Holling is a key thinker in work on resilience theory and the first question he asks of people who want to work on his program is "can you work on islands?"—this is about operationalizing islandness to develop resilience thinking.

Elaine: Is there anyone—and especially Liz and Godfrey—who has any last words for tonight?

Godfrey: It's been wonderful and better than I thought it might be. Even though many of us didn't necessarily know each other, and we come from different disciplines, it has been unbelievably coherent. I'm pleasantly surprised at how this has gone. I'm sure we all are chafing at the bit to get flesh onto some of the questions and ideas that perhaps need some more thought and articulation.

Elizabeth: And I want to thank everybody also for the ideas, provocations, and different approaches drawn from a wide range of experiences and contexts; it has been incredibly important, so: thank you.

Elaine: My heartfelt thanks to all, as well. Many fascinating and crucial questions and ideas about islands and about why and how we study them—with and for whom and to what ends! So, we close with an opening, which seems really apt.

Chapter 9

Practicing

What Does It Mean to Apply the "Knowing" of Island and Archipelagic Studies?

Godfrey Baldacchino and Elaine Stratford

Praxis: the synthesis of theory and practice seen as a basis for or condition of political and economic change. [But also] Techne: an art, skill, or craft; a technique, principle, or method by which something is achieved or created. [And] Phronesis: wisdom personified. (OED)

The application of what we know about islands and archipelagos has significant reach and scope, and *effective* application involves, we suggest, judiciously engaging praxis, techne, and phronesis. After all, who would not aspire to be useful, adept, and wise?

Strangely enough, explanatory powers derived from (small) island-based research and the scrutiny that attends it are often more readily applied to large, nonisland habitats than to other islands, in peer-to-peer fashion. Note that here we mean small in both areal size (for example, Malta) and/or population base (for example, lutruwita/Tasmania, where degrees of separation are slight, despite the island's large land area). And note, too, that we distinguish between doing, as examined earlier, and practicing, considered here. Our first focus in chapter 7 was on methodology and method and our second focus, in this chapter, is on how island and archipelagic studies and/or studies of islands and archipelagos gain effect in the world because of the application of thought, technique, and critique.

Source: Jean-Yves Vigneau.

133

Much has been written about lessons *from* islands, rather than *about, with,* and *for* them; as we noted in the introduction, too often they are reduced to *mise-en-scènes*—mere backdrops to agendas shaped elsewhere. Practice as we conceive it in this chapter would change that equation, but challenges need to be overcome—and many are shaped by asymmetrical power relations the characteristics of which we have aired throughout the book.

Residents of island places may want, be expected, and be encouraged to write on, and conduct research about, their own islands. There are many instances of where, for instance, they have mobilized under the banner of citizen science or social science, sometimes of their own volition and sometimes with institutional support (Petridis et al., 2017; Teasdale & Teasdale, 2022; University of Tasmania, 2022). Some involve funded multinational collaborations to advance citizen science on mosquito surveillance in the Solomon Islands to mitigate the "risk of disease transmission and allow pinpointed response activities" (Craig, 2022, n.p.). Yet, research *for* islanders *about* islands and islanders may not command interest deemed sufficiently large by market standards set by publishers on the basis of specific financial models and expected returns.

Skewed power relations continue to thwart much Indigenous scholarship (Baldacchino, 2004). In Australia, First Nations' peoples envision living "in a world in which Aboriginal and Torres Strait Islander knowledge and cultures are recognized, respected, celebrated, and valued" (AIATSIS, 2022, n.p.). Stringent requirements are in place to ensure ethical conduct in relation to Indigenous research (NHMRC, 2018, n.p.):

> Researchers planning to do any type of research involving Aboriginal and Torres Strait Islander peoples must consult and follow the advice in the most contemporary versions of *Ethical conduct in research with Aboriginal and Torres Strait Islander Peoples and communities: Guidelines for researchers and stakeholders* and *Keeping research on track II* as well as the *Guidelines for Ethical Research in Australian Indigenous Studies (GERAIS)* produced by the Australian Institute of Aboriginal and Torres Strait Islander Studies. These guidelines embody the best standards of ethical research and human rights and seek to ensure that research with and about Aboriginal and Torres Strait Islander peoples follows a process of meaningful engagement and reciprocity between the researcher and the individuals and/or communities involved in the research.

However, challenges remain—involving questions about the extent to which non-Indigenous scholars should engage without first being invited and about how Indigenous scholars inside Western university systems are positioned. In this respect, Corrinne Sullivan's (2020) research on Sydney sex workers from Aboriginal backgrounds shows that Indigenous scholars who may assume they have "insider" status in communities may not be seen as such by those they seek to work with and for. In some ways, her findings parallel those outlined earlier in the book in relation to insider/outside tensions in island studies, especially where Indigeneity pertains.

Likewise, in Canada, Indigenous scholars are practicing what Michael Hart (2010, p. 1) has called "radical Indigenism"—in his case by working "with Cree peoples in north central Turtle Island, also referred to as North America [in order to include] worldviews, Indigenous knowledge, Indigenous knowledge of helping, and research from an Indigenous stance." The call he makes for radically reshaping research practices is also reflected in more recent efforts to show how Canadian researchers are seeking to balance "individual and collective rights, [uphold] culturally-grounded ethical principles, and [ensure] community driven and self-determined research" (Hayward et al., 2021, p. 403). At the same time, at least one systematic review of the literature provides valuable guidance based in *rapprochement*, itself a form of wise practice. In that review, Alexandra Drawson and colleagues (2017, p. 17) conclude that

> using an Indigenous method necessitates an Indigenous methodology, but . . . an Indigenous methodology could be utilized with strictly Western methods. For example, if a researcher was planning to use a talking circle method, then *they must approach the entirety of their research with an Indigenous methodology*, but a researcher employing an overall Indigenous methodology *could do so while using Western methods, such as surveys*. What is *important* is that the Indigenous community involved has the ability to *determine* the direction and approaches that are preferred. (emphasis added)

Arguably, such concerns and considerations prevail everywhere; whether they are magnified on islands is moot, however, and that is a debate not likely to be solved any time soon.

Of late, the Internet and the World Wide Web, digital publishing (including blogging), and open access reforms have helped to democratize somewhat the availability and dissemination of island and Indigenous knowledges. So have international movements such as the Declaration on Research Assessment (DORA, 2022, n.p.). Constituted in 2012 in San Francisco at one annual meeting of the American Society for Cell Biology, the declaration is a "worldwide initiative covering all scholarly disciplines and all key stakeholders including funders, publishers, professional societies, institutions, and researchers." Among other initiatives, DORA tracks the ways in which we collectively deal with Indigenous research challenges—how we practice our craft in the terms defined at the start of the chapter. In one blog, for example, the focus is on the radical revitalization of the Australian and New Zealand Standard Research Classification in 2019 (DORA, 2021). Prior to that review, Aboriginal, Torres Strait Islander, Māori, and

Pacific Peoples research was all but invisible. Belated but welcome redress has addressed that gap. At the same time, the point is made that Indigenous and islander research remains unfairly subjected to Western quantitative metrics related to, for example, citations and funding. More informed practices are needed to better value such research for its community impacts and intrinsic worth.

It is common to treat "the island" instrumentally: for example, as a harbinger of events or shifts somewhere else or as a space to observe early manifestations of what is yet to come elsewhere. So conceived, "the island" serves as a convenient and manageable petri dish, with its arguably simpler internal dynamics and seemingly impenetrable borders to enclose any unwelcome outcomes and reduce risks of contamination—but with significant potential to replicate discoveries and escalate their impacts. The opinion that islands are "so splendidly splitable into PhD topics" still applies (Spate, 1978, p. 42). Island residents remain objects of "the gaze" of nonislanders—including academics, filmmakers, journalists, and tourists (Urry & Larsen, 2011). This gaze seems especially gripped by the dramatic impacts of, or adaptations to, climate change on islands. Struggling for media, donor, or investor visibility, one is tempted to ask what choices residents of (small) islands have (Baldacchino & Kelman, 2014). And yet, there are powerful examples of both the reversal of that gaze and the deployment of new scopic regimes to advance radical practices by islanders and for island places and the solid, liquid, and aerial spaces between them. So, for instance, Jaimey Faris (2019, n.p.) adds value to work done by Jetñil-Kijiñer and Niviâna by pointing out that they use their positions to critique "the continuity between colonial and environmental *scopic regimes* that, taken together, stymie climate change imaginaries" (emphasis added). Johannes Riquet (2019) also does much useful work to point to such reversals.

Much is needed to continue to refine practices in island and archipelagic studies in order to radicalize their potential. In what follows, we critically review some of ways in which "the island" is used as a stage in ways that ultimately may not serve us well enough. We consider practices in studies of island biogeography, cultural inquiry, social intimacy and interaction, and place branding and identity, to briefly flag certain limitations.

PRACTICING ISLAND NATURAL HISTORY, PHILOSOPHY, AND BIOGEOGRAPHY

Island diversity has led to scientific investigations that have vastly expanded our knowledge of biogeography. Such sustained inquiry has often been founded on or supported by fieldwork and data collection *in situ*, although digitization of spatial data has transformed how fieldwork is both conceived and conducted (Lowy Institute, 2012). Those investigations in the field on islands have advanced our understandings of and capacities to make forecasts about: the numbers and types of species one might find; the existence of endemic species and their vulnerability to non-natives; dwarfism, gigantism, and evolutionary changes in species size; the effects on "pristine" habitats of invasive species—including humans; the effects of extreme weather events; and the overall dynamics of species arrivals and extinctions in enisled locales (Kueffer et al., 2016).

The earliest practical applications of what are now island and archipelagic studies involved natural history and philosophy, alongside surveying, mapping, and paintings of species and landscapes as ways by which to capture these under the imperial gaze (Allen, 2021; Kennedy, 2012; Ritvo, 1997). General knowledge of an island's geological age, size and topography, location, climate, and degree of isolation from other islands and the closest mainland is enough to provide rough estimates of the relative number and diversity of species. It was already observed in the eighteenth century that the "small size of the island, together with its vast distance from either the eastern or western continent, did not admit of a great variety of animals" (Forster, 1777/2000, p. 156). Much of what was gleaned via natural history and philosophy informs island biology and biogeography (see Nunn, 2021, especially Chapter 4).

And so, one can expect more species to dwell on: larger islands than smaller ones; those closer to the mainland (and what is likely to be their species pool) than those that are further away; those that are high and have rugged terrain than those that are flat and barely above sea level. At the same time, one is more likely to find a larger proportion of endemic species on more isolated islands than on near islands. The "species-area" relationship has been expressed mathematically as $S = cAz$, where S is the number of species; A is the area of the habitat under scrutiny; z is the slope of the "species-area" relationship when using logarithmic scales on both the horizontal and vertical axes of the graph; and c is a constant (Gooriah et al., 2020). These measuring practices are meant to hold, especially when observing islands that occupy the same general location and share a common history (especially of non-native interventions, including humans), climate (including rainfall patterns), and geology (such as lava versus limestone versus coral atoll). The precepts that inform such practices still influence city planners and conservation strategists when it comes to, for example, designing parks and ecological corridors in urban spaces (Dondina et al., 2016). And core principles underpinning this (quasi-mechanistic) model originated in the equilibrium theory of island biogeography, according to which the number of species on an island at any point in time is the net outcome between immigration and extinction dynamics (MacArthur & Wilson, 1963, 1967).

There is, however, keen debate on some of the model's basic implications. In what has been termed the SLOSS debate ("single large" or "several small" sites), the superiority of a single large reserve suggested by the model as against two or more smaller ones has been questioned. The query arises because, if a population at one small reserve in a system of several reserves becomes extinct, then individuals from other small reserves can recolonize it; this would be impossible with a large but single reserve (Tjørve, 2010). These are vital questions, since preserving enough habitat in order to save as many species as possible from extinction is a fundamental tenet of environmental management.

The notion of island species pool as being a balance of immigration and extinction also belies the openness of many islands to trans-territorial connections. So, for example, island ports are critical interfaces with the outside world and depend on imports and trade, and often on immigrant skilled labor; no wonder then that most island capital cities are indeed ports. And island seas and oceans are frequently recipients of invasive aquatic species that travel in ships' ballast tanks. Given this susceptibility to invasives, and waves of species movements over time, islands are, like mainlands, also messy spaces to explore any purported species "balance" (Potter, 2007).

However, there are also exceptions to the observation that openness to trans-territorial connections prevails. Jamie Kirkpatrick (2022, n.p.) has shown this powerfully in work about conservation connectivity across the Bass Strait separating lutruwita/Tasmania from the Australian mainland. On the basis of decades-long research in biogeography, he has established that "there is a negligible millennium-scale isolation effect of Bass Strait on compositional variation in *E. regnans* forest." However, he also found "a definite lesser effect on species composition differences of disjunctions within states than between them, indicating that water barriers might be more effective than land barriers." And he points out that, while on land, "there may be possibilities for steppingstones for dispersal of wet forest species between locally moist situations, options [are] less available in Bass Strait with its very scattered, small, dry islands."

Either way, the point to be made here is that biogeography and associated fields continue to have immense importance as practices that shape island and archipelagic futures. The key will be to ensure that methodological approaches stay open to innovation, exception, and cross-fertilization with other fields. Some of that openness was perhaps more apparent in past centuries when disciplinary boundaries were more fluid, and, for example, surveyors were artists and scientists all in one. And we make that observation cautiously, noting that those same individuals were also constituting partial systems of knowledge production and limited engagement with marginalized people—Indigenous knowledge holders, women, and those from precarious backgrounds not least among them. Priya Satia (2020) is outstanding in her exposition of the ways in which the discipline of history has also been complicit in those absences and silences. Nevertheless, some of the promised cross-fertilization is alive and well and in the now, as exemplified by, for example, work by Patrick Nunn and Margaret Cook (2022), who weave together archaeological and mythological sources of evidence in a discussion about the creation of islands.

PRACTICES IN CULTURAL ANTHROPOLOGY AND ALLIED FIELDS

Evolutionary scientists may have been the first to visit islands for scientific purposes; but anthropologists have not been far behind. They were especially keen to visit the Pacific, that massive segment of the planet that was the last to be settled by those who became its Indigenous populations and then later invaded and colonized by Europeans. It was therefore expected to hold on best to relictual social mores and practices. Here were abundant examples of self-contained island "laboratories," many of which were compact and homogeneous in their smallness and imputed simplicity. It was assumed that they would, therefore, be easy to understand under the penetrating gaze of both amateur and professional researchers.

And so, a long procession of cultural specialists—anthropologists perhaps first among them—came to study the peoples of small islands, notably in the Pacific but also in the Caribbean, in the Indian Ocean, and elsewhere. Again, those studies did not start in a disciplinary isolation. Rather, they were informed by an enormous swell of interest in what we now know as the imperial-colonial project that itself was undergirded by rapid technological change in international postal and telegraphic services, steam shipping, or growing levels of literacy and interest in news. By way of rough example, a search of the British Library's online Newspaper Archive in June 2022 lists over 33,000 instances of "anthropology" or "anthropologist" just between 1850 and 1899; there was just one reference between 1700 and 1749 and just over 1,800 references between 2000 and 2022. The same archive has 1,166 references to "Pacific" between 1700 and 1749, a staggering 2,346,200 between 1850 and 1899, and 14,446 between 2000 and 2022. The arts, too, played a powerful role in influencing the anthropological gaze; there was significant aesthetic force in, for instance, paintings of Tahitians by Paul Gauguin (1848–1903), and that is but one well-known example. Intentionally or otherwise, responses to such chronicles generated among home publics lurched between considering islanders noble savages, exemplars of the residents of an "Eden without apples" bereft of the emptiness and ennui of life in the West, and viewing them as the last vestiges of tradition (Edmond & Smith, 2003), "primitives" doomed to be overwhelmed by modernity and caricatured most cruelly (Smith, 1960). As one of us has noted elsewhere, in 1871 in *The Descent of Man*, Darwin:

> mounts an argument about those higher faculties and links them to the differential vigour of certain races. Invoking a hierarchy that now is galling, he asks "how little can the hard-worked wife of a degraded Australian savage [*sic*], who uses hardly any abstract words and cannot count above four, exert her self-consciousness, or reflect on the nature of her own existence? A corollary of his embedded answer—which is that she can neither exert or reflect—is that she is unfit and under-developed; the parent stem is flawed. (Stratford, 2019, p. 60)

In what perhaps remains the most famous—and deeply problematic—anthropological work, *Coming of Age in Samoa*, Margaret Mead documented her perceptions of the behavior of 50 female islanders, allegedly untainted by cultural contact, untouched by progress, and enjoying sexual freedoms. Mead (1928/2001) was not interested in Samoans *per* se; they were handy exponents of a "simpler civilization" and used by her to constitute forms of scientific analysis and interpretation to dispute and disprove a prevailing hypothesis that adolescence is a period of turmoil and stress irrespective of cultural context. With her eagerness to publish, perhaps to please her German-born supervisor and mentor and "father of modern American anthropology" Franz Boas (1858–1942), and goaded by William Morrow, her publisher, Mead (1901–1978) ended up reinforcing the erotic island paradise stereotype. This might explain her book's enduring status as a bestseller (Côté, 2000) and also the justifiable offence Samoans have taken in her depiction of Samoan adolescent sexuality (Isaia, 1999).

Again, the overarching insight to be drawn from these observations is that cultural fields such as anthropology, but also human geography, sociology, or political science—all of which have specific takes on social and cultural milieux that have been highly problematic—have shaped island and archipelagic pasts. How they are engaged in supporting island and archipelagic futures will depend in some measure on the various methodological choices that are made. Inventive, creative, collaborative, and ethical practices are central to those choices. There is compelling evidence for hope in these fields of practice, especially with respect to decolonizing agendas, novel approaches to research design, staunch opposition to the imperialist project, and similar strategies and tactics.

PRACTICES HIGHLIGHTING SOCIAL INTIMACY AND INTERACTION

Mead's major works involved participant observation among the islanders of Tàū, in what is now American Samoa: 600 persons scattered over seven villages. In such small settlements, social environments tend to be characterized by pervasive personal connections and overlapping role relationships (Benedict, 1967). Whether or not they like or dislike each other is irrelevant: small island inhabitants generally know each other very well, too well, and are compelled to deal with each other on multiple occasions and while fulfilling different societal roles (Cica, 2005; Lowenthal, 1987). These dealings are, we suggest, also forms of practice, and they can be informed or visceral, based on artful and skillful techniques, and on wise counsel, or they can be otherwise. That observation holds, no matter where one is. But an abiding question continues to be whether, how, to what extent, and with what effects such practices matter more on (small) islands, and how one might even go about establishing that methodologically and with "right" ends in mind. Either way, as Enright (2013, n.p.) observes, within the "enclosed and entangled world of island society, no one [is] given the freedom of being a stranger." Citizens of small, often island, societies have detailed knowledge about each other's personal lives, and "learn to get along, like it or not, with one another, knowing that they are likely to renew and reinforce relationships with the same persons in a variety of contexts over a whole lifespan" (Baldacchino, 1997, p. 77). Such "multiple role relationships" are ubiquitous in a social matrix where the threshold of intimacy is low (Ott, 2000, p. 5). As a result, professional interactions slide and morph imperceptibly into personal ones, and vice versa: trends that are often described (by outsiders) in terms of clientelism, patronage, or nepotism (Hassall, 2019; May & Tupouniua, 1980).

It has been claimed that "intimacy" and ensuing expressions of social cohesiveness and clannishness foster a social milieu friendlier, more harmonious, and more oriented to consensus (Srebrnik, 2004) than may be evident off islands. Small island societies, we are told, are naturally charged with "a spirit of fellowship and community" associated with "feelings of tolerance and understanding" (Anckar, 2002, pp. 386–87). Yet, social intimacy can also generate profound antagonism, hostility, pique, and long-standing feuds. But, because individuals who do not like each other must also repeatedly interact and engage, such antagonism may be subtle, nuanced, and subdued. Again, subversive practices via embodied or discursive regimes, for example, are not exclusive to islands (Dean, 1999; Hajer, 2006; Scott, 1987), but *are* they concentrated on islands? So, in rethinking island methodologies what would any answer to that question—yes, no, perhaps—require and of whom in any inquiry that might follow?

Out of this context develops a complex situation of so-called managed intimacy (Bray, 1991; Lowenthal, 1972), in which citizens are forced to downplay or mitigate open conflict. That tendency is often marked in relation to those practices that inform democratic processes, and that has been studied both statistically and qualitatively (Anckar, 2008; Veenendaal, 2018), pointing to a welcome alertness to the value of mixed-method approaches to these challenging questions. Some commentators also suggest that island social-psychological contexts breed "dissimulation, a guardedness that one can never be completely divested of without fear of negative consequences" (Spiteri, 2016, p. 300). The result of such dynamics could well be a *prima facie* "concerted social harmony" (Sutton, 2007, p. 204) and the prevalence of strong pressures to conform to "dominant cultural codes" (Baldacchino, 2012; Stratford, 2006b).

And so, social intimacy may be linked to a semblance of harmony and consensus, but those characteristics may typify carefully coded and managed façades that obscure deep-seated personal conflicts, subtly handled and/or stoically borne. Indeed, individuals from small island societies who openly voice their opposition or dissent run the risk of social exclusion and ostracism (Alonso-Bello et al., 2020; Presterudstuen, 2019). As a result of the closeness between citizens and politicians and the politicization of society, small island communities can be remarkably polarized along party or other social or ethnic lines. Especially among island groups with deep social divisions or divisive practices with respect to ethnic, religious, and linguistic pluralism, the risk of vicious conflict looms large (Austin, 2000, p. 61). In culturally heterogeneous island *states*—including Cyprus, Fiji, Ireland, Solomon Islands, Trinidad & Tobago, and Vanuatu—violent conflicts have occurred, and social tensions between groups occasionally resurface. Particularly in archipelagic units that bind multiple small islands into a single jurisdiction, island-based national-ism and separatist sentiments may also cause upheaval and a risk of secession or of state breakdown (Baldacchino, 2005; Hepburn & Baldacchino, 2013). Situations on subnational island jurisdictions pose both similar and dissimilar challenges (Ferdinand et al., 2020; Karlsson, 2009; Stratford, 2006a).

We should therefore not be surprised to note that major theories about small group behavior have emerged from the studies (by outsiders) of such tight island social universes. British social scientist John Barnes (1954) pio-neered the use of the concept of "social network" following his research in the small Norwegian parish of Bremnes on Bømlo island, Norway. Dutch anthropologist Jeremy Boissevain (1974) perfected his understanding of the mechanics of network theory, and the instrumental and manipulative construction and nurturing of "friends of friends," from his observations in Malta. More recently, feminist scholars have provided vivid examples of the ways in which network and assemblage thinking can enrich the application of methodologies among particular communities: Marina Karides (2015) in relation to Lesvos among the Greek islands and Sonja Boon and colleagues (2018) in terms of the "land and sea-scapes" of Newfoundland. Then there is work by Eleonora Diamanti and Paolo Favero (2022) in respect of the "symbiotic assemblages" formed via social digital practices that reach out into the waters and connect with aquatic creatures—thereby productively and inventively stretching the meanings of social relations in ways that account for commitments to a more-than-human ontology. These (methodological) practices matter, and they are exciting to witness as they unfold.

PRACTICES RELATED TO PLACE BRANDING AND IDENTITY

Small island economies striving for export competitiveness may face impediments: scarcity of local raw materials, limited and finite domestic markets, and the absence of economies of scale. These hindrances may then conspire to render locally manufactured goods ill-fit to compete with similar products developed in larger locations (Briguglio, 1998). Two classic solutions to this quandary are, first, a focus on exporting services that, being intangible, are not straddled with the weight, volume, and logistic headaches of material goods; and, second, a focus on promoting specific manufactures that command unassailable niches and remain attractive purchases in spite of being relatively more costly. For the first, the most successful pursuits for small island jurisdictions have included tourism, offshore finance, shipping registries, rentier incomes, and internet-based services such as e-gaming. For the second, handicraft, local foods and beverages, and souvenirs appeal to tourist markets and succeed because they align with images and representations of place and locality and thus avoid external competition.

At the same time, there are significant moves afoot to bring together major financial organizations, entrepreneurs, and island communities to circumvent these impediments, move beyond the two classic solutions, and forge novel methodologies and practices that support islanders to innovate (Island Innovation, 2022). A significant number of such possibilities exist in the virtual world. In the internet age, branding has become a sophisticated industry since reputation and its associated risks have become key factors when considering consumer or investor behavior. Hence the resort to brand strategies to guide governments, economic development agencies, and private sector organizations to work together to design and romance credible brand portfolios to lift the economic fortunes of specific jurisdictions using names, symbols, logos, and other graphics and also experiences and emotional outcomes (Govers & Go, 2009).

One powerful example of the kind of collaborative practice to which we have just referred is based in lutruwita/Tasmania, where Brand Tasmania is a body corporate constituted as an independent statutory authority. It is the first such organization in Australia to be created under legislation—the Brand Tasmania Act (2018), which binds the Crown. One implicit intent is to ensure that Tasmanians are seen not as mendicants to the mainland and nation-state but as communities in place who recognize the power of the island's brand as part of identity formation and transformation. In this sense, Brand Tasmania's objects exemplify decades of debate about and refinements to how that place and its people are understood (on which, see Ripoll González & Gale, 2020).

More explicitly, under section 7 of the Act, the objects of the Authority are:

(a) ensure that a Tasmanian Brand, which *differentiates and enhances* Tasmania's appeal and *national and international competitiveness*, is developed, maintained, protected, and promoted; and
(b) ensure that Tasmania's *image and reputation locally, nationally, and internationally* are strengthened; and
(c) ensure that the Tasmanian Brand is nurtured, enhanced, and promoted as a key *asset* of the Tasmanian community. (emphasis added)

It is noteworthy, too, that, under section 8, the Authority's functions include having:

(c) to promote the Tasmanian Brand by creating, coordinating, managing, developing and supporting promotional and marketing activities that—

    (i) strengthen Tasmania's *image and reputation*; and
    (ii) enhance the attractiveness of Tasmania as a place in which to live, work, study, visit, *invest or trade*; and
    (iii) *maximise* the profile, and the competitive position, of Tasmanian goods, services, experiences and products in local, national and international *markets*;

(d) to identify *risks* to the reputation of the Tasmanian Brand and to develop mitigation or contingency plans in relation to that risk. (emphasis added)

That such assemblages of praxis, technical expertise, governmental oversight, and multisectoral engagements exist is striking in and of itself. Equally remarkable is the fact that the words used on Brand Tasmania's (2022) website include isolation, inventiveness, culture, the Bass Strait, the boutique, the bespoke, the extraordinary, struggle, hard work, ingenuity, and unify story but not island—that is conjured into these other terms. But in doing so does Tasmania, *the island, the archipelago*, disappear as such? And what practical implications has that for those doing research t/here and seeking to engage with it on its own (island) rather than merely its subnational terms?

Either way, whether explicit reference to islands is made or not, the brands used to identify with them and that are partially constitutive of them are more successful when they both identify *and* differentiate a location. Conjuring up "Jamaica," say, to a potential tourist audience should not only identify it as part of the Caribbean playground but also speak to its distinction from dozens of Caribbean island tourism destinations. Complementarity is key, or brand dissonance can lead to confusion. Thus, the fun and frolic of Jamaica-as-tourism-destination should be supported, and thus reinforced, by the multiple brand profiles of other things Jamaican—such as rum, biscuits, sauces, Bob Marley/reggae, and Usain Bolt (Johnson & Gentles-Peart, 2019). In their more extreme rendition, brands become simulacra, where their associated symbols and catchphrases and their evocations replace reality: suggesting, for example, that one may "know" Jamaica even without visiting it (Baudrillard, 1994).

Islands have been the stuff of branding long before the concept found its way into management schools and contemporary marketing discourse. Five hundred years ago, it was claimed that one could harvest cod from the rich waters off the island of Newfoundland (now, part of Canada) simply by lowering a basket into the sea (Baldacchino, 2016b). Earlier, in the tenth century CE, Eric the Red (c. 950–1003) is reported in old Icelandic sagas to have named the "new" territory that he "discovered," *Greenland*, in order to attract "settlers" there. Of course, as Juno Berthelsen points out, Inuit cultures have much longer, rightful claims over that space, and part of the innovations to be had in rethinking island methodologies involves rethinking how those places are branded—hence his engagement in activities to remove statues of the Danish missionary Hans Egede, labors redolent of the 2015 *Rhodes Must Fall* movement (Berthelsen, 2020a, 2020b, 2021). Indeed, Greenland today is increasingly known by its Indigenous name: Kalaallit Nunaat.

Islands are powerful brands in part because enduring traditions hold islands as pivotal in the economic, political, religious, and social life of, for example, the Mediterranean and then Atlantic worlds. That central position is evident in myth, iconography, and narratives of/from islands that have powerful functions in mainland cultures and in cross-cultural exchanges related to, for example, ningyo, sirens, and mermaids among Japanese, Portuguese, and Dutch sailors trading icons to protect them on sea voyages from one island to another, and from island to mainland (Castiglioni, 2021; see also Campbell & Moyers, 1988). Often marginalized or erased by such pursuits are traditional, Indigenous, and subaltern voices—women, children, the elderly, ethnic minorities, or immigrants—whose voices and representations may sully, weaken and unhinge the brand from its focus, and wrest the myth from its masculine roots, as Sarah Nicholson (2011) has adeptly pointed out in relation to Joseph Campbell's near dominance over mythology studies. As one outcome, islanders can find themselves left to grapple with glossy covers over what are sometimes deeply troubled places with dark secrets (Birkett, 1997).

As another outcome, among islanders living amidst archipelagos, any differences and similarities *between* islands may be transformed into a "contrived complementarity" that encourages island hopping (Baldacchino & Ferreira, 2016). This process of aestheticization can be undertaken with the collusion of islanders keen to protect and nudge along their islands' appeal as small island tourist economies (McElroy & Parry, 2010). But it cannot disguise other forms of island migration based on, for example, degrading conditions (Roland & Curtis, 2020) or urban bias (Naidu & Vaike, 2016).

In sum, the effects on identity formation and transformation of place branding demand that significant care be taken in how its practices are designed and deployed, and in how scholars, policy makers, and practitioners address the powers that adhere to their respective roles and voices. As Robyn Mayes (2008, p. 124) nailed it, place branding "is a powerful and ubiquitous practice deployed around the globe. Parallel to its acceptance and development as a distinct discipline is an understanding that place branding as responsible practice offers the means to achieve widespread economic, social and cultural benefits." But that understanding, she argues, is not just about reflection but also about generative practices to ensure place branding (for islands and archipelagos not least) is "a force for good." In our view, that agenda invites more in the way of methodological innovation and engagement. In no small measure, and beyond all the drama and trauma that essentializes island vulnerability—and perhaps its imputed corollary, resilience—islanders lead their own, normal lives. The island citizens of Tonga do not go about their daily lives anxious about the next eruption of Hunga Tonga–Hunga Ha'apai; as much as Barbadians do not consciously anticipate a powerful hurricane; and Mauritians another tanker striking their coral reef. Economies of scope and the resort to polyvalency and broad skill sets, practiced at home and away from home, mitigate the excessive dependency on a few export industries. Like Leopold Bloom in James Joyce's Ulysses—another islander—there is epic even in the mundane (Joyce, 1922). Sometimes (island) place is just that, and to be celebrated as such.

So, there we have it. An introduction, eight ensuing chapters, and eight verbs to contemplate in venturing forth: to value, be, know, speculate, guide, do, converse, and practice. The field is open, we hope, for many more forays into deep consideration of rethinking island methodologies, and we look forward to witnessing what happens next. But enough for now.

References

Abadia, O., & Porr, M. (2021). *Ontologies of rock art: Images, relational approaches, and Indigenous knowledges*. London and New York: Routledge.

Adams-Hutcheson, G. (2017). Spatialising skin: Pushing the boundaries of trauma geographies. *Emotion, Space and Society*, 24(Supp. C), 105–12. https://doi.org/10.1016/j.emospa.2016.03.002

Agius, K., Sindico, F., Sajeva, G., & Baldacchino, G. (2022). "Splendid isolation": Embracing islandness in a global pandemic. *Island Studies Journal*, 17(1), 44–65. https://doi.org/10.24043/isj.163

AIATSIS (Australian Institute of Aboriginal and Torres Strait Islander Studies) (2022). Home>About. https://aiatsis.gov.au/about-aiatsis

Ajakaye, J. E., & Ogunniyi, S. O. (2021). 21st-Century multidisciplinary collaboration in research in library. *Library Philosophy and Practice (e-journal)*. https://digitalcommons.unl.edu/libphilprac/6228

Alessio, D., & Renfro, W. (2021). Building empires litorally in the South China Sea: Artificial islands and contesting definitions of imperialism. *International Politics*. https://doi.org/10.1057/s41311-021-00328-x

Alexander, J. (1988). The new theoretical movement. In N. J. Smelser (Ed.), *Handbook of sociology* (pp. 77–101). Thousand Oaks, London, New Delhi: SAGE.

Allen, C. (Ed.). (2021). *A companion to Australian art*. Wiley Blackwell. https://onlinelibrary.wiley.com/doi/pdf/10.1002/9781118767979#page=137

Alonso-Bello, E., Santana-Vega, L., & Feliciano-García, L. (2020). Employability skills of unaccompanied immigrant minors in Canary Islands. *Journal of New Approaches in Educational Research (NAER Journal)*, 9(1), 15–27. https://www.learntechlib.org/p/216729/

Anckar, C. (2008). Size, islandness, and democracy: A global comparison. *International Political Science Review*, 29(4), 433–59. https://doi.org/10.1177/0192512108095722

Anckar, D. (2002). Why are small island states democracies? *The Round Table: Commonwealth Journal of International Affairs*, 91(365), 375–90. https://doi.org/10.1080/0035853022000010344

147

Anderson, B., & Wylie, J. (2009). On geography and materiality. *Environment and Planning A: Economy and Space*, *41*(2), 318–35. https://doi.org/10.1068/a3940

Anguera, M. T., Blanco-Villaseñor, A., Losada, J. L., Sánchez-Algarra, P., & Onwuegbuzie, A. J. (2018, February). Revisiting the difference between mixed methods and multimethods: Is it all in the name? *Quality & Quantity*, *52*, 2757–70. https://doi.org/10.1007/s11135-018-0700-2

Appadurai, A. (1996). *Modernity at large: Cultural dimensions of globalization*. Minneapolis: University of Minnesota Press.

Archibald, J. (2008). An indigenous storywork methodology. In J. G. Knowles & A. L. Cole (Eds.), *Handbook of the arts in qualitative research: Perspectives, methodologies, examples, and issues* (pp. 371–85). Thousand Oaks, London, New Delhi: SAGE. https://dx.doi.org/10.4135/9781452226545

Argent, N. (2021). Adaptive capacities and social resilience on Kangaroo Island: Beyond the staples trap. *Geographical Research*, *59*(3), 378–93. https://doi.org/10.1111/1745-5871.12469

Armstrong, D., & Stratford, E. (2009). Thoughts on scale, land use, and opportunities for good governance: A tale of two sub-national island jurisdictions. In G. Baldacchino, L. Felt, & R. M. Greenwood (Eds.), *Remote control: Governance lessons for and from small, insular, and remote regions* (pp. 187–207). St. Johns, Newfoundland: ISER Books.

Arnall, A. (2022). Where land meets sea: Islands, erosion and the thing-power of hard coastal protection structures. *Environment and Planning E: Nature and Space*. https://doi.org/10.1177/25148486221101461

Austin, D. (2000). Contested islands. *The Round Table: Commonwealth Journal of International Affairs*, *89*(353), 59–63. https://doi.org/10.1080/750459456

Bacon, J. (2003, February 6). *Building a culture of peace through tourism: A global perspective*. Second Global Summit on Peace through Tourism.

Baker, C. M., & Bode, M. (2021). Recent advances of quantitative modelling to support invasive species eradication on islands. *Conservation Science and Practice*, *3*(2), e246. https://doi.org/10.1111/csp2.246

Baldacchino, G. (1997). *Global tourism and informal labour relations: The small scale syndrome at work*. London and New York: Routledge.

Baldacchino, G. (1998). The other way round: Manufacturing as an extension of services in small island states. *Asia Pacific Viewpoint*, *39*(3), 267–79. https://doi.org/10.1111/1467-8373.00069

Baldacchino, G. (2004). The coming of age of island studies. *Tijdschrift voor Economische en Sociale Geografie*, *95*(3), 272–83. https://doi.org/10.1111/j.1467-9663.2004.00307.x

Baldacchino, G. (2005). Editorial: Islands—objects of representation. *Geografiska Annaler: Series B, Human Geography*, *87*(4), 247–51, https://doi.org/10.1111/j.0435-3684.2005.00196.x

Baldacchino, G. (2006a). Islands, island studies, island studies journal. *Island Studies Journal*, *1*(1), 3–18. https://doi.org/10.24043/isj.185

Baldacchino, G. (2006b). Innovative development strategies from non-sovereign island jurisdictions? A global review of economic policy and governance practices. *World Development*, *34*(5), 852–67. https://doi.org/10.1016/j.worlddev.2005.10.004

Baldacchino, G. (2007a). Introducing a world of islands. In G. Baldacchino (Ed.), *A world of islands: An island studies reader* (pp. 1–29). Newcastle upon Tyne: Agenda Academic and Institute of Island Studies, University of Prince Edward Island.

Baldacchino, G. (2007b). Islands as novelty sites. *Geographical Review, 97*(2), 165–74. https://doi.org/10.1111/j.1931-0846.2007.tb00396.x

Baldacchino, G. (Ed.). (2007c). *Bridging islands: The impact of fixed links.* Charlottetown, PEI: Acorn Press.

Baldacchino, G. (2008). Studying islands: On whose terms? Some epistemological and methodological challenges to the pursuit of island studies. *Island Studies Journal, 3*(1), 37–56. https://doi.org/10.24043/isj.214

Baldacchino, G. (2010a). Islands and beers: Toasting a discriminatory approach to small island manufacturing. *Asia Pacific Viewpoint, 51*(1), 61–72. https://doi.org/10.1111/j.1467-8373.2010.01414.x

Baldacchino, G. (2010b). Re-placing materiality: A Western anthropology of sand. *Annals of Tourism Research, 37*(4), 763–78. https://doi.org/10.1016/j.annals.2010.02.005

Baldacchino, G. (2010c). Editorial: The island lure. *International Journal of Entrepreneurship & Small Business, 9*(4), 373–78.

Baldacchino, G. (Ed.). (2011a). *Island songs: A global repertoire.* Lanham: Scarecrow Press.

Baldacchino, G. (2011b). Surfers of the ocean waves: Change management, intersectoral migration and the economic development of small island states. *Asia Pacific Viewpoint, 52*(3), 236–46. https://doi.org/10.1111/j.1467-8373.2011.01456.x

Baldacchino, G. (2012a). Come visit, but don't overstay: Critiquing a welcoming society. *International Journal of Culture, Tourism and Hospitality Research, 6*(2), 145–53. http://doi.org/10.1108/17506181211233072

Baldacchino, G. (2012b). Islands and despots. *Commonwealth & Comparative Politics, 50*(1), 103–20. https://doi.org/10.1080/14662043.2012.642119

Baldacchino, G. (Ed.). (2013). *The political economy of divided islands: Unified geographies, multiple polities.* Amsterdam: Springer.

Baldacchino, G. (Ed.). (2016a). *Archipelago tourism: Policies and practices.* London and New York: Routledge.

Baldacchino, G. (2016b, September 27). On the branding and reputation of islands. *Place Brand Observer.* https://placebrandobserver.com/branding-islands/

Baldacchino, G. (2018a). Preface. In G. Baldacchino (Ed.), *The Routledge international handbook of island studies* (pp. xix–xxxv). London and New York: Routledge.

Baldacchino, G. (2018b). Seizing history: Development and non-climate change in Small Island Developing States. *International Journal of Climate Change Strategies and Management, 10*(2), 217–28. https://doi.org/10.1108/IJCCSM-02-2017-0037

Baldacchino, G. (2020). How far can one go? How distance matters in island development. *Island Studies Journal, 15*(1), 25–42. https://doi.org/10.24043/isj.70

Baldacchino, G. (2021a). Extra-territorial quarantine in pandemic times. *Political Geography, 85.* https://doi.org/10.1016/j.polgeo.2020.102302

Baldacchino, G. (2021b). Island tourism experience. In R. Sharpley (Ed.), *Handbook on the tourist experience* (pp. 498–507). 4 Volumes. London and New York: Routledge.

Baldacchino, G., & Clark, E. (2013). Guest editorial introduction: Islanding cultural geographies. *cultural geographies, 20*(2), 129–34. https://doi.org/10.1177/1474474012469594

Baldacchino, G., & Ferreira, E. C. D. (2016). Contrived complementarity: Transport logistics, official rhetoric and inter-island rivalry in the Azorean archipelago. In G. Baldacchino (Ed.), *Archipelago tourism: Policies and practices* (pp. 85–102). Farnham, UK: Ashgate.

Baldacchino, G., & Kelman, I. (2014). Critiquing the pursuit of island sustainability: Blue and green, with hardly a colour in between. *Shima, 8*(2), 1–21. https://www.shimajournal.org/issues/v8n2/c.-Baldacchino-&-Kelman-Shima-v8n2-1-21.pdf

Baldacchino, G., & Khamis, S. (2018). Island brands and branding. In G. Baldacchino (Ed.), *The Routledge international handbook of island studies* (pp. 368–80). London and New York: Routledge.

Baldacchino, G., & Starc, N. (2021). The virtues of insularity: Pondering a new chapter in the historical geography of islands. *Geography Compass, 15*(12). https://doi.org/10.1111/gec3.12596

Ballantyne, R. M. (1857). *The coral island: A tale of the Pacific Ocean*. Edinburgh: T. Nelson.

Barnes, J. A. (1954). Class and committees in a Norwegian island parish. *Human Relations, 7*(1), 39–58. https://doi.org/10.1177/001872675400700102

Barrie, J. M. (1911). *Peter Pan; or, the boy who wouldn't grow up; or, Peter and Wendy*. London: Charles Scribner's Sons.

Barth, F. (1969). Introduction. In F. Barth (Ed.), *Ethnic groups and boundaries: The social organization of culture difference* (pp. 9–38). Boston: Little, Brown & Company.

Barthes, R. (1990). *The fashion system*. (M. Ward & R. Howard, Trans.). Berkeley: University of California Press.

Baruah, M. (2022). *Slow disaster: Political ecology of hazards and everyday life in the Brahmaputra Valley, Assam*. London and New York: Routledge.

Bates, S. (2022, January 15). Tonga volcano plume reached the mesosphere. NASA Earth Laboratory. https://go.nasa.gov/3zVLPVi

Baudrillard, J. (1994). *Simulacra and simulation*. Lansing: University of Michigan Press.

Baum, T. G. (1997). The fascination of islands: A tourist perspective. In D. G. Lockhart & D. Drakakis-Smith (Eds.), *Island tourism: Problems and perspectives* (pp. 21–35). London: Mansell.

Baum, T. G., Hagen-Grant, L., Jolliffe, L., Lambert, S., & Sigurjonsson, B. (2000). Tourism and cold water islands on the North Atlantic. In G. Baldacchino & D. Milne (Eds.), *Lessons in the political economy of small islands: The resourcefulness of jurisdiction* (pp. 214–29). London: Macmillan.

Bawaka Country, Suchet-Pearson, S., Wright, S., Lloyd, K., Tofa, M., Sweeney, J., Burarrwanga, L., Ganambarr, R., Ganambarr-Stubbs, M., & Ganambarr, B. (2019). Goŋ Gurtha: Enacting response-abilities as situated co-becoming. *Environment and*

Planning D: Society and Space, 37(4), 682–702. https://journals.sagepub.com/doi/full/10.1177/0263775818799749

Beck, C., & Gleyzon, F-X. (2016). Deleuze and the event(s). *Journal for Cultural Research, 20*(4), 329–33, http://doi.org/10.1080/14797585.2016.1264770

Beer, G. (1989). Discourses on the island. In F. Amrine (Ed.), *Literature and science as modes of expression* (pp. 1–27). Alphen aan den Rijn: Kluwer Academic Publishers.

Belcher, W. (2019). *Writing your journal article in twelve weeks, 2nd edition.* Chicago: University of Chicago Press.

Benchley, P. (1974). *Jaws: A novel.* New York: Ballantine Books.

Benedict, B. (1967). *Problems of smaller territories.* London: University of London and Athlone Press.

Benítez-Rojo, A. (1996). *The repeating island: The Caribbean and the postmodern perspective.* Durham, NC: Duke University Press.

Benjamin, L., & Thomas, A. (2016). 1.5 to stay alive? AOSIS and the long term temperature goal in the Paris Agreement. *SSRN Electronic Journal.* https://papers.ssrn.com/sol3/papers.cfm?abstract_id=3392503

Berthelsen, J. (2020a). Facebook post, June 22.

Berthelsen, J. (2020b). Facebook post, July 25.

Berthelsen, J. (2021, January 18). Greenlandic student: We do not erase history by taking down the statue of Hans Egede. We create history. *Politiken.*

Bertram, G., & Watters, R. (1985). The MIRAB economy in South Pacific microstates. *Pacific Viewpoint, 26*(3), 497–519. https://doi.org/10.1111/apv.263002

Bessell, S. (2021). Childhood and belonging over time: Narratives of identity across generations on Tasmania's east coast. *Children's Geographies.* https://doi.org/10.1080/14733285.2021.1985431

Bioy Casares, A. (1940). *La invención de Morel [The invention of Morel].* Editorial Losada.

Bird, A. (2002). Thomas Kuhn. In E. N. Zalta (Ed.), *The Stanford Encyclopedia of Philosophy* (spring edition). https://plato.stanford.edu/entries/thomas-kuhn/

Birkett, D. (1997). *Serpent in paradise.* New York: Doubleday.

Blaim, A. (2020). Islands as laboratories in early modern literature and beyond. *Tekstualia, 2*(6), 5–16. https://doi.org/10.5604/01.3001.0014.5175

Blair, R. (2014). Heritage watch. *Marrickville Heritage Society Newsletter, 30*(7), 2.

Blake, W. (1803?). Auguries of innocence. https://www.poetryfoundation.org/poems/43650/auguries-of-innocence

Blomgren, O. (2021). Thinking with and from archipelagos in global humanistic studies. *Worlds enough and time: Towards a comparative Global Humanities.* Seminar, November 12. MIT, Boston. https://comparativeglobalhumanities.mit.edu/speakers/olga-blomgren/thinking-with-and-from-archipelagos-in-global-humanistic-studies/

Blum, H. (2010). The prospect of Oceanic Studies. *Publications of the Modern Language Association of America, 125*(3), 670–77. https://www.jstor.org/stable/25704464

Blum, H. (2013). Introduction: Oceanic studies. *Atlantic Studies, 10*(2), 151–55. https://doi.org/10.1080/14788810.2013.785186

Bogdan, R. C., & Biklen, S. K. (2007). *Qualitative research for education: An introduction to theory and methods,* 5th edition. London: Pearson.

Boissevain, J. (1974). *Friends of friends: Networks, manipulations and coalitions.* Oxford: Blackwell.

Bolon, C. (2018). 1.5 to stay alive: The influence of AOSIS in international climate negotiations. *E-International Relations.* https://bit.ly/3NgQwfr

Bongie, C (1998). *Islands and exiles: The Creole identities of post/colonial literature.* Redwood City: Stanford University Press.

Bonnemaison, J. (1994). *The tree and the canoe: History and ethnogeography of Tanna.* Honolulu: University of Hawai'i Press.

Bonner, R. (2006, February 17). Tokelau: Islanders reject independence. *New York Times.* https://nyti.ms/3mLFGU3

Bonnett, A. (2020). *Elsewhere: A journey into our age of islands.* Chicago: University of Chicago Press.

Boon, S., Butler, L., & Jeffries, D. (2018). *Autoethnography and feminist theory at the water's edge.* London: Palgrave Macmillan.

Booth, K., Ragaini, B. S., & Hardy, A. (2021). A Mona effect: How place discourse constitutes culture-led change. *Geographical Research, 59*(1), 16–28. https://doi.org/10.1111/1745-5871.12431

Bourdieu, P. (1991). *Language and symbolic power.* Cambridge, MA: Harvard University Press.

Bowen, D., Zubair, S., & Altinay, L. (2017). Politics and tourism destination development: The evolution of power. *Journal of Travel Research, 56*(6), 725–43. https://doi.org/10.1177/0047287516666719

Bradshaw, M., & Williams, S. (2002). Scales, lines and minor geographies: Whither King Island. *Geographical Research, 37*(3), 248–67. https://doi.org/10.1111/1467-8470.00082

Brand Tasmania (2022) About Brand Tasmania. https://tasmanian.com.au/brand-tasmania/

Brand Tasmania Act (2018). Tasmanian Parliament. https://www.legislation.tas.gov.au/view/html/asmade/act-2018-037

Brathwaite, E. K. (1975). Caribbean man in space and time. *Savacou,* (11–12), 1–11.

Bray, M. (1991). *Making small practical: The organisation and management of ministries of education in small states.* London: Commonwealth Secretariat.

Briguglio, L. P. (1998). Small country size and returns to scale in manufacturing. *World Development, 26*(3), 507–15. https://doi.org/10.1016/S0305-750X(97)10059-6

Briguglio, L., Byron, J., Moncada, S., & Veenendaal, W. (Eds.). (2020). *Handbook of governance in small states.* London and New York: Routledge.

Brinklow, L. (2021). *My island's the house I sleep in at night.* Hobart: Walleah Press.

Brinklow, L. (2022). Studying islandness through the language of art. *Geographical Research.* https://doi.org/10.1111/1745-5871.12534

Brookfield, H. (1990). An approach to islands. In W. Beller, P. d'Ayala, & P. Hein (Eds.), *Sustainable development and environmental management of small islands* (pp. 23–33). Nashville: Parthenon Publishing.

Brunhes, J. (1920/1971). *Human geography: An attempt at a positive classification* (I. C. LeCompte, Trans.). London: George C. Harrap.

Brunsdon, C. (2016). Quantitative methods I: Reproducible research and quantitative geography. *Progress in Human Geography*, *40*(5), 687–96. https://doi.org/10.1177/0309132515599625

Business Wire (2020). Grand theft auto online. https://bwnews.pr/39yzRpI

Campbell, J., & Moyers, B. (1988). *The power of myth.* New York: Doubleday.

Canavan, B. (2014). Sustainable tourism: Development, decline and de-growth. Management issues from the Isle of Man. *Journal of Sustainable Tourism*, *22*(1), 127–47. https://doi.org/10.1080/09669582.2013.819876

Capistrano, R. (2010). Indigenous peoples, their livelihoods and fishery rights in Canada and the Philippines: Paradoxes, perspectives and lessons learned. United Nations. https://bit.ly/3QHoWe3

Caricom Today (2020, July 9). Beckles calls for a high-level international reparations summit. https://today.caricom.org/2020/07/09/beckles-calls-for-high-level-international-reparations-summit/

Carlquist, S. (1974). *Island biology.* New York: Columbia University Press.

Carlsen, J., & Butler, R. (Eds.). (2011). *Island tourism: Towards a sustainable perspective.* Wallingford: CABI.

Carson, R. (1951/2003). *The sea around us.* Oxford: Oxford University Press.

Carter, G. (2020). Pacific island states and 30 years of global climate change negotiations. In C. Klöck, P. Castro, F. Weiler, & L. Ø. Blaxekjær (Eds.), *Coalitions in the climate change negotiations* (pp. 73–90). London and New York: Routledge.

Carter, J., & Hollinsworth, D. (2022). Governing extension and extending governance for Pacific organic farming. *Geographical Research.* https://doi.org/10.1111/1745-5871.12542

Carter, P. (2019). *Decolonizing governance: Archipelagic thinking.* London and New York: Routledge.

Carter, S. M., & Little, M. (2007). Justifying knowledge, justifying method, taking action: Epistemologies, methodologies, and methods in qualitative research. *Qualitative Health Research*, *17*(10), 1316–28. https://doi.org/https//:doi.org/10.1177/1049732307306927

Casarino, C. (2002). *Modernity at sea: Melville, Marx, Conrad in exile.* Minneapolis: University of Minnesota Press.

Casey, E. S. (1997). *The fate of place: A philosophical history.* Berkeley: University of California Press.

Cassinelli, E. (2012). Favignana, Italy. In G. Baldacchino (Ed.), *Extreme heritage management: Policies and practices from island territories* (pp. 134–51). New York: Berghahn Books.

Castiglioni, A. (2021). The human-fish. *Japanese Journal of Religious Studies*, *48*(1), 1–44. https://www.jstor.org/stable/27039930

Catungal, J. P., & Dowling, R. (2021). Power, subjectivity, and ethics in qualitative research. In I. Hay & M. Cope (Eds.), *Qualitative research methods in human geography* (pp. 18–39). Toronto: Oxford University Press.

Chan, N. (2018). "Large ocean states": Sovereignty, small islands, and marine protected areas in global oceans governance. *Global Governance: A Review of Multilateralism and International Organizations*, *24*(4), 537–55. https://doi.org/10.1163/19426720-02404005

Chandler, D., & Pugh, J. (2020a). Islands and the rise of correlational epistemology in the Anthropocene: Rethinking the trope of the "canary in the coalmine." *Island Studies Journal, 16*(1), 209–28. http://doi.org/10.24043/isj.119

Chandler, D., & Pugh, J. (2020b). Islands of relationality and resilience: The shifting stakes of the Anthropocene. *Area, 52*(1), 65–72. https://doi.org/10.1111/area.12459

Chandler, D., & Reid, R. (2019). *Becoming Indigenous: Governing imaginaries in the Anthropocene*. London: Rowman & Littlefield.

Chiblow, S. (2021). An Anishinaabe research methodology that utilizes Indigenous intelligence as a conceptual framework exploring humanity's relationship to n'bi (water). *International Journal of Qualitative Methods*. https://doi.org/10.1177/16094069211058017

Chilisa, B. (2019). *Indigenous research methodologies, 2nd edition*. Thousand Oaks, London, New Delhi: SAGE.

Christie, A. (1939). *And then there were none*. London: Collins Crime Club.

CIA (2021). The world factbook. US Central Intelligence Agency. https://www.cia.gov/the-world-factbook/

Cica, N. (2005). Turbo Tassie. *Island, 101*, 6–17.

Cica, N. (2013). The cracks are how the light gets in: Does Tasmania need an intervention? *Griffith Review, Tasmania: The Tipping Point, 39*, 9–19. https://search.informit.org/doi/abs/10.3316/ielapa.105763300876419

Clapham, K., Hasan, H., Fredericks, B., Bessarab, D., Kelly, P., Harwood, V., Senior, K., Longbottom, M., & Dale, E. (2021, October). Digital support for Indigenous research methodologies. *Australasian Journal of Information Systems, 25*. https://doi.org/10.3127/ajis.v25i0.2885

Clare, N. (2019, November). Can the failure speak? Militant failure in the academy. *Emotion, Space and Society, 33*. https://doi.org/10.1016/j.emospa.2019.100628

Clark, E., Johnson, K., Lundholm, E., & Malmberg, G. (2007). Gentrification and space wars. In G. Baldacchino (Ed.), *A world of islands: An island studies reader* (pp. 483–512). Newcastle upon Tyne: Agenda Academic and Institute of Island Studies, University of Prince Edward Island.

Clark, J., Laing, K., Leat, D., Lofthouse, R., Thomas, U., Tiplady, L., & Woolner, P. (2017). Transformation in interdisciplinary research methodology: The importance of shared experiences in landscapes of practice. *International Journal of Research & Method in Education, 40*(3), 243–56. http://doi.org/10.1080/1743727X.2017.1281902

Clayton, D. (1999). *Islands of truth: The imperial fashioning of Vancouver Island*. Vancouver: University of British Columbia Press.

Cliff, A., & Haggett, P. (1984). Island epidemics. *Scientific American, 250*(5), 110–17. https://www.jstor.org/stable/24969374

Cohen, M. (Ed.). (2021). *A cultural history of the sea, volumes 1–6*. London: Bloomsbury.

Coleman, R. (2017). A sensory sociology of the future: Affect, hope and inventive methodologies. *The Sociological Review, 65*(3), 525–43. https://doi.org/10.1111/1467-954X.12445

Conkling, P. (2007). On islanders and islandness. *Geographical Review*, *97*(2), 191–201. http://www.jstor.org/stable/30034161

Connell, J. (2003). Island dreaming: The contemplation of Polynesian paradise. *Journal of Historical Geography*, *29*(4), 554–81. https://doi.org/10.1006/jhge.2002.0461

Connell, J. (2021). COVID-19 and tourism in Pacific SIDS: Lessons from Fiji, Vanuatu and Samoa? *The Round Table: The Commonwealth Journal of International Affairs*, *110*(1), 149–58. https://doi.org/10.1080/00358533.2021.1875721

Corbett, J., Xu Y-C., & Weller. P. (2021). *International organisations and small states: Participation, legitimacy and vulnerability*. Bristol: Bristol University Press.

Côté, J. E. (2000). The Mead–Freeman controversy in review. *Journal of Youth and Adolescence*, *29*(5), 525–38. http://doi.org/10.1023/A:1005172012716

Cottrell, J. R., & Cottrell, S. P. (2020). In spaces in between–from recollections to nostalgia: Discourses of bridge and island place. *Island Studies Journal*, *15*(2), 273–90. https://doi.org/10.24043/isj.133

Courchamp, F., Hoffmann, B. D., Russell, J. C., Leclerc, C. & Bellard, C. (2014). Climate change, sea-level rise, and conservation: Keeping island biodiversity afloat. *Trends in Ecology & Evolution*, *29*(3), 127–30. https://doi.org/10.1016/j.tree.2014.01.001

Craig, A. (2022). Citizen science for enhanced arboviral-carrying mosquito surveillance in low resource Pacific island settings. In Academy of the Social Sciences in Australia>News>Grants>2021 Australia-France Social Science Collaborative Research Program winners announced. https://socialsciences.org.au/news/2021-australia-france-social-science-collaborative-research-program-winners-announced/

Crane, R., & Fletcher, L. M. (2017). *Island genres, genre islands: Conceptualisation and representation in popular fiction*. London: Rethinking the Island Series, Rowman & Littlefield International.

Creswell, J. W. (2015). *Research design: Qualitative, quantitative, and mixed methods approaches, 4th edition*. Thousand Oaks, London, New Delhi: SAGE.

Crosby, A. (1986). *Ecological imperialism: The biological expansion of Europe: 900–1900*. Cambridge: Cambridge University Press.

da Sousa Correa, D., & Owens, W. R. (2009). *The handbook to literary research*. London and New York: Routledge.

Darwin, C. (1859/1997). *On the Origin of Species*. London: Wordsworth Editions.

Darwin, C. (1871). *The descent of Man and selection in relation to sex in two volumes with illustrations*. London: John Murray, Albemarle Street.

Davis, R. A. (2003). Coastal geology. In R. A. Meyers (Ed.), *Encyclopedia of physical science and technology* (Geology, pp. 123–58). Amsterdam: Elsevier. https://doi.org/10.1016/B0-12-227410-5/00113-7

De Bono, E. (2017). *Six thinking hats*. London: Penguin.

De Castro, E. V. (2015). Who is afraid of the ontological wolf? Some comments on an ongoing anthropological debate. *The Cambridge Journal of Anthropology*, *33*(1), 2–17.

De Lauretis, T. (1984). *Alice doesn't: Feminism, semiotics, cinema*. Bloomington: Indiana University Press.

De Vries, J., Yanotti, M., Verdouw, J., Jacobs, K., & Flanagan, K. (2021). The Tasmanian housing market: Update 2020–2021. Hobart: University of Tasmania, Housing and Community Research Unit.

Dean, M. (1999). *Governmentality: Power and rule in modern society*. Thousand Oaks, London, New Delhi: SAGE.

Defoe, Daniel (1719). *The life and strange surprizing adventures of Robinson Crusoe: of York, mariner: Who lived eight and twenty years, all alone in an un-inhabited island on the coast of America, near the mouth of the great river of Oroonoque; . . . Written by himself*. Oxford Text Archive. http://hdl.handle.net/20.500.12024/K061280.000

Deleuze, G. (1997). *Bartleby; or, the formula in essays critical and clinical*. (D. W. Smith and M. A. Greco, Trans.). Minneapolis: University of Minnesota Press.

Deleuze, G. (2004). Desert islands. In *Desert islands and other texts 1953–1974* (pp. 9–14). (M. Taormina, Trans.). Los Angeles: Semiotext(e) Foreign Agents Series.

Deleuze, G., & Guattari, F. (1987). *A thousand plateaus* (B. Massumi, Trans.). Minneapolis: University of Minnesota Press.

DeLoughrey, E. (2001). "The litany of islands, the rosary of archipelagoes": Caribbean and Pacific archipelagraphy. *ARIEL: A Review of International English Literature, 32*(1), 21–52. https://journalhosting.ucalgary.ca/index.php/ariel/article/view/34394/28430

DeLoughrey, E. (2009). *Routes and roots*. Honolulu: University of Hawai'i Press.

DeLoughrey, E. (2013). The myth of isolates: Ecosystem ecologies in the nuclear Pacific. *cultural geographies, 20*(2), 167–84. https://doi.org/10.1177/1474474012463664

DeLoughrey, E. (2017). Submarine futures of the Anthropocene. *Comparative Literature 69*(1), 32–44. https://doi.org/10.1215/00104124-3794589

DeLoughrey, E. (2019a). *Allegories of the Anthropocene*. Durham, NC: Duke University Press. https://library.oapen.org/handle/20.500.12657/24899

DeLoughrey, E. (2019b). Toward a critical ocean studies for the Anthropocene. *English Language Notes, 57*(1), 21–36. https://doi.org/10.1215/00138282-7309655

DeLoughrey, E., & Flores, T. (2020). Submerged bodies: The tidalectics of representability and the sea in Caribbean art. *Environmental Humanities, 12*(1), 132–66. https://doi.org/10.1215/22011919-8142242

Denzin, N., & Lincoln, Y. (2005). Introduction: The discipline and practice of qualitative research. In N. Denzin & Y. Lincoln (Eds.), *The SAGE handbook of qualitative research methods, 3rd edition* (pp. 1–32). Thousand Oaks, London, New Delhi: SAGE.

Depraetere, C. (1991). NISSILOG: Base des données des îles de plus de 100 km2. Presentation at 17th Pacific Science Congress, Honolulu, MSDOS computer program and unpublished manuscript. Editions de l'OSTROM.

Depraetere, C. (2008). The challenge of nissology: A global outlook on the world archipelago. Part 1: Scene setting the world archipelago. *Island Studies Journal, 3*(1), 3–16. https://doi.org/10.24043/isj.212

Derrida, J. (2010). *The beast and the sovereign. Volume 1* (Eds. M. Lisse, M-L. Mallett, & G. Michaud & Trans. G. Bennington). Chicago: University of Chicago Press.

Deschenes, P. J., & Chertow, M. (2004). An island approach to industrial ecology: Towards sustainability in the island context. *Journal of Environmental Planning and Management, 47*(2), 201–17. https://doi.org/10.1080/0964056042000209102

Di Castri, F., & Balaji, V. (Eds.). (2002). *Tourism, biodiversity and information.* Kerkwerve: Backhuys.

Diamanti, E., & Favero, P. S. (2022). Octopuses, remoras, and surfers: Speculative stories from the offline space of digital circulation in Cuba. *Feminist Media Studies.* https://doi.org/10.1080/14680777.2022.2042831

Dodds, R., & Butler, R. (Eds.). (2019). *Overtourism: Issues, realities and solutions.* Berlin: Walter de Gruyter.

Dondina, O., Kataoka, L., Orioli, V., & Bani, L. (2016). How to manage hedgerows as effective ecological corridors for mammals: A two-species approach. *Agriculture, Ecosystems & Environment, 231*(1), 283–90. https://doi.org/10.1016/j.agee.2016.07.005

Donne, J. (1624/2001). Meditation 17: Devotions upon emergent occasions. In D. Donoghue (Ed.), *The complete poetry and selected prose of John Donne.* New York: Modern Library.

DORA (Declaration on Research Assessment) (2021). Updates on recognizing and supporting Indigenous research from New Zealand and Australia. https://sfdora.org/2021/04/27/updates-on-recognizing-and-supporting-indigenous-research-from-new-zealand-and-australia/

DORA (Declaration on Research Assessment) (2022). About DORA. https://sfdora.org/about-dora/

Drawson, A. S., Toombs, E., & Mushquash, C. J. (2017). Indigenous research methods: A systematic review. *International Indigenous Policy Journal, 8*(2). http://doi.org/10.18584/iipj.2017.8.2.5

Drozdzewski, D., & Birdsall, C. (2019). Advancing memory methods. In *Doing memory research* (pp. 1–20). London: Palgrave Macmillan.

Druckman, D., & Donohue, W. (2020). Innovations in social science methodologies: An overview. *American Behavioral Scientist, 64*(1), 3–18. https://doi.org/10.1177/0002764219859623

Easthope, H., & Gabriel, M. (2008). Turbulent lives: Exploring the cultural meaning of regional youth migration. *Geographical Research, 46*(2), 172–82. https://doi.org/10.1111/j.1745-5871.2008.00508.x

Edmond, R., & Smith, V. (Eds.) (2003). *Islands in history and representation.* London and New York: Routledge.

Enright, J. (2013). *Fire knife dancing* (Audio book). Newburyport, MA: Thomas and Mercer.

EuroStat (2021). Glossary: Island region. https://ec.europa.eu/eurostat/statistics-explained/index.php?title=Glossary:Island_region

Fabinyi, M. (2008). Dive tourism, fishing and marine protected areas in the Calamianes Islands, Philippines. *Marine Policy, 32*(6), 898–904. https://doi.org/10.1016/j.marpol.2008.01.004

Fair, H. (2022). Playing with the Anthropocene: Board game imaginaries of islands, nature, and empire. *Island Studies Journal, 17*(1), 85–101. https://doi.org/10.24043/isj.165

Faire, L., & Gunn, S. (2012). *Research methods for history.* Edinburgh: Edinburgh University Press.

Farbotko, C., McMichael, C., Dun, O., Ransan-Cooper, H., McNamara, K. E., & Thornton, F. (2018). Transformative mobilities in the Pacific: Promoting adaptation and development in a changing climate. *Asian and the Pacific Policy Studies,* *5*(3), 393–407. https://doi.org/10.1002/app5.254

Farbotko, C., Stratford, E., & Lazrus, H. (2016). Climate migrants and new identities? The geopolitics of embracing or rejecting mobility. *Social & Cultural Geography,* *17*(4), 533–52. https://doi.org/10.1080/14649365.2015.1089589

Farbotko, C., Watson, P., Kitara, T., & Stratford, E. (2022). Decolonising methodologies: Emergent learning in island research. *Geographical Research.* https://doi.org/10.1111/1745-5871.12519

Faris, J. H. (2019). Sisters of ocean and ice: On the hydro-feminism of Kathy Jetñil-Kijiner and Ana Niviâna's Rise: From one island to another. *Shima, 13*(3). http://doi.org/10.21463/shima.13.2.08

Ferdinand, M., Oostindie, G., and Veenendaal, W. (2020). A global comparison of non-sovereign island territories: The search for "true equality." *Island Studies Journal,* *15*(1), 43–66. https://doi.org/10.24043/isj.75

Firth, R. (1936/1983). *We, the Tikopia: A sociological study of kinship in primitive Polynesia.* Redwood City: Stanford University Press.

Fischer, S. R. (2012). *Islands: From Atlantis to Zanzibar.* London: Reaktion Books.

Fischer, S. R. (2013). *A history of the Pacific Islands.* London: Macmillan International Higher Education.

Fitzhugh, B., & Hunt, T. L. (1997). Introduction: Islands as laboratories: Archaeological research in comparative perspective. *Human Ecology, 25*(3), 379–83. http://www.jstor.org/stable/4603248

Fitzpatrick, S. M., Thompson, V. D., Poteate, A. S., Napolitano, M. F., & Erlandson, J. M. (2016). Marginalization of the margins: The importance of smaller islands in human prehistory. *Journal of Island and Coastal Archaeology, 11*(2), 155–70. https://doi.org/10.1080/15564894.2016.1192568

Flanagan, R. (2004, July 22). The selling-out of Tasmania. *The Age Newspaper.*

Fletcher, L. M. (2011). ". . . some distance to go": A critical survey of Island Studies. In E. DeLoughrey (Ed.), Special issue: The literature of postcolonial islands. *New Literatures Review, (47–48)*, 17–34. https://search.informit.org/doi/pdf/10.3316/ielapa.201206208

Fletcher, L. M. (2008). Reading the news: Pitcairn Island at the beginning of the 21st century. *Island Studies Journal, 3*(1), 57–72. https://doi.org/10.24043/isj.215

Fletcher, L. M. (2008). Reading the news: Pitcairn Island at the beginning of the 21st century. *Island Studies Journal, 3*(1), 57–72. https://islandstudiesjournal.org/files/ISJ-3-1-2008-Fletcher-FINAL.pdf

Flint, V. I. J. (2017). *The imaginative landscape of Christopher Columbus.* Princeton: Princeton University Press.

Forster, G. (1777/2000). *A voyage around the world: Book I, Chapter VIII* (Ed. N. Thomas & O. Berghof). Honolulu: University of Hawai'i Press.

Foucault, M. (1967/1984). Of other spaces: Utopias and heterotopias. *Architecture / Mouvement/ Continuité,* October, 1–9 (J. Miskowiec, Trans., and later published in *Diacritics, 16*(1), 22–27. https://doi.org/10.2307/464648)

Foucault, M. (1969/2002). *The archaeology of knowledge* (A. M. Sheridan Smith, Trans.). London and New York: Routledge.

Frambach, J. M., van der Vleuten, C. P. M., & Durning, S. J. (2013). AM last page: Quality criteria in qualitative and quantitative research. *Academic Medicine, 88*(4), 552. https://journals.lww.com/academicmedicine/toc/2013/04000

Freeman, C., Ergler, C., Kearns, R., & Smith, M. (2021). Covid-19 in New Zealand and the Pacific: Implications for children and families. *Children's Geographies, 20*(4), 1–10. https://doi.org/10.1080/14733285.2021.1907312

Frølunde, L., Hee Pedersen, C., & Pedersen, M. (2017). Unravelling the workings of difference in collaborative inquiry. *Departures in Critical Qualitative Research, 6*(1), 30–51. https://doi.org/10.1525/dcqr.2017.6.1.30

Führer, M. (2020). Albert the Great. In E. N. Zalta (Ed.), *The Stanford Encyclopedia of Philosophy* (summer edition). https://plato.stanford.edu/archives/sum2020/entries/albert-great/

Gair, S. (2012). Feeling their stories: Contemplating empathy, insider/outsider positionings and enriching qualitative research. *Qualitative Health Research, 22*(1), 134–43. https://doi.org/10.1177/1049732311420580

Galvan, J. L., & Galvan, M. C. (2017). *Writing literature reviews: A guide for students of the social and behavioral sciences*. London and New York: Routledge.

Garcia, L. F., Abel, M., Perrin, M., & dos Santos Alvarenga, R. (2020). The GeoCore ontology: a core ontology for general use in geology. *Computers & Geosciences, 135*, 104387.

Geertz, C. (1973). *The interpretation of cultures: Selected essays*. New York: Basic Books.

George, L., Tauri, J., & Macdonald, L. T. A. o. T. (2020). *Indigenous research ethics claiming research sovereignty beyond deficit and the colonial legacy*. Bingley: Emerald Insight. http://doi.org/10.1108/S2398-6018202006

George, S., Duran, N., & Norris, K. (2014). A systematic review of barriers and facilitators to minority research participation among African Americans, Latinos, Asian Americans, and Pacific Islanders. *American Journal of Public Health, 104*(2), e16–e31. https://doi.org/10.2105/AJPH.2013.301706

Getty, L. J. (2021). *Islands and captivity in popular culture: A critical study of film, television and literature*. Jefferson, NC: McFarland.

Gillis, J. R. (2004). *Islands of the mind: How the human imagination created the Atlantic world*. London: Palgrave Macmillan.

Gillis, J. R. (2012). *The human shore: Seacoasts in history*. Chicago: University of Chicago Press.

Gillis, J. R. (2013). The Blue Humanities: In studying the sea, we are returning to our beginnings. *Humanities 34*(3). www.neh.gov/humanities/2013/mayjune/feature/the-blue-humanities.

Gillis, J. R., & Lowenthal, D. (2009). Islands. Special issue. *The Geographical Review, 97*(2), iii–iv. https://doi.org/10.1111/j.1931-0846.2007.tb00394.x

Ginoza, A., Alexander, R., DeLoughrey, E., Randall, J. E., Hatano, S., & Karimata, S. (2020). Prospects for critical island studies. In A. Ginoza (Ed.), *The challenges of island studies* (pp. 95–116). Singapore: Springer. https://doi.org/10.1007/978-981-15-6288-4_7

Głomb, K. (2021, February). How to improve eyewitness testimony research: Theoretical and methodological concerns about experiments on the impact of emotions on memory performance. *Psychological Research*, *86*, 1–11. https://doi.org/10.1007/s00426-021-01488-4

Golding, W. (1954). *Lord of the flies*. London: Faber and Faber.

Gooriah, L. D., Davidar, P., & Chase, J. M. (2020). Species–area relationships in the Andaman and Nicobar Islands emerge because rarer species are disproportionately favored on larger islands. *Ecology and Evolution*, *10*(14), 7551–59. https://doi.org/10.1002/ece3.6480

Gosden, C., & Pavlides, C. (1994). Are islands insular? Landscape vs. seascape in the case of the Arawe Islands, Papua New Guinea. *Archaeology in Oceania*, *29*(3), 162–71. https://doi.org/10.1002/arco.1994.29.3.162

Goss, J., & Wesley-Smith, T. (2010). *Remaking area studies: Teaching and learning across Asia and the Pacific*. Honolulu: University of Hawai'i Press.

Government of Canada (2021). Canada Research Chairs. https://www.chairs-chaires.gc.ca/home-accueil-eng.aspx

Govers, R., & Go, F. (2009). *Place branding: Glocal, virtual and physical identities, constructed, imagined and experienced*. London: Palgrave Macmillan.

Gracio, F. (2014, March 17). Scientists can't claim to be neutral about their discoveries. *The Conversation*. https://theconversation.com/scientists-cant-claim-to-be-neutral-about-their-discoveries-23798

Grosz, E. (2007). Deleuze, Bergson and the concept of life. *Revue Internationale De Philosophie*, *241*, 287–300. https://www.cairn.info/revue-internationale-de-philosophie-2007-3-page-287.htm

Grove, R. H. (1995). *Green imperialism: Colonial expansion, tropical island Edens and the origins of environmentalism, 1600–1860*. Cambridge: Cambridge University Press.

Grydehøj, A. (2008). Branding from above: Generic cultural branding in Shetland and other islands. *Island Studies Journal*, *3*(2), 175–98. https://doi.org/10.24043/isj.221

Grydehøj, A. (2011). "It's a funny thing that they were all bad men": Cultural conflict and integrated tourism policy in Shetland, UK. *International Journal of Tourism Anthropology*, *1*(2), 125–40. https://doi.org/10.1504/IJTA.2011.040430

Grydehøj, A. (2014). Guest editorial introduction: Understanding island cities. *Island Studies Journal*, *9*(2), 183–90. https://doi.org/10.24043/isj.300

Grydehøj, A. (2018). Hearing voices: Colonialism, outsider perspectives, island and Indigenous issues, and publishing ethics. *Island Studies Journal*, *13*(1), 3–12. https://doi.org/10.24043/isj.54

Grydehøj, A., & Kelman, I. (2017). The eco-island trap: Climate change mitigation and conspicuous sustainability. *Area*, *49*(1), 106–13. https://doi.org/10.1111/area.12300

Grydehøj, A., Bevacqua, M. L., Chibana, M., Nadarajah, Y., Simonsen, A., Su, P., Wright, R., & Davis, S. (2021, March). Practicing decolonial political geography:

Island perspectives on neocolonialism and the China threat discourse. *Political Geography, 85.* https://doi.org/10.1016/j.polgeo.2020.102330

Guba, E. G., & Lincoln, Y. S. (1989). *Fourth generation evaluation.* Thousand Oaks, London, New Delhi: SAGE.

Gugganig, M., & Klimburg-Witjes, N. (2021). Island imaginaries: Introduction to a special section. *Science as Culture, 30*(3), 321–41. https://doi.org/10.1080/09505 431.2021.1939294

Guglielmucci, F., Monti, M., Franzoi, I. G., Santoro, G., Granieri, A., Billieux, J., & Schimmenti, A. (2019). Dissociation in problematic gaming: A systematic review. *Current Addiction Reports, 6*(1), 1–14. https://doi.org/10.1007/s40429-019-0237-z

Hajer, M. A. (2006). Doing discourse analysis: Coalitions, practices, meaning. In M. van den Brink & T. Metze (Eds.), *Words matter in policy and planning: Discourse theory and method in the social sciences* (pp. 65–74). Amsterdam: Netherlands Geographical Studies.

Haraway, D. J. (1988). Situated knowledges: The science question in feminism and the privilege of partial perspective. *Feminist Studies, 14*(3), 575–99. https://doi. org/10.2307/3178066

Harman, G. (2009). *Prince of networks: Bruno Latour and metaphysics.* Melbourne: Re-Press.

Harman, G. (2018). *Object oriented ontology: A new theory of everything.* London: Penguin.

Harrison, R. P. (2010). *The dominion of the dead.* Chicago: University of Chicago Press.

Hart, M. A. (2010). Indigenous worldviews, knowledge, and research: The development of an Indigenous research paradigm. *Journal of Indigenous Voices in Social Work, 1*(1), 1–16. http://hdl.handle.net/10125/12527

Hassall, G. (2019). Law, culture, and corruption in the Pacific Islands. In C. Riffel and R. Burke (Eds.), *New Zealand Yearbook of International Law* (pp. 9–28). Amsterdam: Brill. https://doi.org/10.1163/9789004387935_003

Hau'ofa, E. (1993). Our sea of islands. In E. Waddell, V. Naidu, & E. Hau'ofa (Eds.), *A new Oceania: Rediscovering our sea of islands* (pp. 2–18). Suva: School of Social and Economic Development, University of the South Pacific and Beake House.

Hau'ofa, E. (1998). The ocean in us. *The Contemporary Pacific, 10*(2), 391–410. https://www.jstor.org/stable/23706895

Haugeland, J. (2005). Reading Brandom, reading Heidegger. *European Journal of Philosophy, 13*(3), 421–28. https://doi.org/10.1111/j.1468-0378.2005.00237.x

Hay, P. (2006). A phenomenology of islands. *Island Studies Journal, 1*(1), 19–42. https://islandstudiesjournal.org/files/ISJ-1-1-2006-Hay-pp19–42.pdf

Hay, P. (2013). What the sea portends: A reconsideration of contested island tropes. *Island Studies Journal, 8*(2), 209–32. https://doi.org/10.24043/isj.283

Hayward, A., Sjoblom, E., Sinclair, S., & Cidro, J. (2021). A new era of Indigenous research: Community-based Indigenous research ethics protocols in Canada. *Journal of Empirical Research on Human Research Ethics, 16*(4), 403–17. https://doi. org/10.1177/15562646211023705

Hayward, P. (2012). Aquapelagos and aquapelagic assemblages. *Shima: The International Journal of Research into Island Cultures, 6*(1), 1–10. https://www.shimajournal.org/issues/v6n1/c.-Hayward-Shima-v6n1-1-11.pdf

Heath, C. (2000). Configuring action in objects: From mutual space to media space. *Mind, Culture, and Activity, 7*(1–2), 81–104. http://doi.org/10.1080/10749039.2000.9677649

Heidegger. M. (1927/2010). *Being and time* (J. Stambaugh & Revision D. J. Schmidt, Trans.). New York: SUNY Press.

Hennessy, E. (2018). The politics of a natural laboratory: Claiming territory and governing life in the Galápagos Islands. *Social Studies of Science, 48*(4), 483–506. https://doi.org/10.1177/0306312718788179

Hepburn, E., & Baldacchino, G. (Eds.). (2013). *Independence movements in subnational island jurisdictions*. London and New York: Routledge.

Hessler, S. (2018) *Tidalectics: Imagining an oceanic worldview through art and science*. Boston: MIT Press.

Heywood, P. (2017). Ontological turn. In F. Stein (Ed.), *The Cambridge Encyclopedia of Anthropology*. http://doi.org/10.29164/17ontology

Higginbottom, G. M. A., & Serrant-Green, L. (2005). Developing culturally sensitive skills in health and social care with a focus on conducting research with African Caribbean communities in England. *The Qualitative Report, 10*(4), 662–86. http://www.nova.edu/ssss/QR/QR10-4/higginbottom.pdf

Higgins, M., & Kim, E-J. A. (2019). Decolonizing methodologies in science education: Rebraiding research theory-practice-ethics with Indigenous theories and theorists. *Cultural Studies of Science Education, 14*(3). http://doi.org/10.1007/s11422-018-9862-4

Hodgson, B. (2001). *Hippolyte's island: An illustrated novel*. San Francisco: Chronicle Books.

Holbraad, M., & Pedersen, M. A. (2017). *The ontological turn: An anthropological exposition*. Cambridge: Cambridge University Press.

Hopkins, P. (2019). Social geography I: Intersectionality. *Progress in Human Geography, 43*(5), 937–47. https://doi.org/10.1177/0309132517743677

Houbert, J. (1985). Settlers and natives in decolonization: The case of New Caledonia. *The Round Table: Commonwealth Journal of International Affairs, 74*(295), 217–29. https://doi.org/10.1080/00358538508453703

Howitt, R. (2022). Ethics as first method: Reframing geographies at an(other) ending-of-the-world as co-motion. *Environment and Planning F, 1*(1), 82–92. https://doi.org/10.1177/26349825221082167

Howitt, R., & Stevens, S. (2005). Cross-cultural research: Ethics, methods, and relationships. In I. Hay (Ed.), *Qualitative research methods in geography, 2nd edition* (pp. 30–50). Oxford: Oxford University Press.

Howkins, A., Dudley, M., Coates, P., Badcoe, T., Brice, S., Flack, A., Publicover, L., Stone, R., & Would, A. (2019). An excursion in the environmental humanities: Some thoughts on fieldwork, collaboration, and disciplinary identity following a day trip to the Island of Lundy. *Green Letters, 23*(1), 39–53. https://doi.org/10.1080/14688417.2019.1593211

Hubbard, D. K., Rogers, C. S., Lipps, J. H., & Stanley, G. D. (Eds.). (2016). *Coral reefs at the crossroads*. Amsterdam: Springer.

Huijbens, E. H. (2021). The emerging earths of climatic emergencies: On the island geography of life in modernity's ruins. *Geografiska Annaler: Series B, Human Geography, 103*(2), 1–15. https://doi.org/10.1080/04353684.2021.1873072

Hummel-Colla, C. L. (2019). Doling out colonialism: Refiguring archival memory of settler colonialism in the Hawai'i an Islands. *InterActions: UCLA Journal of Education and Information Studies, 15*(2), unpaginated. http://dx.doi.org/10.5070/D4152040294

Hurst, A. (2017). Post-structuralism. In E. O'Brian (Ed.), *Oxford Bibliographies: Literary and critical theory.* http://doi.org/10.1093/obo/9780190221911-0008

Husband, D. (2015, October 25). Teresia Teaiwa: You can't paint the Pacific with just one brush stroke. E-tangata. https://e-tangata.co.nz/korero/you-cant-paint-the-pacific-with-just-one-brush-stroke/

Hymer, S. (1971). Robinson Crusoe and the secret of primitive accumulation. Growth, profits and property: Essays in the revival of political economy. *Monthly Review Press.* https://monthlyreview.org/2011/09/01/robinson-crusoe-and-the-secret-of-primitive-accumulation/

Ibn Tufajl (1180?). *Hajj Ibn Yaqzan [The improvement of human reason by Hajj Ibn Yaqzan].* Original in Arabic. The author.

Iglesias, G., & Carballo, R. (2011). Wave resource in El Hierro: An island towards energy self-sufficiency. *Renewable Energy, 36*(2), 689–98. https://doi.org/10.1016/j.renene.2010.08.021

International Small Islands Studies Association (2022). Objectives. https://www.isisa.org/index.php?c=isisa-objectives

Isaia, M. (1999). *Coming of age in anthropology: Margaret Mead and paradise.* Irvine, CA: Universal Publishers.

Island Innovation (2022). About us. https://islandinnovation.co/

Island Innovation (2022). Island finance forum 2022. https://islandinnovation.co/finance-forum-2022/

Iturralde-Vinent, M.A., García-Casco, A., Rojas-Agramonte, Y., Proenza, J. A., Murphy, J. B., & Stern, R. J. (2016). The geology of Cuba: A brief overview and synthesis. *GSA Today, 26*(10), 4–10. http://doi.org/10.1130/GSATG296A.1.4–10

Jackson, L. C. (2021, November 15). Cop26: Pacific delegates condemn "monumental failure" that leaves islands in peril. *The Guardian.* https://www.theguardian.com/world/2021/nov/15/cop26-pacific-delegates-condemn-monumental-failure-that-leaves-islands-in-peril

Jackson, M. (2013). Plastic islands and processual grounds: Ethics, ontology, and the matter of decay. *cultural geographies, 20*(2), 205–24. https://doi.org/10.1177/1474474012454998

Jackson, M., & Della Dora, V. (2009). "Dreams so big only the sea can hold them": Man-made islands as anxious spaces, cultural icons, and travelling visions. *Environment and Planning A: Economy and Space, 41*(9), 2086–2104. https://doi.org/10.1068/a41237

Jackson, P. (2000). Rematerializing social and cultural geography. *Social & Cultural Geography, 1*(1), 9–14, http://doi.org/10.1080/14649369950133449

Jameson, F. (1998). *The cultural turn: Selected writings on the postmodern, 1983–1998.* New York: Verso.

Jaumotte, H. (2022, June 17). Tristan to participate in The Queen's Platinum Jubilee beacons. *Tristan da Cunha Community News*. https://bit.ly/3HYIPtq

Jetñil-Kijiñer, K. (2016). Statement and poem: "Dear Matafela Peinam." United Nations Climate Summit. https://www.kathyjetnilkijiner.com/videos-featuring-kathy/

Jetñil-Kijiñer, K. (2022). Poet, performer, educator. https://www.kathyjetnilkijiner.com/

Jetñil-Kijiñer, K., & Niviâna, A. (2018). *Rise: From one island to another*. https://www.kathyjetnilkijiner.com/videos-featuring-kathy/

Johnson, H., & Gentles-Peart, K. (Eds.). (2019). *Brand Jamaica: Reimagining a national image and identity*. Lincoln, NE: University of Nebraska Press.

Johnson, R., & Blair, A. (1983). *Logical self-defence, 2nd edition*. Toronto: McGraw-Hill Ryerson.

Johnson, R. B., Onwuegbuzie, A. J., & Turner, L. A. (2007). Toward a definition of mixed methods research. *Journal of Mixed Methods Research*, *1*(2), 112–33. https://doi.org/10.1177/1558689806298224

Johnston, B. (2021). Seongapdo, South Korea: The real-life Squid Game island nobody wants to talk about. *Traveller*. https://www.traveller.com.au/seongapdo-island-south-korea-the-reallife-squid-game-island-nobody-wants-to-talk-about-h20pgb

Joyce, J. (1922). *Ulysses*. Paris: Shakespeare and Company.

Kallis, G., Stephanides, P., Bailey, E., Devine-Wright, P., Chalvatzis, K., & Bailey, I. (2021, November). The challenges of engaging island communities: Lessons on renewable energy from a review of 17 case studies. *Energy Research & Social Science*, *81*. https://doi.org/10.1016/j.erss.2021.102257

Kane, S. C. (2018). Floodplains: Where sheets of water intersect: Infrastructural culture from flooding to hydropower in Winnipeg, Manitoba. In K. Peters, P. E. Steinberg, & E. Stratford (Eds.), *Territory beyond terra* (Chapter 7). London: Rowman & Littlefield International.

Kaplinsky, R. (1983). Prospering at the periphery: A special case? In R. Cohen (Ed.), *African islands and enclaves* (pp. 195–216). Thousand Oaks, London, New Delhi: SAGE.

Kapstein, H. (2017). *Postcolonial nations, islands, and tourism: Reading real and imagined spaces*. London: Rethinking the Island Series. Rowman & Littlefield International.

Karides, M. (2015). An island feminism: Convivial economics and women's cooperatives of Lesvos. In E. Stratford (Ed.), *Island geographies: Essays and conversations* (pp. 78–96). London and New York: Routledge.

Karlsson, A. (2009). Sub-national island jurisdictions as configurations of jurisdictional powers and economic capacity: Nordic experiences from Åland, Faroes and Greenland. *Island Studies Journal*, *4*(2), 139–62. https://doi.org/10.24043/isj.232

Kearns, R. (2021). Narrative and metaphors in New Zealand's efforts to eliminate COVID-19. *Geographical Research*, *59*(3), 324–30. https://doi.org/10.1111/1745-5871.12492

Kennedy, D. (2012). The great arch of empire. In M. Hewitt (Ed.), *The Victorian world* (pp. 57–72). London and New York: Routledge.

Kinane, I. (2016). *Theorising literary islands: The island trope in contemporary Robinsonade narratives.* London: Rethinking the Island Series. Rowman & Littlefield International.

King, R. (1993). The geographical fascination of islands. In D. G. Lockhart, D. Drakakis-Smith, & J. Schembri (Eds.), *The development process in small island states* (pp. 13–37). London and New York: Routledge.

King, R. (2009). Geography, islands and migration in an era of global mobility. *Island Studies Journal*, *4*(1), 53–84. https://doi.org/10.24043/isj.228

Kirkpatrick, J. B. (2022). A lesson from Bass Strait on connectivity conservation. *Geographical Research.* https://doi.org/10.1111/1745-5871.12540

Kitchin, R., & Tate, N. (2000). *Conducting research in human geography: Theory, methodology and practice.* London and New York: Routledge.

Klöck, C., & Nunn, P. D. (2019). Adaptation to climate change in small island developing states: A systematic literature review of academic research. *Journal of Environment & Development*, *28*(2), 196–218. https://doi.org/10.1177/1070496519835895

Koch, C. (1958), *The boys in the island.* Sydney: Angus & Robertson.

Kreft, H., Jetz, W., Mutke, J., Kier, G. & Barthlott, W. (2007). Global diversity of island floras from a macroecological perspective. *Ecology Letters*, *11*(2), 116–27. https://doi.org/10.1111/j.1461-0248.2007.01129.x

Kueffer, C., Drake, D., & Fernández-Palacios, J. M. (2016). *Island biology.* Oxford: Oxford University Press.

Kueffer, C., & Kinney, K. (2017). What is the importance of islands to environmental conservation? *Environmental Conservation*, *44*(4), 311–22. https://doi.org/10.1017/S0376892917000479

Kuhn, T. (1962/1970). *The structure of scientific revolutions.* Chicago: University of Chicago Press.

Kutschera, U. (2003). A comparative analysis of the Darwin-Wallace papers and the development of the concept of natural selection. *Theory in Biosciences*, *122*(4), 343–59. https://doi.org/10.1078/1431-7613-00094

Kydd-Williams, R. (2019). Ethical issues of insider/outsider interviewing: Qualitative research in Grenada, a Caribbean island. *Ethics and Social Welfare*, *13*(4), 424–33. https://doi.org/10.1080/17496535.2019.1685788

LaFlamme, A. G. (1983). The archipelago state as a societal subtype. *Current Anthropology*, *24*(3), 361–62. https://doi.org/10.1086/203006

Landes, D. S. (1998). *The wealth and poverty of nations: Why some are so rich and some so poor.* New York: W. W. Norton.

Latour, B. (2005). *Reassembling the social: An introduction to actor-network-theory.* Oxford: Oxford University Press.

Latour, B., and Woolgar, S. (1986). *Laboratory life: The construction of scientific facts, 2nd edition, with an introduction by J. Salk.* Princeton: Princeton University Press.

Lawrence, D. H. (1928). The man who loved islands. In *The tales of D. H. Lawrence. Volume 2* (pp. 917–39). London: Heinemann.

Lees, L. (2002). Rematerializing geography: The "new" urban geography. *Progress in Human Geography*, *26*(1), 101–12. https://doi.org/10.1191/0309132502ph358pr

Lehane, D. (2010). *Shutter island.* New York: Harper Collins.

Levinson, S. C. (2008). Landscape, seascape and the ontology of places on Rossel Island, Papua New Guinea. *Language Sciences, 30*(2–3), 256–90. https://doi.org/10.1016/j.langsci.2006.12.032

Lewis, V. A. (1974). The Bahamas in international politics: Issues arising for an archipelago state. *Journal of Interamerican Studies and World Affairs, 16*(2), 131–52. https://doi.org/10.2307/174734

Llenín-Figueroa, B. (2022). *Affect, archive, archipelago: Puerto Rico's sovereign Caribbean lives*. London: Rethinking the Island Series. Rowman & Littlefield International.

Lochrie, K. (2006). Sheer wonder: Dreaming Utopia in the Middle Ages. *Journal of Medieval and Early Modern Studies, 36*(3), 493–516. https://doi.org/10.1215/10829636-2006-002

Lockhart, D. G. (1997). Islands and tourism: An overview. In D. G. Lockhart & D. Drakakis-Smith (Eds.), *Island tourism: Problems and perspectives* (pp. 3–20). London: Mansell.

Lockhart, D. G., Drakakis-Smith, D., & Schembri, J. (Eds.). (1993). *The development process in small island states*. London and New York: Routledge.

Long, H. (2014). An empirical review of research methodologies and methods in creativity studies (2003–2012). *Creativity Research Journal, 26*(4), 427–38. https://doi.org/10.1080/10400419.2014.961781

Losos, J. B., & Ricklefs, R. E. (Eds.). (2010). *The theory of island biogeography revisited*. Princeton: Princeton University Press.

Love, H. (2013). Close reading and thin description. *Public Culture, 25*(3 71), 401–34.

Lowenthal, D. (1972). *West Indian societies*. Oxford: Oxford University Press.

Lowenthal, D. (1987). Social features. In C. Clarke & A. Payne (Eds.), *Politics, security and development in small states* (pp. 26–49). London: Allen and Unwin.

Lowy Institute (2012, November 21). Digital islands: How the Pacific ICT revolution is transforming the region. https://www.lowyinstitute.org/publications/digital-islands-how-pacific-ict-revolution-transforming-region

Lucieer, A., & van der Werff, H. (2007, July). Panchromatic wavelet texture features fused with multispectral bands for improved classification of high-resolution satellite imagery. In *2007 IEEE International Geoscience and Remote Sensing Symposium* (pp. 5154–57). https://doi.org/10.1109/IGARSS.2007.4424022

Lyotard, J-F. (1988). *The differend: Phrases in dispute* (G. Van Den Abbele, Trans.). Manchester: Manchester University Press.

MacArthur, R. H., & Wilson, E. O. (1963). An equilibrium theory of insular zoogeography. *Evolution, 17*(4), 373–87. https://doi.org/10.2307/2407089

MacArthur, R. H., & Wilson, E. O. (1967). *The theory of island biogeography*. Princeton: Princeton University Press.

MacLeod, A. (1989). The return. In *The lost salt gift of blood*. Toronto: McClelland and Stewart.

Maddern, J. F. (2008). Spectres of migration and the ghosts of Ellis Island. *cultural geographies, 15*(3), 359–81. http://cgj.sagepub.com/content/15/3/359.short

Malatesta, S., Schmidt di Friedberg, M., Zubair, S., Bowen, D., & Mohamed, M. (Eds.). (2021). *Atolls of the Maldives: Nissology and geography*. London: Rethinking the Island Series, Rowman & Littlefield International.

Malinowski, B. (1922). *Argonauts of the western Pacific*. London: G. Routledge & Sons.

Manathunga, C., Carter, J., & Raciti, M. (2022). Towards decolonisation and transformation in universities: Foregrounding Indigenous and transcultural knowledge systems and communities. In S. S. E. Bengtsen & R. E. Gildersleeve (Eds.), *Transformation of the university: Hopeful futures for higher education* (pp. 92–108). London and New York: Routledge.

Marland, P. (2022). *Ecocriticism and the island: Readings from the British-Irish archipelago*. London: Rethinking the Island Series, Rowman & Littlefield International.

Marshall, J. (2008). *Tides of change on Grand Manan Island: Culture and belonging in a fishing community*. Montreal: McGill-Queen's University Press.

Martin, P. C., Nunn, P. D., Tokainavatu, N., Thomas, F., Leon, J., & Tindale, N. (2019). Last-millennium settlement on Yadua Island, Fiji: Insights into conflict and climate change. *Asian Perspectives*, *58*(2), 316–30. https://doi.org/10.1353/asi.2019.0018.

Martinich, A. P., & Stroll, A. (no date). Epistemology. *Britannica*. https://www.britannica.com/topic/epistemology

Mason, J. (2018). *Qualitative researching, 3rd edition*. Thousand Oaks, London, New Delhi: SAGE.

Massey, D. (2011) Imagining the field. In M. Pryke, G. Rose & S. Whatmore (Eds.), *Using Social Theory: Thinking Through Research*. SAGE. https://dx.doi.org/10.4135/9780857020253

Matheson, K., Pawson, C., & Clegg, P. (2020). Anonymity versus advocacy: Challenges and pitfalls of ethical island research. *The Round Table: Commonwealth Journal of International Affairs*, *109*(6), 720–29. https://doi.org/10.1080/00358533.2020.1849500

Mawyer, A. (2021). Floating islands, frontiers, and other boundary objects on the edge of Oceania's futurity. *Pacific Affairs*, *94*(1), 123–44. https://doi.org/10.5509/2021941123

Maxwell-Stewart, H. (2015). Convict labour extraction and transportation from Britain and Ireland, 1615–1870. In C. G. De Veto & A. Lichtenstein (Eds.), *Global Convict Labour* (pp. 168–98). Amsterdam: Brill.

Maxwell-Stewart, H. (2016). The rise and fall of penal transportation. In P. Knepper & A. Johansen (Eds.), *The Oxford handbook of the history of crime and criminal justice*. Oxford: Oxford University Press. https://doi.org/10.1093/oxfordhb/9780199352333.013.33

May, R., & Tupouniua, S. (1980). The politics of small island states. In R. T. Shand (Ed.), *The island states of the Pacific and Indian Oceans: Anatomy of development* (pp. 419–37). Canberra: Australian National University (ANU) Press.

Mayer, R. E. (1999). Fifty years of creativity research. In R. J. Sternberg (Ed.), *Handbook of creativity* (pp. 449–60). Cambridge: Cambridge University Press.

Mayes, R. (2008) A place in the sun: The politics of place, identity and branding. *Place Branding and Public Diplomacy, 4*(2), 124–35. https://doi.org/10.1057/pb.2008.1

McCall, G. (1994). Nissology: The study of islands. *Journal of the Pacific Society, 17*(2–3), 1–14.

McCall, G. (1996). Clearing confusion in a disembedded world: The case for nissology. *Geographische Zeitschrift, 84*(2), 74–85. https://www.jstor.org/stable/27818741

McChesney, K., & Aldridge, J. (2019). Weaving an interpretivist stance throughout mixed methods research. *International Journal of Research and Method in Education, 42*(3), 225–38. https://doi.org/10.1080/1743727X.2019.1590811

McElroy, J. L., & Parry, C. E. (2010). The characteristics of small island tourist economies. *Tourism and Hospitality Research, 10*(4), 315–28. https://www.jstor.org/stable/23745403

McLennan, S., Forster, M., & Hazou, R. (2022). Weaving together: Decolonising global citizenship education in Aotearoa New Zealand. *Geographical Research, 60*(1), 86–99. https://doi.org/10.1111/1745-5871.12484

McMahon, E. (2003). The gilded cage: From utopia to monad in Australia's island imaginary. In R. Edmond & V. Smith (Eds.), *Islands in history and representation* (pp. 190–202). London and New York: Routledge.

McMahon, E. (2005). Encapsulated space: The paradise-prison of Australia's island imaginary. *Southerly, 65*(1), 20–30. https://search.informit.org/doi/abs/10.3316/informit.432634255068032

McMahon, E. (2010). Australia, the island continent: How contradictory geography shapes the national imaginary. *Space and Culture, 13*(2), 178–87. https://doi.org/10.1177/1206331209358224

McMahon, E. (2013a). Archipelagic space and the uncertain future of national literatures. *Journal of the Association for the Study of Australian Literature, 13*(2), n.p. https://openjournals.library.sydney.edu.au/index.php/JASAL/article/view/9860

McMahon, E. (2013b). Reading the planetary archipelago of the Torres Strait. *Island Studies Journal, 8*(1), 55–66. https://doi.org/10.24043/isj.276

McMahon, E. (2016). *Islands, identity and the literary imagination.* Anthem Press.

McMahon, E., (2019). *Islands, identity and the literary imagination.* London: Anthem Press.

McMahon, E., & André, B. (2018). Literature and the literary gaze. In G. Baldacchino (ed.), *The Routledge international handbook of island studies* (pp. 296–311). London and New York: Routledge. https://doi.org/10.4324/9781315556642

McMillan, K. (2019). *Contemporary art and unforgetting in colonial landscapes: Islands of empire.* London: Palgrave Macmillan.

Mead, M. (1928/2001). *The coming of age in Samoa: A psychological study of primitive youth for western civilisation.* New York: William Morrow/Harper Collins.

Mead, M. (1934/2002). *Kinship in the Admiralty islands.* Piscataway: Transaction Publishers.

Minter, P. (2015). Kath Walker (Oodgeroo Noonuccal), Judith Wright and decolonised transcultural ecopoetics in Frank Heimans' "Shadow Sister." *Sydney Studies in English*, *41*, 61–74. https://openjournals.library.usyd.edu.au/index.php/SSE/article/view/10048

More, T. (1516). *Utopia: On the best form of a commonwealth and on the new island of Utopia* (C. E. Miller, Trans. Kindle edition). New Haven, CT: Yale University Press.

Morozov, E. (2013). *To save everything, click here: The folly of technological solutionism*. New York: Public Affairs.

Moscovici, D. (2017). Environmental impacts of cruise ships on island nations. *Peace Review*, *29*(3), 366–73. https://doi.org/10.1080/10402659.2017.1344580

Moss, P. (Ed.). (2001). *Placing autobiography in geography*. Syracuse: Syracuse University Press.

Mountz A. (2011). The enforcement archipelago: Detention, haunting, and asylum on islands. *Political Geography*, *30*(3), 118–28. https://doi.org/10.1016/j.polgeo.2011.01.005

Mühlhäusler, P., & Stratford, E. (1999). Speaking of Norfolk Island: From dystopia to utopia? In R. King & J. Connell (Eds.), *Small worlds, global lives: Islands and migration* (pp. 213–34). London: Pinter.

Müller, M., & Schurr, C. (2016). Assemblage thinking and actor-network theory: Conjunctions, disjunctions, cross-fertilisations. *Transactions of the Institute of British Geography*, *41*(3), 217–29. https://doi.org/10.1111/tran.12117

Nadarajah, Y., & Grydehøj, A. (2016). Island studies as a decolonial project (Guest Editorial Introduction). *Island Studies Journal*, *11*(2), 437–46. http://doi/org/10.24043/isj.360

Nadarajah, Y., Burgos Martinez, E. E., Su, P., & Grydehøj, A. (2022). Critical reflexivity and decolonial methodology in island studies: Interrogating the scholar within. *Island Studies Journal*, *17*(1), 3–25. http://doi.org/10.24043/isj.380

Naidu, V., & Vaike, L. (2016). Internal migration in the Pacific Islands: A regional overview. *Journal of Pacific Studies*, *35*(3), 91–110. http://jps.library.usp.ac.fj/

NHMRC (National Health and Medical Research Council) (2018). National Statement on Ethical Conduct in Human Research (2007, updated). Canberra: Australian Government. NHMRC. https://www.nhmrc.gov.au/about-us/publications/national-statement-ethical-conduct-human-research-2007-updated-2018

Nicholson, S. (2011). The problem of woman as hero in the work of Joseph Campbell. *Feminist Theology*, *19*(2), 182–93. https://doi.org/10.1177/0966735010384331

Nunn, P. (1994). *Oceanic islands*. Oxford: Blackwell.

Nunn, P. (2021). *Worlds in shadow: Submerged lands in science, memory and myth*. London: Bloomsbury.

Nunn, P., & Cook, M. (2022). Island tales: Culturally-filtered narratives about island creation through land submergence incorporate millennia-old memories of post-glacial sea-level rise. *World Archaeology*. http://doi.org/10.1080/00438243.2022.2077821

Nuttall, M. (2009). Living in a world of movement: Human resilience to environmental instability in Greenland. In S. A. Crate & M. Nuttall (Eds.), *Anthropology and climate change: From encounters to actions* (19 pp.). London and New York: Routledge. https://doi.org/10.4324/9781315434773

Okihiro, G. Y. (2010). Unsettling the imperial sciences. *Environment & Planning D: Society and Space, 28*(5), 745–58. https://doi.org/10.1068/d7210

Olwig, K. F. (2003). "Transnational" socio-cultural systems and ethnographic research: Views from an extended field site. *International Migration Review, 37*(3), 787–811. https://doi.org/10.1111/j.1747-7379.2003.tb00158.x

Olwig, K. R. (2007). Are islanders insular? A personal view. *Geographical Review, 97*(2), 175–90. https://doi.org/10.1111/j.1931-0846.2007.tb00397.x

Online Etymology Dictionary (2022). Paradigm. https://bit.ly/3tey4xl

Oregon Progress Board. (1989). Oregon shines.

Oregon Progress Board. (1997). Oregon shines II. Updating Oregon's strategic plan. A report to the people of Oregon.

Oswald, D., Sherratt, F., & Smith, S. (2014). Handling the Hawthorne effect: The challenges surrounding a participant observer. *Review of Social Studies, 1*(1), 53–73. https://doi.org/10.21586/ross0000004

Ott, D. (2000). *Small Is democratic: An examination of state size and democratic development*. New York: Garland.

Oxford English Dictionary.

Pala. C. (2020, August 10). Kiribati's president's plans to raise islands in fight against sea-level rise. *The Guardian*. https://www.theguardian.com/world/2020/aug/10/kiribatis-presidents-plans-to-raise-islands-in-fight-against-sea-level-rise

Parent, T. (2014). Knowing-wh and embedded questions. *Philosophy Compass, 9*(2), 81–95. http://doi.org/10.1111/phc3.12104

Patke, R. S. (2018). *Poetry and Islands: Materiality and the Creative Imagination*. London: Rethinking the Island Series, Rowman & Littlefield International.

Pedersen, C. (2021). *Crafting collaborative research methodologies: Leaps and bounds in interdisciplinary inquiry*. London and New York: Routledge.

Perera, S. (2009). *Australia and the insular imagination: Beaches, borders, boats, and bodies*. London: Palgrave Macmillan.

Perera, S., & Pugliese, J. (2021). Geographies of violence: Island prisons, prison islands, black sites. *From the European South, 9*, 85–97. https://researchers.mq.edu.au/files/178999333/Publisher_version.pdf

Perez, C. S. (2020). "The ocean in us": Navigating the Blue Humanities and diasporic Chamoru Poetry. *Humanities, 9*(3), 66 (11 pp.). https://doi.org/10.3390/h9030066

Perez, C. S. (2021). Thinking (and feeling) with Anthropocene (Pacific) islands. *Dialogues in Human Geography, 11*(3), 429–33. https://doi.org/10.1177/20438206211017453

Péron, F. (2004). The contemporary lure of the island. *Tijdschrift voor Economische en Sociale Geografie, 95*(3), 326–39. https://doi.org/10.1111/j.1467-9663.2004.00311.x

Peters, K., & Steinberg, P. E. (2019). The ocean in excess: Towards a more-than-wet ontology. *Dialogues in Human Geography, 9*(3), 293–307. https://doi.org/10.1177/2043820619872886

Petridis, P., Fischer-Kowalski, M., Singh, S. J., & Noll, D. (2017). The role of science in sustainability transitions: Citizen science, transformative research, and experiences from Samothraki island, Greece. UWSpace. http://hdl.handle.net/10012/11995

Philip, L. J. (1998). Combining quantitative and qualitative approaches to social research in human geography—an impossible mixture? *Environment and Planning A: Economy and Space, 30*(2), 261–76. https://doi.org/10.1068/a300261

Pilkey, O. J., Cooper, A. G., & Lewis, D. A. (2009). Global distribution and geomorphology of fetch-limited barrier islands. *Journal of Coastal Research, 25*(4), 819–37. https://doi.org/10.2112/08-1023.1

Pithouse-Morgan, K., Pillay, D., & Naicker, I. (2021). Autoethnography as/in higher education. In A. E. Adams, S. Holman Jones, & C. Ellis (Eds.), *Handbook of autoethnography* (pp. 215–27). London and New York: Routledge.

Pleijel, C. (2015). How to read an island. European Small Island Network. https://europeansmallislands.com/how-to-read-an-island/

Poole, M. O. (1937, February 28). Historic islands at New York's door. *New York Times.* https://www.nytimes.com/1937/02/28/archives/historic-islands-at-new-yorks-front-door.html

Potter, S. (2007). The quarantine protection of sub-Antarctic Australia: Two islands, two regimes. *Island Studies Journal, 2*(2), 177–92. https://doi.org/10.24043/isj.206

Povinelli, E. (1995). Do rocks listen? The cultural politics of apprehending Australian Aboriginal labor. *American Anthropologist, 97*(3), 505–18. http://www.jstor.org/stable/683270

Prasad, N. (2004). Escaping regulation, escaping convention: Development strategies in small economies. *World Economics, 5*(1), 41–65. https://ssrn.com/abstract=721443

Presterudstuen, G. H. (2019). Understanding sexual and gender diversity in the Pacific Islands. In J. Ravulo, T. Mafile'o, & D. B. Yeates (Eds.), *Pacific social work* (pp. 161–71). London and New York: Routledge.

Pugh, J. (2020). The aesthetics of island space: Perception, ideology, geopoetics. *Island Studies Journal, 15*(2), 387–390.

Pugh, J., & Chandler, D. (2021). *Anthropocene islands: Entangled worlds.* London: University of Westminster Press.

Pwerte Marnte Marnte Aboriginal Corporation (2022). Aboriginal Art & Culture. Alice Springs Australia > Our country. https://www.aboriginalart.com.au/culture/tourism2.html

Quammen, D. (2012). *The song of the dodo: Island biogeography in an age of extinctions.* New York: Random House.

Radcliffe-Brown, A. R. (1922/1948). *The Andaman islanders: A study in social anthropology.* New York: Free Press.

Randall, J. E. (2021). *An introduction to island studies.* London: Rowman & Littlefield International.

Randolph, S., Coakley, T., & Shears, J. (2018). Recruiting and engaging African-American men in health research. *Nurse Researcher, 26*(1), 8–12. http://doi.org/10.7748/nr.2018.e1569

Ratuva, S. (2021). COVID 19, communal capital and the moral economy: Pacific Islands responses. *Cultural Dynamics, 33*(3), 194–97. https://doi.org/10.1177/09213740211014312

Redfield, P. (2000). *Space in the tropics: From convicts to rockets in French Guiana.* Berkeley: University of California Press.

Reed, A. (2021, April 7). Getting to the source. The importance of field research. United States Institute of Peace. https://bit.ly/3QNliQd

Reichenbach, M. (2020, December 29). Green island. *ATZ Worldwide, 123*(3). https://link.springer.com/article/10.1007/s38311-020-0622-1

Ren, C., & Mahadevan, R. (2018) "Bring the numbers and stories together": Valuing events. *Annals of Tourism Research, 72*(1), 75–84. https://doi.org/10.1016/j.annals.2018.06.008

Rentschler, R., Lehman, K., & Filais, I. (2018). A private entrepreneur and his art museum: How MONA took Tasmania to the world. In L. Lazzeretti & M. Vecco (Eds.), *Creative industries and entrepreneurship: Paradigms in transition from a global perspective* (pp. 136–55). Cheltenham: Edward Elgar. https://doi.org/https://doi.org/10.4337/9781786435927.00014

Richardson, M. (2018). Climate trauma, or the affects of the catastrophe to come. *Environmental Humanities, 10*(1), 1–19. https://doi.org/10.1215/22011919-4385444

Richmond, B. M. (1993). Development of atoll islets in the central Pacific. In *Proceedings of the 7th International Coral Reef Congress Volume 2* (pp. 1185–94). Guam: University of Guam Press.

Ripoll González, L., & Gale, F. (2020). Place branding as participatory governance? An interdisciplinary case study of Tasmania, Australia. *SAGE Open, 10*(2), https://doi.org/10.1177/2158244020923368

Riquet, J. (2019). *The aesthetics of island space: Perception, ideology, geopoetics.* Oxford: Oxford University Press.

Ritvo, H. (1997). *The platypus and the mermaid, and other figments of the classifying imagination.* Cambridge, MA: Harvard University Press.

Roberts, B. R. (2021). *Borderwaters: Amid the archipelagic states of America.* Durham, NC: Duke University Press.

Robinson, M. (2016, June 6) Marilynne Robinson on fear. BBC News World Service. *Heart and Soul.* www.bbc.co.uk/programmes/p03nbzwg

Rodman, M. (1992). Empowering place: Multilocality and multivocality. *American Anthropologist, 94*(3), 640–56. http://www.jstor.org/stable/680566

Roland, H. B., & Curtis, K. J. (2020). The differential influence of geographic isolation on environmental migration: A study of internal migration amidst degrading conditions in the central Pacific. *Population and Environment, 42*(2), 161–82. https://doi.org/10.1007/s11111-020-00357-3

Ronström, O. (2013). Finding their place: Islands as locus and focus. *cultural geographies, 20*(2), 153–65. https://doi.org/10.1177/1474474012445446

Royle, S. A. (2002). *Geography of islands.* London and New York: Routledge.

Runco, M. A., & Albert, R. S. (2010). Creativity research: A historical view. In J. C. Kaufman & R. J. Sternberg (Eds.), *The Cambridge handbook of creativity* (pp. 3–19). Cambridge: Cambridge University Press. https://doi.org/10.1017/CBO9780511763205.003

Ryan, L., Debenham, J., Pascoe, W., Smith, R., Owen, C., Richards, J., Gilbert, S. Anders, R., Usher, K., Price, D., Newley, J., Brown, M., Le, L. H., & Fairbairn,

H. (2022). Colonial frontier massacres in Australia, 1788–1930. https://c21ch.newcastle.edu.au/colonialmassacres/

Salk, J. (2013) Introduction. In B. Latour and S. Woolgar, *Laboratory life: The construction of scientific facts*. Princeton University Press, pp.11–14.

Saramago, J. (1986/1994). *A jangada de pedra [The stone raft]*. Editorial Caminho.

Satia, P. (2020). *Time's monster: History, conscience and Britain's empire*. London: Penguin.

Sayre, R., Noble, S., Hamann, S., Smith, R., Wright, D., . . . & Reed, A. (2019). A new 30 metre resolution global shoreline vector and associated global islands database for the development of standardised ecological coastal units. *Journal of Operational Oceanography*, *12*(Supp. 2), S47–S56. https://doi.org/10.1080/17558 76X.2018.1529714

Schott, C. (2015). Digital immersion for sustainable tourism education: A roadmap to virtual fieldtrips. In G. Moscardo & P. Benckendorff (Eds.), *Education for sustainability in tourism* (pp. 213–27). Berlin: Springer. http://doi.org/10.1007/978-3-662-47470-9_14

Schröter, M., & Taylor, C. (Eds.). (2018). *Exploring silence and absence in discourse: Empirical approaches*. London: Palgrave Macmillan.

Scott, H. (2020, November). Nature's laboratories, fiction's fantasies: The ecocritical significance of islands. *Academia Letters*, Article 32. https://doi.org/10.20935/al32

Scott, J. (2014). Tautology. In *A dictionary of sociology*. Oxford University Press.

Scott, J. C. (1987, July). Everyday forms of resistance. *Copenhagen Journal of Asian Studies*, *4*, 33–62. http://rauli.cbs.dk/index.php/cjas/article/view PDFInterstitial/1765/1785

Selwyn, P. (1980). Smallness and islandness. *World Development*, *8*(12), 945–51. https://doi.org/10.1016/0305-750X(80)90086-8

Semple, E. C. (1911). *Influences of the geographic environment*. London: Constable.

Shakespeare, W. (first performed 1611). *The tempest*. http://shakespeare.mit.edu/tempest/full.html

Shalini, R. T. (2009). Economic cost of occupational accidents: Evidence from a small island economy. *Safety Science*, *47*(7), 973–79. https://doi.org/10.1016/j.ssci.2008.10.021

Sharples, C. (2006). Indicative mapping of Tasmanian coastal vulnerability to climate change and sea-level rise: Explanatory report. Vol. 2. Tasmanian Government Department Primary Industries, Water and Environment.

Sheller, M. (2022). The end of flying: Coronavirus, confinement, academic (im)mobilities ad me. In K. Bjørkdahl & A. S. Franco Duharte (Eds.), *Academic flying and the means of communication* (pp. 53–77). London: Palgrave Macmillan. https://doi.org/10.1007/978-981-16-4911-0_3

Shin, H., & Jin, Y. (2021). The politics of forgetting: Unmaking memories and reacting to memory-place-making. *Geographical Research*, *59*(3), 439–51. https://doi.org/10.1111/1745-5871.12467

SICRI (Small Island Cultural Research Initiative) (2022, May 11). Podcast interview with Elaine Stratford. https://www.sicri.net/island-conversations-elaine

Simpson M. (2020, January). For a prefigurative pandemic politics: Disrupting the racial colonial quarantine. *Political Geography, 84.* http://doi/org/10.1016/j. polgeo.2020.102274

Smith, B. (1960). *European vision and the South Pacific, 1768–1850: A study in the history of art and ideas.* Oxford: Clarendon Press.

Smith, B. (1999). An introduction to ontology. In D. Peuquet, B. Smith, & B. Brogaard (Eds.), *The ontology of fields. Report of a specialist meeting held under the auspices of the Varenius Project.* Bar Harbor, Maine: NCGIA

Smith, L. T. (1999). *Decolonizing methodologies: Research and Indigenous peoples.* Dunedin: University of Otago Press and Zed Books.

Smith, L. T. (2005). On tricky ground: Research the Native in the age of uncertainty. In N. Denzin and Y. Lincoln (Eds.), *The SAGE handbook of qualitative research methods, 3rd edition* (pp. 85–108). Thousand Oaks, London, New Delhi: SAGE.

Smith, L. T., Maxwell, T. K., Puke, H., & Temara, P. (2016). Indigenous knowledge, methodology and mayhem: What is the role of methodology in producing indigenous insights? A discussion from Mātauranga Māori. *Knowledge Cultures, 4*(3), 131–56. https://www.ceeol.com/search/article-detail?id=411005

Smithers S. G., & Hopley D. (2011). Coral cay classification and evolution. In D. Hopley & S. G. Smithers (Eds.), *Encyclopedia of modern coral reefs.* Amsterdam: Springer, Encyclopedia of Earth Sciences Series. https://doi. org/10.1007/978-90-481-2639-2_6

Somerville, A. T. P. (2012). *Once were pacific: Māori connections to oceania.* University of Minnesota Press.

Spate, O. H. K. (1978). The Pacific as an artefact. In N. Gunsson (Ed.), *The changing Pacific: Essays in honour of H. E. Meade* (pp. 32–45). Oxford: Oxford University Press.

Sperling, K. (2017, May). How does a pioneer community energy project succeed in practice? The case of the Samsø Renewable Energy Island. *Renewable and Sustainable Energy Reviews, 71,* 884–97. https://doi.org/10.1016/j.rser.2016.12.116

Spiteri, S. (2016). Developing a national quality culture for further and higher education in a microstate: The case of Malta. *Malta Review of Educational Research, 10*(2), 297–313. https://www.um.edu.mt/library/oar//handle/123456789/20786

Srebrnik, H. (2004). Small island nations and democratic values. *World Development, 32*(2), 329–41. https://doi.org/10.1016/j.worlddev.2003.08.005

Stake, R. (1995). *The art of case study research.* Thousand Oaks, London, New Delhi: SAGE.

Stalker, L. H., & Burnett, K. (2016). Good work? Scottish cultural workers' narratives about working and living on islands. *Island Studies Journal, 11*(1), 193–208. https://doi.org/10.24043/isj.342

Starc, N. (2020a). Introduction. In *The notion of near islands: The Croatian Archipelago* (pp. 1–12). London: Rethinking the Island Series, Rowman & Littlefield International.

Starc, N. (Ed.). (2020b). *The notion of near islands: The Croatian archipelago.* London: Rethinking the Island Series, Rowman & Littlefield International.

Steinberg, P. E. (2001). *The social construction of the ocean.* Cambridge: Cambridge University Press.

Steinberg, P. E. (2005). Insularity, sovereignty and statehood: The representation of islands on portolan charts and the construction of the territorial state. *Geografiska Annaler: Series B, Human Geography*, *87*(4), 253–65. https://doi.org/10.1111/j.0435-3684.2005.00197.x

Steinberg, P. E., & Peters, K. (2015). Wet ontologies, fluid spaces: Giving depth to volume through oceanic thinking. *Environment and Planning D: Society and Space*, *33*(2), 247–64.

Stephens, M., and Martínez-San Miguel, Y. (Eds.) (2020). *Contemporary archipelagic thinking: Towards new comparative methodologies and disciplinary formations*. London: Rethinking the Island Series, Rowman & Littlefield International.

Steup, M., & Neta, R. (2020). Epistemology. In E. N. Zalta (Ed.), *The Stanford Encyclopaedia of Philosophy*. https://plato.stanford.edu/archives/fall2020/entries/epistemology/

Storlazzi, C., Gingerich, S., Van Dongeren, A., Cheriton, O., Swarzenski, P., Quataert, E., Voss, C., Field, D. W., Annamalai, H., Piniak, G. & McCall, R. (2018). Most atolls will be uninhabitable by the mid-21st century because of sea-level rise exacerbating wave-driven flooding. *Science Advances*, *4*(4). http://doi.org/10.1126/sciadv.aap9741

Strange, C., & Kempa, M. (2003). Shades of dark tourism: Alcatraz and Robben Island. *Annals of Tourism Research*, *30*(2), 386–405. https://doi.org/10.1016/S0160-7383(02)00102-0

Stratford, E. (2003). Flows and boundaries: Small island discourses and the challenge of sustainability, community and local environments. *Local Environment*, *8*(5), 495–99. https://doi.org/10.1080/1354983032000143653

Stratford, E. (2006a). Isolation as disability and resource: Considering sub-national island status in the constitution of the "New Tasmania." *The Round Table: Commonwealth Journal of International Affairs*, *95*(386), 575–88. https://doi.org/10.1080/00358530600929933

Stratford, E. (2006b). Technologies of agency and performance: Tasmania Together and the constitution of harmonious island identity. *Geoforum*, *37*(2), 273–86.

Stratford, E. (2008). Islandness and struggles over development: A Tasmanian case study. *Political Geography*, *27*(2), 160–75. https://doi.org/doi:10.1016/j.polgeo.2007.07.007

Stratford, E. (2012). Vantage points: Observations on the emotional geographies of heritage. In G. Baldacchino (Ed.), *Extreme heritage management: Policies and practices from island territories* (pp. 1–20). New York: Berghahn Books.

Stratford, E. (2013). Guest editorial introduction. The idea of the archipelago: Contemplating island relations. *Island Studies Journal*, *8*(1), 3–8. https://doi.org/10.24043/isj.272

Stratford, E. (2015a). A critical analysis of the impact of Island Studies Journal: Retrospect and prospect. *Island Studies Journal*, *10*(2), 139–62. https://doi.org/10.24043/isj.324

Stratford, E. (2015b). "Dear Prime Minister" . . . Mapping island children's political views on climate change. In M. Benwell & P. Hopkins (Eds.), *Children, Young People and Critical Geopolitics* (pp. 123–38). Aldershot: Ashgate.

Stratford, E. (2015c). *Geographies, mobilities, and rhythms over the life-course: Adventures in the interval*. London and New York: Routledge (Chapter 3).

Stratford, E. (Ed.). (2016). *Island geographies: Essays and conversations*. Routledge.

Stratford, E. (2017). Imagining the archipelago. In M. A. Stephens & B. R. Roberts (Eds.), *Archipelagic American Studies: Decontinentalizing the study of American culture* (pp. 74–94). Durham, NC: Duke University Press.

Stratford, E. (2019). *Home, nature, and the feminine ideal: Geographies of the interior and of empire*. London: Rowman & Littlefield International.

Stratford, E. (2020). Disciplinary formations, creative tensions, and certain logics in archipelagic studies. In M. A. Stephens & Y. Martínez-San Miguel (Eds.), *Archipelagic thinking: Towards new comparative methodologies and disciplinary formations* (pp. 51–64). London: Rethinking the Island Series, Rowman & Littlefield International.

Stratford, E., & Bradshaw, M. (2021). Rigorous and trustworthy: Qualitative research design. In I. Hay and M. Cope (Eds.), *Qualitative research methods in human geography* (pp. 92–106). Toronto: Oxford University Press.

Stratford, E., & Howell, S. (2007). *Webbing the Islands Project*. Hobart: University of Tasmania and the Ian Potter Fund.

Stratford, E., & Jaskolski, M. (2004). In pursuit of sustainability? Challenges for deliberative democracy in a Tasmanian local government. *Environment and Planning B: Planning & Design, 31*(2), 311–324. https://doi.org/10.1068/b2944

Stratford, E., & Langridge, C. (2012). Critical artistic interventions into the geopolitical spaces of islands. *Social & Cultural Geography, 13*(7), 821–43. https://doi.org/ online http://dx.doi.org/10.1080/14649365.2012.728615

Stratford, E., & Low, N. (2013). Young islanders, the meteorological imagination, and the art of geopolitical engagement. *Children's Geographies, 13*(2), 164–80. https://doi.org/10.1080/14733285.2013.828454

Stratford, E., & Low, N. (2015). Young islanders, the meteorological imagination and the art of geopolitical engagement. *Children's Geographies, 13*(2), 164–80. https:// doi.org/10.1080/14733285.2013.828454

Stratford, E., Armstrong, D., & Jaskolski, M. (2003). Relational spaces and the geopolitics of community participation in two Tasmanian local governments: A case for agonistic pluralism? *Transactions of the Institute of British Geographers, 28*(4), 461–72. https://doi.org/10.1111/j.0020-2754.2003.00104.x

Stratford, E., Baldacchino, G., McMahon, E., Farbotko, C., & Harwood, A. (2011a). Envisioning the archipelago. *Island Studies Journal, 6*(2), 113–30. https://doi.org/10.24043/isj.253

Stratford, E., McMahon, E., Farbotko, C., Jackson, M., & Perera, S. (2011b). Review Forum. Reading Suvendrini Perera's "Australia and the Insular Imagination." *Political Geography, 30*(6), 329–38. http://doi.org/10.1016/j.polgeo.2011.06.001

Sullivan, C. (2020). Who holds the key? Negotiating gatekeepers, community politics, and the "right" to research in Indigenous spaces. *Geographical Research, 58*(4), 344–54. https://doi.org/10.1111/1745-5871.12415

Sutton, P. K. (2007). Democracy and good governance in small states. In E. Kisanga & S. J. Danchie (Eds.), *Commonwealth small states: Issues and prospects* (pp. 201–17). London: Commonwealth Secretariat.

Szadziewski, H. (2021). Everyday geoeconomics: The belt and road initiative in Oceania. *Geographical Research, 59*(3), 483–88. https://doi.org/10.1111/1745-5871.12473

Taitingfong, R. I. (2020). Islands as laboratories: Indigenous knowledge and gene drives in the Pacific. *Human Biology, 91*(3), 179–188. https://doi.org/10.13110/humanbiology.91.3.01

Tambassi, T. (2021). From the philosophies of geographies to the applied ontology of geography. In *The philosophy of geo-ontologies: Applied ontology of geography* (pp. 3–20). Amsterdam: Springer. https://doi.org/10.1007/978-3-030-78145-3_1

Tashakkori, A., & Teddie, C. (Eds.) (2010). *The SAGE handbook of mixed methods in social and behavioral research, 2nd edition*. Thousand Oaks, London, New Delhi: SAGE.

Taylor, J. R., & Van Every, E. J. (2000). *The emergent organization: Communication as its site and surface*. Mahwah, NJ: Erlbaum.

Taylor-Bragge, R. (Iowendjeri Boonwurrung), Whyman, T. (Paakantji-Ngiyampaa), & Jobson, L. (2021). *People Needs Country*: The symbiotic effects of landcare and wellbeing for Aboriginal peoples and their countries. *Australian Psychologist, 56*(6), 458–71. http://doi.org/10.1080/00050067.2021.1983756

Teaiwa, K. (2014). *Consuming Ocean Island: Stories of people and phosphate from Banaba*. Bloomington: Indiana University Press.

Teaiwa, T. (2007). To island. In G. Baldacchino (Ed.), *A world of islands: An island studies reader* (p. 514). Newcastle upon Tyne: Agenda Academic and Institute of Island Studies, University of Prince Edward Island.

Teasdale, J. I., & Teasdale, G. R. (2022). Incidental researchers: Investigating islands from the inside out. *Geographical Research*. https://doi.org/10.1111/1745-5871.12530

Terrell, J. E. (2020). Metaphor and theory in island archaeology. *Journal of Island and Coastal Archaeology, 17*. https://doi.org/10.1080/15564894.2020.1830892

The Economist (2003, May 17). On the world's rich list. The Economist Group, p. 33.

The World Bank (2020). GNI per capita, Atlas method (current US$). https://data.worldbank.org/indicator/NY.GNP.PCAP.CD

Thomas, S. (2009). Nissopoesis: Visuality and aesthetics in poetic inquiry. In M. Prendergast, C. Leggo, & P. Sameshima (Eds.), *Poetic inquiry: Vibrant voices in the social sciences* (pp. 127–32). Rotterdam: Sense Publishers.

Thrift, N. J. (2011). Lifeworld Inc.: And what to do about it. *Environment & Planning D: Society and Space, 29*(1), 5–26. https://doi.org/10.1068/d0310

Timans, R., Wouters, P., & Heilbron, J. (2019). Mixed methods research: What it is and what it could be. *Theory and Society, 48*(2), 193–216. https://doi.org/10.1007/s11186-019-09345-5

Tjørve, E. (2010). How to resolve the SLOSS debate: Lessons from species-diversity models. *Journal of Theoretical Biology, 264*(2), 604–12. https://doi.org/10.1016/j.jtbi.2010.02.009

To, L. S., Bruce, A., Munro, P., Santagata, E., MacGill, I., Rawali, M., & Raturi, A. (2021). A research and innovation agenda for energy resilience in Pacific Island Countries and Territories. *Nature Energy, 6*(12), 1098–1103. https://doi.org/10.1038/s41560-021-00935-1

Tobi, H., & Kampen, J. K. (2018, May). Research design: The methodology for interdisciplinary research framework. *Quality & Quantity 52*, 1209–25. https://doi.org/10.1007/s11135-017-0513-8

Todd, Z. (2016). An Indigenous feminist's take on the ontological turn: "Ontology" is just another word for colonialism. *Journal of Historical Sociology, 29*(1), 4–22. http://doi.org/10.1111/johs.12124

Tsavdaroglou, C., & Kaika, M. (2022). Refugees' caring and commoning practices against marginalisation under COVID-19 in Greece. *Geographical Research, 60*(2), 232–40. https://doi.org/10.1111/1745-5871.12522

United Nations (1994a). Agenda 21: Sections 17 and 18. United Nations Conference on Environment and Development (UNCED). Rio de Janeiro, Brazil. https://www.un.org/esa/dsd/agenda21/res_agenda21_17.shtml

United Nations (1994b). Barbados Programme of Action. https://sustainabledevelopment.un.org/conferences/bpoa1994

United Nations (1999, September 27). General Assembly begins two-day special session to review progress of 1994 Barbados Action Programme. Press Release GA/9610, ENV/DEV/519. https://www.un.org/press/en/1999/19990927.ga9610.doc.html

United Nations (2021). United Nations Convention on the Law of the Sea, Part VIII, Article 121. https://www.un.org/depts/los/convention_agreements/texts/unclos/part8.htm

UNESCO (2022). World Heritage List. https://whc.unesco.org/en/list/&order=property

United States Department of the Interior (n.d.). Global islands explorer. https://rmgsc.cr.usgs.gov/gie/

University of Tasmania (2022). The Tasmania project. https://www.utas.edu.au/community-and-partners/the-tasmania-project

Urry, J., & Larsen, J. (2011). *The tourist gaze 3.0.* Thousand Oaks, London, New Delhi: SAGE.

van Inwagen, P., & Sullivan, M. (2021). Metaphysics. In E. N. Zalta (Ed.), *The Stanford Encyclopedia of Philosophy* (winter edition). https://plato.stanford.edu/archives/win2021/entries/metaphysics/

Vannini, P. (2012). *Ferry Tales: Mobility, place, and time on Canada's west coast.* London and New York: Routledge.

Vannini, P., Baldacchino, G., Guay, L., Royle, S. A., & Steinberg, P. E. (2009). Recontinentalizing Canada: Arctic ice's liquid modernity and the imagining of a Canadian archipelago. *Island Studies Journal, 4*(2), 121–38. https://doi.org/10.24043/isj.231

Veenendaal, W. (2018). Islands of democracy. *Area, 52*(1), 30–37. https://doi.org/10.1111/area.12462

Voirol, B. (2019, May). Decolonization in the field? Basel—Milingimbi back and forth. *TSANTSA. Journal of the Swiss Anthropological Association, 24*, 48–57. https://doi.org/10.36950/tsantsa.2019.24.6903

Vourdoubas, J. (2021). Islands with zero net carbon footprint due to electricity use. The case of Crete, Greece. *European Journal of Environment and Earth Sciences, 2*(1), 37–43. https://doi.org/10.24018/ejgeo.2021.2.1.116

Walcott, D. (1992, December 7). Nobel lecture: The Antilles: Fragments of epic memory. https://www.nobelprize.org/prizes/literature/1992/walcott/lecture/

Walcott, D. (2014). *Omeros*. New York: Farrar, Straus and Giroux.

Wallace, A. R. (1869). *The Malay Archipelago, the land of the orang-utan and the bird of paradise: a narrative of travel with studies of man and nature*. London: Macmillan.

Walshe, R. A., & Foley, A. M. (2021). Learning from the archives of island jurisdictions: Why and how island history should inform disaster risk reduction and climate action. *Small States & Territories*, 4(2), 205–30. https://www.um.edu.mt/library/oar/handle/123456789/83376

Wang, P., & Roberts Briggs, T. M. (2015). Storm-induced morphology changes along barrier islands and poststorm recovery. In J. F. Shroder, J. T. Ellis, & D. Sherman (Eds.), *Coastal and marine hazards, risks, and disasters* (pp. 271–306). Amsterdam: Elsevier. https://doi.org/10.1016/B978-0-12-396483-0.00010-8

Watts, R. (2000). Islands in comparative constitutional perspective. In G. Baldacchino & D. Milne (Eds.), *Lessons from the political economy of small islands: The resourcefulness of jurisdiction* (pp. 23–29). London: Macmillan.

Weaver-Hightower, R. (2007). *Empire islands: Castaways, cannibals, and fantasies of conquest*. Minneapolis: University of Minnesota Press.

Weick, K. E., Sutcliffe, K. M., & Obstfeld, D. (2005). Organizing and the process of sensemaking. *Organization Science*, 16(4), 409–21. https://doi.org/10.1287/orsc.1050.0133

Wennecke, C. W., Jacobsen, R. B., & Ren, C. (2019). Motivations for Indigenous island entrepreneurship: Entrepreneurs and behavioural economics in Greenland. *Island Studies Journal*, 14(2), 43–60. https://doi.org/10.24043/isj.99

West, J. (2013). Obstacles to progress. *Griffith Review. Tasmania: The Tipping Point*, 39. https://www.griffithreview.com/articles/obstacles-to-progress/

Whatmore, S. (2006). Materialist returns: Practising cultural geography in and for a more-than-human world. *cultural geographies*, 13(4), 600–9. https://doi.org/10.1191/1474474006cgj377oa

Wheatley, N. (2013, July3). Fatima Island: Memories of little surprises. *The Leader*. https://bit.ly/3yp7Bj9

Williams, S., Anders, R., Vreugdenhil, R., & Byrne, J. (2022). Indigenising the curriculum: Transcending Australian geography's dark past. *Geographical Research*, 60(1), 100–12. https://doi.org/10.1111/1745-5871.12504

Withers, C. W. J. (2011). Geography's narratives and intellectual history. In J. Agnew & D. Livingstone (Eds.), *The SAGE handbook of geographical knowledge* (pp. 39–50). London: SAGE. http://doi.org/10.4135/9781446201091.n3

Witze, A. (2022, February 9). Why the Tongan eruption will go down in the history of volcanology. *Nature News Feature*. https://doi.org/10.1038/d41586-022-00394-y

World Health Organization (2022). Ensuring ethical standards and procedures for research with human beings. https://www.who.int/activities/ensuring-ethical-standards-and-procedures-for-research-with-human-beings

Yamamoto, L., & Esteban, M. (2010). Vanishing island states and sovereignty. *Ocean and Coastal Management*, 53(1), 1–9. https://doi.org/https://doi.org/10.1016/j.ocecoaman.2009.10.003

Yilmaz, K. (2013). Comparison of quantitative and qualitative research traditions: Epistemological, theoretical, and methodological differences. *European Journal of Education, 48*(2), 311–25. https://doi.org/10.1111/ejed.12014

Young, L. B. (1999). *Islands: Portraits of miniature worlds.* New York: W. H. Freeman & Company.

Yusoff, K. (2015). Queer coal: Genealogies in/of the blood. *Philosophia, 5*(2), 203–29. https://www.pdcnet.org/sophia/content/sophia_2015_0005_0002_0203_0229

Yusoff, K. (2019). *A billion Black Anthropocenes or none.* Minneapolis: University of Minnesota Press.

Zubair, S., & Bowen, D. (2021). New waves: The guest house dilemma. In S. Malatesta, M. Schmidt di Friedberg, S. Zubair, D. Bowen, & M. Mohamed (Eds.), *Atolls of the Maldives: Nissology and geography* (pp. 125–44). London: Rethinking the Island Series, Rowman & Littlefield International.

Index

Aborigines and the aboriginal. *See* Indigenous peoples and issues
absence, 15, 90, 143. *See also* silence
abstraction. *See* reason and reasoning
academic practice, 13, 23, 26–27, 35, 38, 86, 88, 97, 100, 115, 125, 127–28
Africa, 10, 14, 48
analysis. *See* reason and reasoning
Antarctica, 10, 14
Anthropocene, 6, 10, 12, 18, 40, 52, 54, 63–64, 114, 119, 128. *See also* climate and climate change
Aotearoa/New Zealand, 10, 18, 28, 86, 135
aquatic, the/aquapelago, 6, 42–43, 46, 56, 63, 138, 142. *See also* water[s]
archipelagic, the, 5–10, 23, 27, 37, 46, 54, 59, 64–65, 90, 100, 106–10, 114–18, 127, 133–42
archipelagos, 2–6, 9–10, 12–15, 19, 21, 25, 30–31, 35–37, 40–48, 54–63, 66–69, 71, 73, 76–79, 81, 85–91, 94–96, 100–3, 118, 130, 133, 146
archives and libraries, 7, 94, 99, 108, 139. *See also* museums
area [dimension]. *See* space and spatiality
Asia, 10, 14, 117; China, 29–30, 126; India, 115, 126; Indonesia, 8, 10, 31, 77; Japan, 9–10, 29, 49, 79; Philippines, 8, 10
assemblage. *See* theory
assessment, 27, 38, 39, 52, 53, 77, 94, 100, 119. *See also* evaluation
assumptions. *See* reason and reasoning
Australia, 2, 4, 6, 9, 10, 16, 17, 26, 28, 36, 55–58, 62, 64, 78–79, 87, 129, 134, 143
axiology. *See* theory

Baldacchino, Godfrey, 113–31 and *passim*
Baruah, Mitul, 113–31
behavior, 26, 67, 77, 89, 121, 140–43. *See also* perception[s]
body, the, 14, 36, 67, 84, 98, 123
boundaries, 7–9, 12, 15–16, 42, 57–58, 60, 95, 101, 109, 138
bridge, 10, 22, 29–30, 62, 66, 105, 122–23; causeway, 8, 22; tunnel, 10, 22, 66
Britain, 6, 48, 66. *See also* United Kingdom

Canada, 4, 6, 10, 16, 23, 60, 66, 79, 83, 122, 135, 145
Caribbean, 8, 10, 11, 27–29, 38, 44, 47, 90, 114, 122, 124, 127, 139, 145

About the Authors

Elaine Stratford is a cultural and political geographer professor at the University of Tasmania. She is editor-in-chief of *Geographical Research* and a deputy editor of *Island Studies Journal*. Elaine co-leads Rowman & Littlefield's *Rethinking the Island* series with Godfrey Baldacchino and Elizabeth McMahon. In 2021, Elaine was recognized by the Institute of Australian Geographers for outstanding services to the discipline of geography, receiving the Griffith Taylor Medal.

Godfrey Baldacchino is professor of sociology, University of Malta, and Malta ambassador-at-large for islands and small states. He was Canada Research Chair in Island Studies (2003–2013) and UNESCO Co-Chair in Island Studies and Sustainability (2016–2020) at the University of Prince Edward Island, Canada—as well as president of the International Small Islands Studies Association (2014–2022). He is the founding editor of *Island Studies Journal* and *Small States & Territories* journal.

Elizabeth McMahon is professor of literature in the School of the Arts and Media, University of New South Wales, Australia. She researches across the related domains of literary studies and island studies, the subject of her award-winning monograph, *Islands and the Literary Imagination* (Anthem Press, 2016). She is editor of *Southerly*, Australia's oldest literary journal.

www.ingramcontent.com/pod-product-compliance
Lightning Source LLC
Chambersburg PA
CBHW030650270326
41929CB00007B/297